Standard
COMPANION DEVOTIONS®

*I am he that liveth, and was dead;
and, behold, I am alive for evermore,
Amen; and have the keys of hell and of death.*
—Revelation 1:18

Volume 6

PUBLISHING
Bringing The Word to Life

Cincinnati, Ohio

All Scripture quotations, unless otherwise indicated, are taken from the HOLY BIBLE, NEW INTERNATIONAL VERSION®. NIV®. Copyright © 1973, 1978, 1984 by International Bible Society. Used by permission of Zondervan. All rights reserved.

Where noted, Scripture quotations are from the following, used with permission from the copyright holders, all rights reserved:

King James Version (KJV), public domain.
New American Standard Bible (NASB), © 1960, 1962, 1963, 1971, 1972 by The Lockman Foundation, La Habra CA.
The Living Bible (TLB), © 1971 by Tyndale House Publishers, Wheaton, IL.
The New King James Version (NKJV), Copyright © 1982 by Thomas Nelson, Inc.
Holy Bible, New Living Translation (NLT), © 1996 by Tyndale House Publishers, Wheaton, IL.
The Revised Standard Version of the Bible (RSV) copyrighted 1946, 1952, 1971, 1973 by the Division of Christian Education of the National Council of the Churches of Christ in the United States of America.
New Century Version® *(NCV)* © 1986, 1988, 1999 by Thomas Nelson, Nashville, Tennessee.

• *The Lion, The Witch, and the Wardrobe* by C.S. Lewis copyright © C.S. Lewis Pte. Ltd. 1950. Extract reprinted with permission.
• *Mere Christianity* by C.S. Lewis copyright © C.S. Lewis Pte. Ltd. 1950. Extract reprinted with permission.

Gary Allen, *editor*
Margaret Williams, *editor*
Jonathan Underwood, *senior editor*

The "Spotlight" and "Search the Word" features were written by the following: Cheryl Frey and Ronald G. Davis

Cover by DesignTeam.

Published by Standard Publishing, Cincinnati, Ohio
www.Standardpub.com
Copyright © 2008 by Standard Publishing.
All rights reserved. No part of this book may be reproduced in any form, except for brief quotations in reviews, without the written permission of the publisher.

Topics based on the Home Daily Bible Readings, International Sunday School Lessons.
© 2008 by the Committee on the Uniform Series. Printed in the U.S.A.

September

BIRTH OF A NEW COMMUNITY

*You are the people of God;
. . . you have received mercy.*
—1 Peter 2:10

Photo © Comstock

September 1

Surprise Witness

"I will be quick to testify against sorcerers, adulterers and perjurers, against those who defraud laborers of their wages, who oppress the widows and the fatherless, and deprive aliens of justice, but do not fear me," says the Lord Almighty (Malachi 3:5).

Scripture: Malachi 3:1-5

Song: *"Thus Speaks the Lord to Wicked Men"*

From this meditation today, I will pray . . .

Adoration _____

Confession _____

Thanksgiving _____

Supplication _____

From this meditation today, I will . . .

Think _____

Say _____

Do _____

I love intense courtroom scenes in movies. I particularly enjoy watching the psychological strategies unfold as each attorney attempts to prove the innocence of his or her client. The best part is when it appears the "evil" attorney is about to win, but at the last possible moment, the "good" attorney calls a surprise witness to the stand. Brand new testimony then wins the day!

It often seems as if the evil in our world is going to win, doesn't it? Everywhere we look, sin abounds. And those who flagrantly parade their sin, without any fear of the Lord, sometimes appear to be doing better at life than those who pursue righteousness and honor God. But at the last moment, God will call himself as a surprise witness against all evil, finally bringing justice to His people. Now that's a dramatic conclusion!

Dear Father, *remind me that those who appear to be getting away with evil will one day have to answer to You. May I never compare myself with others but only look to You as my standard and guide. In Jesus' name, amen.*

September 1–7. **Reneé Gray-Wilburn,** *of Colorado Springs is a wife and mother of three who runs a writing and editorial service called A Way with Words.*

SPOTLIGHT
Next Week's Lesson

Evil is a mind-set; repentance is the necessary remedy.

September 2

Paid in Full

Speak tenderly to Jerusalem, and proclaim to her . . . that her sin has been paid for
(Isaiah 40:2).

I'll never forget the day when my parents made their final house payment. Our family had a huge "Paid in Full" party, complete with a mortgage-burning bonfire! This was truly a joyous occasion for my parents. After being indebted to the bank for 30 years, they were finally free.

Since the fall of Adam thousands of years ago, humankind has been in debt. This is not a debt we can pay back with our finances, good deeds, or even our lives. And it won't go away in a mere 30 years! It exists because of our sin nature, and there isn't a thing we can do about it on our own.

Thankfully, though, God didn't leave us on our own. He sent His Son, Jesus, to set us free from our sin debt. He actually *became* sin for us so we could become righteous in God's sight (see 2 Corinthians 5:21). And when He hung on the cross, He declared, "It is finished" (John 19:30). It's time to celebrate, brothers and sisters in Christ. Our debt has been paid in full!

Thank You, Dear Father, for sending Jesus to pay the price for my sin. Because of Your love for me, You have marked my debt "paid in full." Help me never to forget the extent of the debt I owed—and what it cost You to free me from it. Through Christ the Lord, amen.

Scripture: Isaiah 40:1-5
Song: *"Free at Last"*

From this meditation today, I will pray . . .

Adoration _____

Confession _____

Thanksgiving _____

Supplication _____

From this meditation today, I will . . .

Think _____

Say _____

Do _____

SEARCH THE WORD

No sweeter words exist for the debtor: "Paid in Full!"

September 3

Only One Thing Will Remain

*The grass withers and the flowers fall,
but the word of our God stands forever* (Isaiah 40:8).

Scripture: Isaiah 40:6-11
Song: *"Thy Word Is Like a Garden, Lord"*

From this meditation today, I will pray . . .
Adoration _____
_____
_____

Confession _____
_____
_____

Thanksgiving _____
_____
_____

Supplication _____
_____
_____

From this meditation today, I will . . .
Think _____
_____
_____

Say _____
_____
_____

Do _____
_____
_____
_____

It's been said that nothing is certain but death and taxes. Yet one day even those will cease. Everything we can see or think of on this earth will be gone. God promises to do away with the earth and Heaven that currently exist in order to replace them with new versions (see Matthew 24:35 and 2 Peter 3:13). The only thing that will remain is God's Word.

Throughout the ages certain persons have tried desperately to snuff out the Word of God. In many countries today, to preach—or even to read the Bible—means putting your very life in danger. And in America there's an increasing effort to remove God's Word from the public eye. But God has declared that His Word will stand "forever." We know that it has and will.

Knowing this, let us place our trust in it. We can't afford to gamble our future on the passing things of this world. Instead, rely on the sure foundation of the Word of our God. It is a piece of Heaven come to us and it can, as well, bring us to Heaven.

Dear Lord, *help me live my days in light of eternity. Show me where I have placed too much value on things that will one day disappear, and help me to put my trust in You and Your precious Word alone. I pray this prayer in the name of Jesus, my merciful Savior and Lord. Amen.*

SPOTLIGHT
Next Week's Lesson

John the Baptizer had one key word from God: "Repent!" It hasn't changed.

September 4

What Kind of Tree Are You?

Produce fruit in keeping with repentance
(Matthew 3:8).

Several years ago, my husband and I moved into a rental home in California. We had a few trees in our yard, but since we moved in the middle of winter (and because neither of us are tree experts), we had no idea what kind they were. But once spring came and we could see their fruit, we no longer had to wonder; a tree that produces oranges, for instance, is . . . an orange tree.

Every day, the people we live with, work with, and hang out with are watching to see what kind of fruit we produce. They may not listen to our words about Christ, but once they see fruit that offers them a glimpse of genuine spiritual life, they'll no doubt become interested in our Savior. After all, who can resist the true love, peace, and joy that Jesus offers?

When we first came to God, He gave us the fruit of His Spirit. It's now up to us to keep producing the fruit of good works to reflect the greatness of God's saving work in us. Thus others will see our fruit and know what kind of "tree" we are—a tree of life, sent by God.

Father God, *thank You for giving me the fruit of Your Spirit that I might be an example of Christ to others. May others be drawn to You by Your work of grace in me. And when I fail, keep me from discouragement while giving me the courage to come to You in repentance and renewed hope. In the name of Jesus, Lord and Savior of all, I pray. Amen.*

SEARCH THE WORD
Few people know all trees by name . . . but the Christian tree is obvious in the forest of worldliness.

Scripture: Matthew 3:4-10
Song: *"O to Be Like Thee"*

From this meditation today, I will pray . . .

Adoration _____
_____
_____

Confession _____
_____
_____

Thanksgiving _____
_____
_____

Supplication _____
_____
_____

From this meditation today, I will . . .

Think _____
_____
_____

Say _____
_____
_____

Do _____
_____
_____

September 5

Can't Buy Love

A voice from heaven said, "This is my Son, whom I love; with him I am well pleased" (Matthew 3:17).

Scripture: Matthew 3:11-19

Song: *"O How I Love Jesus"*

From this meditation today, I will pray...

Adoration _____

Confession _____

Thanksgiving _____

Supplication _____

From this meditation today, I will...

Think _____

Say _____

Do _____

I vividly remember each of my children as they were in their infancy. I spent my days (and nights) feeding them, cleaning them, and holding them. They couldn't do anything for themselves, let alone serve me! Yet, I loved each one immensely.

Jesus was 30 years old when He began His ministry. Until then, He didn't really "do" anything for God. He simply loved His Father with all His being. Jesus' baptism marked the start of His "official" ministry, but the Father's proclamation of His love for Jesus came *before* Jesus began serving Him. God was well pleased with Jesus just because He was His Son, not because of what He did.

It is true of us, as well. God loves us because of who we are, not because of what we do. You see, we are *creatures who need love;* that is the deepest truth of who we are. So God loves us.

Now that my children are older, they do things for me because they love me, not to earn my love. Let us have the same attitude toward our heavenly Father, whose unconditional regard for us is always free.

Dear Lord, *thank You for Your unconditional love toward me. Out of gratitude, may I serve You with all my strength. In Jesus' name, amen.*

SPOTLIGHT
Next Week's Lesson

Jesus is the only one who did not need to repent to please God.

September 6

You Belong

Once you were not a people, but now you are the people of God
(1 Peter 2:10).

As a youngster, Jeremy spent most of his years in and out of foster homes. He'd stay with a family for a time, then for different reasons, the family would have to give him up. After a while Jeremy felt constantly rejected and abandoned, sensing he had nowhere to belong. Then, when Jeremy was 12, a family adopted him for good. He finally received the love and sense of belonging he'd searched for throughout childhood.

Perhaps you can relate to Jeremy. Maybe you were raised in a broken home and felt as if you never had a "real" family. Or maybe you've been deeply betrayed or hurt as an adult and can't seem to find anywhere to go for help. God wants you to know that He has adopted you into His family.

At one time, we were all like Jeremy: on our own, without a sense of purpose, and nowhere to go for the unconditional love we so desperately needed. But as children of God, we're now His people, called into His family, and given a new destiny. Like Jeremy, we can now say, "I belong here."

Thank You, Lord, that You have chosen me as Your own. Help me to remember that no matter what I may go through or how alone I might feel, You are always there for me. Through Christ I pray. Amen.

SEARCH THE WORD
Hosea had a sad task: to name a child "Lo-Ammi . . . not my people" (Hosea 1:9). But Christians can say, "We are God's people."

Scripture: 1 Peter 2:1-10
Song: *"Child of the King"*

From this meditation today, I will pray . . .
Adoration _____
_____
_____

Confession _____
_____
_____

Thanksgiving _____
_____
_____

Supplication _____
_____
_____

From this meditation today, I will . . .
Think _____
_____
_____

Say _____
_____
_____

Do _____
_____
_____

September 7

The Message Is Still the Same

Repent, for the kingdom of heaven is near
(Matthew 3:2).

Scripture: Matthew 3:1-3; Mark 1:1-8
Song: *"Prepare the Way, O Zion"*

From this meditation today, I will pray . . .
Adoration _____
_____
_____
Confession _____
_____
_____
Thanksgiving _____
_____
_____
Supplication _____
_____
_____

From this meditation today, I will . . .
Think _____
_____
_____
Say _____
_____
_____
Do _____
_____
_____
_____

As the years come and go and generations pass, things that were once considered wrong by society have become increasingly acceptable. Part of the reason may be that the Bible has largely been written off as "old-fashioned" and "irrelevant" (even among some preachers). But the truth is, God's Word still speaks to us today, and the message is still the same, regardless of any culture's so-called ethical progress.

John the Baptist proclaimed the message of repentance over 2,000 years ago. The message has not changed in all these years; the kingdom of Heaven is still near. John was letting people know that the Messiah would soon make His first appearance, and they needed to be ready for Him. In our time, we must remember that Jesus is preparing to make His second and final appearance.

Will we be ready for Him? Just like John, we must herald the warning that the kingdom of Heaven is near. We must cry out to sinners and believers alike: Repent; get ready to receive your king!

Heavenly Father, *thank You that Your Word contains timeless truths, that it does not change just because the world changes. Help me to heed Your warning—which is just as relevant today as it was in John the Baptist's day. In the name of my Savior, Jesus Christ, amen.*

SPOTLIGHT
Next Week's Lesson

The kingdom is still as close as repentance and submission.

September 8

Save Me from Myself

*But the more I called to him, the more he rebelled. . . .
I lead Israel along with my ropes of kindness and love*
(Hosea 11:2, 4, *New Living Translation*).

Charles's choices were tearing the family apart. Where was the loving husband and father his family once knew? Years of drinking had changed him, and he was deaf to the cries of his wife and children.

His perilous ways led him down the path of self-destruction. Darkness enveloped him. Yet just when he was about to give up on life, he heard the pleadings of his teenage son in an ultimatum: "Pop, we can't live like this any more. Get help, or get out!" Somewhere inside him the man he had been heard these words of tough love. "Lord, help me!" was his soul-deep response.

That very night a call to Alcoholics Anonymous brought John to their home. Over gallons of coffee and hours of conversation, Charles grabbed hold of a thread of hope. And slowly that rope pulled him from his darkness.

I, too, hear God's calls to me. He still offers the ropes of kindness and love. How can I ignore His invitation to be set free from my dark, painful places?

Father, please don't give up on me. I know deep within my heart that I need Your love. Change my rebellion into openness. In Jesus' name, amen.

Scripture: Hosea 11:1-7
Song: *"Precious Lord, Take My Hand"*

From this meditation today, I will pray . . .

Adoration _____

_____

_____

Confession _____

_____

_____

Thanksgiving _____

_____

_____

Supplication _____

_____

_____

From this meditation today, I will . . .

Think _____

_____

_____

Say _____

_____

_____

Do _____

_____

_____

September 8–14. **Viola Gommer,** *writer and photographer, is a retired nurse educator. She is the wife of a retired minister and a mother of two children.*

SEARCH THE WORD

If you're going to dangle by a rope, make it God's rope of kindness and love.

September 9

Unfailing Presence

Although the world was made through him, the world didn't recognize him when he came. . . . But to all who believed him and accepted him, he gave the right to become children of God (John 1:10, 12, *New Living Translation*).

Scripture: John 1:10-14
Song: *"Savior, Like a Shepherd Lead Us"*

From this meditation today, I will pray . . .
Adoration _____
_____
_____

Confession _____
_____
_____

Thanksgiving _____
_____
_____

Supplication _____
_____
_____

From this meditation today, I will . . .
Think _____
_____
_____

Say _____
_____
_____

Do _____
_____
_____

The doors of the bus opened, and I stepped out into the busy terminal. I searched the waiting crowd for my father, but he wasn't there. I went out to the street to look for him. He wasn't there, either. Soon I was the only person left waiting to be met. Where could he be? He was always on time.

A car was parked across the street, and I noticed the driver waving at someone. He got out of the car and began to walk toward the terminal. The gentleman's stride looked familiar and, as I strained to see the man's face, I realized it was indeed my father. Why didn't I recognize this man whom I had loved my whole life?

He soon told me that his recent eye surgery had transformed his vision, and he'd put aside the glasses he'd worn since childhood. As we hugged he whispered, "Don't worry, I'll still claim you as my daughter."

It is the same with God. He loves us with unfailing love and faithfulness, even when we fail to recognize His presence.

Father God, *forgive me for my blindness to Your constant presence. Help me to see You even in the ordinariness of my days. In Jesus' name, amen.*

SPOTLIGHT
Next Week's Lesson

When Jesus came, He made God's presence more obvious, but God was and is always present.

September 10

From the Heart of a Child

God chose the weak things of the world to shame the strong (1 Corinthians 1:27).

A last-minute phone call brought our three families together, even though the demands of school, work, and church activities often held us hostage. It was unusual for everyone to be able to pull away from responsibilities for a family meal spanning three generations.

There was excitement in the air as we gathered around a table filled with our favorite foods. We stood holding hands, waiting for a blessing to be said. Finally, one of the children said, "Well, who's going to say grace?" No one answered. Then a little voice began, "Thank You, God, for a happy heart, for rain and sunny weather. Thank You, Lord, for our food," he paused, took a deep breath, then continued in a booming voice, "and that we are together! Amen."

"A little child will lead them" says Isaiah 11:6. And my 6-year-old grandson did just that. Not wise or strong by worldly standards, but by God's Spirit, this little boy enabled us to rejoice in the Lord's bounty and grace. It was a lesson in wisdom and gratitude from the heart of a child.

Dear Lord, *I come to You with a grateful heart. Thank You for using those who are open to Your Spirit to teach me lessons in humility. And help me never judge others by their apparent strength or wisdom, for You look at the heart. In the name of Jesus, my merciful Savior and Lord, amen.*

SEARCH THE WORD
Personal weakness doesn't matter . . . if God's strength lies underneath.

Scripture: 1 Corinthians 1:26-31
Song: *"Give Thanks"*

From this meditation today, I will pray . . .

Adoration _____

Confession _____

Thanksgiving _____

Supplication _____

From this meditation today, I will . . .

Think _____

Say _____

Do _____

September 11

Different People, Differing Gifts

Now there are different kinds of spiritual gifts, but it is the same Holy Spirit who is the source of them all
(1 Corinthians 12:4, *New Living Translation*).

Scripture: 1 Corinthians 12:4-13
Song: *"We Are All One in Mission"*

From this meditation today, I will pray...
Adoration _____
_____
_____

Confession _____
_____
_____

Thanksgiving _____
_____
_____

Supplication _____
_____
_____

From this meditation today, I will...
Think _____
_____
_____

Say _____
_____
_____

Do _____
_____
_____
_____

As I waited for the worship service to begin, people were still coming into the sanctuary. I offered thanks to God for each one of them, recalling all the lives they've touched with their kindness and love. One woman prepares meals for an ill neighbor. Our young people go to nursing homes to read and sing for the residents. Another group makes quilts for hospitalized children. The women's study group makes and consecrates prayer shawls for those suffering pain and loss. Men and women go to members' homes to do repairs; no job is too small. Still other members work the food bank, stocking shelves and preparing baskets for needy families.

I thought of one woman in a nursing home who was willing to take prayer requests. She spends part of each day talking to God about those in need of His touch. Her neighbor across the hall telephones people who are housebound, offering encouraging words and a listening ear.

Different people. Differing gifts. Yet, each person is pouring the oils of God's grace over someone's life. Thus God builds His church and transforms the world.

Lord, *I want to follow the examples of my fellow church members in service to You. What gift have You given me? In the name of Jesus, amen.*

SPOTLIGHT
Next Week's Lesson

Jesus' humble beginning was no indication of the breadth of His life and service.

September 12

Remembered and Honored

*Now all of you together are Christ's body,
and each one of you is a separate and necessary part of it
(1 Corinthians 12:27, New Living Translation).*

Our family perpetuates a unique tradition each time we gather to celebrate a special occasion. We hold hands around the table before offering a blessing, and the same question comes forth each time: "Who isn't here with us today?"

We speak the names of dear ones not present. These include family, friends, teachers, neighbors, and ministers who are missing from our circle. Until we say their names, our family circle isn't complete. Our tradition encourages us to remember those who have touched our lives but are now in the presence of the Lord. It is not unusual for tears of gratitude to flow freely for those who have been a part of our life's journey.

Those present and those named are equally important to our lives. They are all indispensable, as they have each gifted us in their own special way. Each is a separate and necessary part of our family, and we need to claim one another to truly be complete. Church is a lot like that too, isn't it?

God, *in the silence of Your presence, I name those in my family and my church whose presence has also gifted my life. I thank You now for the great truth of the communion of the saints. In Christ's name I pray. Amen.*

Scripture: 1 Corinthians 12:14-27
Song: *"Forward Through the Ages"*

From this meditation today, I will pray...

Adoration _____
_____
_____

Confession _____
_____
_____

Thanksgiving _____
_____
_____

Supplication _____
_____
_____

From this meditation today, I will...

Think _____
_____
_____

Say _____
_____
_____

Do _____
_____
_____

SEARCH THE WORD

Necessary. Everyone wants to be necessary, and the body of Christ needs every member.

September 13

Wrapped in Prayer

We ask God to give you a complete understanding of what he wants to do in your lives, and we ask him to make you wise with spiritual wisdom. Then the way you live will always honor and please the Lord, and you will continually do good (Colossians 1:9, 10, *New Living Translation*).

Scripture: Colossians 1:9-14
Song: *"Praying Always"*

From this meditation today, I will pray . . .
Adoration _____
_____
_____

Confession _____
_____
_____

Thanksgiving _____
_____
_____

Supplication _____
_____
_____

From this meditation today, I will . . .
Think _____
_____
_____

Say _____
_____
_____

Do _____
_____
_____
_____

"It's time!" Every school morning my mother's call brought us to the back door. She drew us close to her, asking, "Are you two ready? Do you have any tests or projects due?" Then: "Let's talk to God about your day."

Her prayers asked God to watch over us. She told Him about our tests, projects, and whatever she thought we were worried about that day. She prayed we would please Him, ending by thanking Him for each of her children and the promise their lives held for the future. With the "Amen," my brother and I were out the door and on our way to school.

All my life, Mother's prayers have been with me, wrapping my days in prayer. Through her daily example of faith and prayer, I grew to know God better and better. Now, I pray for my own children and grandchildren. I pray they will learn what God wants them to do with their lives, and that whatever they do will honor and please Him.

Dear Heavenly Father, *thank You for the prayers of my mother. Help me to pray in the same faith-filled way this day. In Jesus' name, amen.*

SPOTLIGHT
Next Week's Lesson

A mother's love is but a shadow of God's love for His Son, especially in His humbled human existence.

September 14

Out of My Darkness

"Joseph, son of David," the angel said, "do not be afraid to go ahead with your marriage to Mary. For the child within her has been conceived by the Holy Spirit" (Matthew 1:20, *New Living Translation*).

The chief operating officer along with the vice president of human resources knocked on my open door. They sat down at my invitation and then turned my life upside down, nearly crushing me with just five words: "Your position has been eliminated." I couldn't believe my ears. I thought I would never be the same again. I felt adrift, discarded.

I couldn't sleep, I wouldn't eat, I didn't want to face my friends and colleagues. The answering machine picked up my messages. All I could do was cry out to God, "Where are You?"

I wonder if that is how Joseph felt? This apparently wasn't his child, but God told him not to be afraid. He must take Mary as his wife, and the child would be special. Joseph trusted God's Word and obeyed His instructions. The child was called Immanuel, "God with us."

Joseph shows me how to deal with disappointment, loss, and pain in my own life. I am to trust God to rescue me. I will not be crushed; He will carry me through.

God, *thank You for Your protective hand as I walk in faith each day. Help me listen for Your instructions—and obey them. In Christ's name, amen.*

Scripture: Matthew 1:18-25; 2:13-15
Song: *"Mary's Boy Child"*

From this meditation today, I will pray . . .
Adoration _____

Confession _____

Thanksgiving _____

Supplication _____

From this meditation today, I will . . .
Think _____

Say _____

Do _____

SEARCH THE WORD

Dark moments—like Joseph's—are devastating . . . unless God's Spirit is present.

September 15

Shalom!

The LORD turn his face toward you and give you peace
(Numbers 6:26).

Scripture: Numbers 6:22-27
Song: *"Wonderful Peace"*

From this meditation today, I will pray . . .

Adoration _____

_____

_____

Confession _____

_____

_____

Thanksgiving _____

_____

_____

Supplication _____

_____

_____

From this meditation today, I will . . .

Think _____

_____

_____

Say _____

_____

_____

Do _____

_____

_____

Peace: a rare commodity these days. Though there seems little the individual can do to bring peace to our troubled world, the believer can know perfect peace in his or her personal world. It's a needed protection from burnout, a condition some consider almost inevitable in our hectic society. Busyness sweeps across even our church congregations like a mighty wind. Programs multiply, and with them the suggestion that truly dedicated Christians will sign up for every cause.

Whatever happened to the simple things, like toasting marshmallows over a campfire for no reason other than friendship? Having lived well past my three score and ten, I can guarantee that you will remember campfire friendships long after the myriad committees and campaigns have faded from mind. Jesus, you recall, took time for a campfire snack by the sea with a few friends, and good work was done. The point is, those who walk close to the Prince of Peace will never burn out.

Lord, grant me peace and serenity in a world obsessed with doing. In the most practical ways, teach me the difference between busyness and servanthood. I thank You, in the name of Jesus. Amen.

SPOTLIGHT
Next Week's Lesson

"Blessed are the peacemakers," for God will give them His peace.

September 15–21. **Lloyd Mattson** is a retired minister and author of Christian camping books. He and his wife, Elsie, live in Duluth, Minnesota.

September 16

The Least Brother

I tell you the truth, whatever you did for one of the least of these brothers of mine, you did for me (Matthew 25:40).

Emilio was small and dark-skinned, with black hair and sparkling eyes. He spoke broken English, but he took his custodial duties in our office seriously, grateful for the job. He lived with his wife and six young children in a third-floor walk-up apartment. He taught a Bible class in their storefront church building.

One day I invited Emilio to our home for Sunday dinner. The family arrived packed into a battered old car. Emilio and I romped outdoors with the rascally youngsters while his petite wife helped Elsie in the kitchen. Dinner was an adventure! Emilio told me this was the first time anyone in America had invited his family to their home for a meal. He insisted on returning the favor. That dinner, too, proved adventurous.

Emilio was the poorest member of our office crew. While everyone treated him kindly, inviting a family with six lively kids for Sunday dinner was . . . inconvenient. But I'm glad we did it. Elsie and I cherish the memory of two memorable meals with a poor immigrant family that so richly blessed us.

Heavenly Father, *teach me the joy of being inconvenienced by serving others in Your name. In fact, fit me with servant sandals for Jesus' sake! In the name of the Father, the Son, and the Holy Spirit, I pray. Amen.*

SEARCH THE WORD
Jesus' face should be seen in slums, in elder care facilities, in war-torn villages, everywhere. Do you see Him?

Scripture: Matthew 25:31-40
Song: *"Freely, Freely"*

From this meditation today, I will pray . . .

Adoration _____

_____

_____

Confession _____

_____

_____

Thanksgiving _____

_____

_____

Supplication _____

_____

_____

From this meditation today, I will . . .

Think _____

_____

_____

Say _____

_____

_____

Do _____

_____

_____

September 17

A Sure Foundation

That house . . . did not fall, because it had its foundation on the rock
(Matthew 7:25).

Scripture: Matthew 7:24-29
Song: *"How Firm a Foundation"*

From this meditation today, I will pray . . .
Adoration _____
_____
_____

Confession _____
_____
_____

Thanksgiving _____
_____
_____

Supplication _____
_____
_____

From this meditation today, I will . . .
Think _____
_____
_____

Say _____
_____
_____

Do _____
_____
_____
_____

An oft-told story from family lore taught me the peril of poor foundations. One of our great uncles, an Old Country fisherman, built a low-roofed cabin on the lee side of Encampment Island on Lake Superior's north shore. On November 28, 1905, a fierce northeaster wind swept down the lake, taking a deadly toll on ships and seamen. Lost in darkness and blinding snow, the 454-foot bulk freighter *Lafayette* struck the cliffs opposite the island and sank. Miraculously, there was no loss of life.

Meanwhile, my great uncle and his family slept, secure in the knowledge that their beach cabin had weathered many a northeaster, protected by a rocky ridge running the length of the small, narrow island.

Then, a strange bumping. The cabin moved! Great-uncle stepped from his bed into icy water to find the cabin's only door jammed. Escaping through a small window, the family sought shelter in the root cellar. By first light they saw the beach was bare, their cabin built on the sand washed away. For the first time in history, waves had breached the island.

Thank You, Lord, that I rest secure on the Rock of Your salvation. And amidst the decisions I'll face today, let me focus on the sure foundation of Your Word, that I may obey it in all things. In Jesus' name, amen.

SPOTLIGHT
Next Week's Lesson

Foolish or wise? Sand or rock?
Jesus' values or the world's values?
All make the decision.

September 18

Brotherly (and Sisterly) Love

*Be devoted to one another in brotherly love.
Honor one another above yourselves* (Romans 12:10).

Two decades ago I had an unlikely friend, Sister Naomi, a godly woman marked by joy and patient faithfulness. She was a teacher, gifted poet, photographer, and naturalist. I found we shared many interests. She came to our home for dinner, and my wife and I dined with her at the priory. During our many conversations, theology never came up.

The dedication of a new addition to our small church building would soon be upon us, and I invited Sister Naomi to display her nature photos throughout the building. She arrived in a subcompact red car bristling with easels bearing a considerable stack of large, mounted photos. On a whim, I asked her to participate in the dedication program. She told three children's stories, the most memorable part of the program. Following the reception, as we loaded her car, Sister Naomi paused. She embraced me and said, "Lloyd, we meet at the cross."

Thus an aging Benedictine nun blessed a Baptist minister, no longer so young. I found a brotherly love existing between us as we sought to honor one another as we honored our Lord.

Thank You, God, *for our unity through Your indwelling Spirit. May I sincerely reach out to all who name Jesus as Savior. Through Him, amen.*

Scripture: Romans 12:9-13
Song: *"I Would Be True"*

From this meditation today, I will pray . . .
Adoration _____
_____
_____

Confession _____
_____
_____

Thanksgiving _____
_____
_____

Supplication _____
_____
_____

From this meditation today, I will . . .
Think _____
_____
_____

Say _____
_____
_____

Do _____
_____
_____

SEARCH THE WORD

*All Christians meet
at the cross, for all must
linger there.*

September 19

My Friend Al

Be willing to associate with people of low position
(Romans 12:16).

Scripture: Romans 12:14-21

Song: *"In the Family of God"*

From this meditation today, I will pray...

Adoration _____

_____

_____

Confession _____

_____

_____

Thanksgiving _____

_____

_____

Supplication _____

_____

_____

From this meditation today, I will...

Think _____

_____

_____

Say _____

_____

_____

Do _____

_____

_____

_____

Al was an ordinary man who seldom took risks. He held the same job in a button factory for many years. Buttons changed with fashion—wood, glass, metal, ceramic, bone, plastic—but Al's particular function never changed. When seniority brought him in line for a foreman's job, he turned it down. Year after year Al carried the same battered lunch bucket with its Thermos®, sandwiches, and New Testament tucked inside.

Al and his wife, Hazel, never missed church services. They learned about Christians in Europe, displaced by war, who were anxiously seeking sponsors so they could start over in America. Al proposed that the church sponsor a German family, but wary of the cost and problems other churches had experienced, the minister deferred action.

Moved by compassion, Al and Hazel tapped their own savings. Within a few weeks a family with two children arrived. They blessed the church for many years, more than paying their way—and all because a cautious man of a "low position" dared to take a blessed risk.

Teach me, dear Father, *that in Your sight we all live on the same level, fully dependent on Your grace. After all, for every human being, the ground is level at the cross. All praise to You, in Christ's name. Amen.*

SPOTLIGHT
Next Week's Lesson

Beatitude values give the correct view of people: all are worthy in His sight.

September 20

Gentle Witness

Always be prepared to give . . . the reason for the hope that you have. But do this with gentleness and respect (1 Peter 3:15).

I would not suggest that our home models the ideals set forth in some Christian writings. Few religious pictures hang on our walls. Our shelves hold varied kinds of books. But our simple faith in Christ and our commitment to one another have kept us married for 64 years. We hope that our lives bear witness to the master, Christ.

Some years ago, a young teen niece spent a few days with us. She came from a large family where faith was not a factor. We were a typical, empty-nest, somewhat retired couple, busy with many things.

We entertained our niece the best that older folks can, but mainly she had to entertain herself. She observed our sometimes disorderly lifestyle. Apart from habitual pre-meal prayer, we made no attempt to involve her in devotions. We lived as we do, whether or not guests were present.

Feedback came a few weeks later, when our niece's foster father phoned. "Know what she said about you? 'They're always smiling!'" Now why should that seem so remarkable?

Dear Lord, help me speak often of You to others, but let me live always for You, letting the light of Your presence shine through me. I pray this prayer in the name of Jesus, my Savior and Lord. Amen.

SEARCH THE WORD

Gentleness and respect open the door for reason . . . and give one a reason for faith.

Scripture: 1 Peter 3:8-15
Song: *"Softly and Tenderly Jesus Is Calling"*

From this meditation today, I will pray . . .
Adoration _____
_____
_____

Confession _____
_____
_____

Thanksgiving _____
_____
_____

Supplication _____
_____
_____

From this meditation today, I will . . .
Think _____
_____
_____

Say _____
_____
_____

Do _____
_____
_____
_____

September 21

Let it Shine!

Let your light shine before men, that they may see your good deeds and praise your Father in heaven (Matthew 5:16).

Scripture: Matthew 5:1-16
Song: *"With Happy Voices Ringing"*

From this meditation today, I will pray...
Adoration _____
_____
_____
Confession _____
_____
_____
Thanksgiving _____
_____
_____
Supplication _____
_____
_____

From this meditation today, I will...
Think _____
_____
_____
Say _____
_____
_____
Do _____
_____
_____
_____

During college years I worked at a rescue mission. One summer evening we were setting up chairs for the nightly street meeting, when a drunken man staggered down the street toward our mission corner. A new volunteer in a straw hat had joined our set-up crew. He caught sight of the man, who seemed about to fall, and rushed to him with a chair. Easing the delirious man down, the volunteer fanned him with his hat, asking whether we should call a doctor.

Some of us smiled. The man was just another skid-row vagrant, hopelessly lost in booze. The volunteer was obviously new to the streets and naive about mission work. Still, I wondered what was going on in the befogged brain of the vagrant, who rarely saw compassion from mission workers hardened by repeated disappointment.

You see, the con schemes are ingenious, promises endless, failure all but inevitable in this type of mission work. So, how easily we forget that God loves alcoholics too, and that we are not responsible for the response to the light, only that we let the light shine. I hope that volunteer never lost his compassion.

Dear Heavenly Father, *help me see the hurting and helpless with eyes of compassion, just as You see them. In the name of Jesus I pray. Amen.*

SPOTLIGHT
Next Week's Lesson
Of all the sermons ever preached, the Sermon on the Mount offers the most light and demands the most from us.

September 22

Wicked Wedges

Fulfil ye my joy, that ye be likeminded, having the same love, being of one accord, of one mind (Philippians 2:2, *King James Version*).

Franklin D. Roosevelt once wrote to a friend about the issue of foreign-born immigrants: "We must remember that any oppression, any injustice, any hatred, is a wedge designed to attack our civilization." He was right. When citizens turn on each other out of hatred, a wedge is driven deep into that society. Such a rift will eventually lead to a collapse of basic civility.

In Philippians 2, Paul wrote to protect the church from the very thing that destroys nations. The first verse reveals the importance of drawing upon our divine resources. Once that's done, the spiritual attitudes of verses 2 through 4 make wedge-making impossible.

Of course, the ultimate inspiration for these unifying traits comes from Christ himself, as seen in verses 5 through 11. Broad, intimate familiarity with Christ's life is the best protection against the mindset that leads to wicked wedges. And that's when the old acronym for JOY is fulfilled: Jesus first, Others second, Yourself last.

Dear Father, *may Your love permeate my heart and heal every division, for Jesus' sake. In His precious name I pray. Amen.*

Scripture: Philippians 2:1-11
Song: *"O Perfect Love"*

From this meditation today, I will pray . . .

Adoration _____

Confession _____

Thanksgiving _____

Supplication _____

From this meditation today, I will . . .

Think _____

Say _____

Do _____

SEARCH THE WORD

Wedges or bridges? That is always the social choice, the Christian choice.

September 22–28. **Richard M. Robinson** *pastors a Baptist church in Denver, Colorado. He also enjoys singing in a male gospel quartet.*

September 23

Back to Basics

Verily I say unto you, Except ye be converted, and become as little children, ye shall not enter into the kingdom of heaven
(Matthew 18:3, *King James Version*).

Scripture: Matthew 18:1-5
Song: *"Victory in Jesus"*

From this meditation today, I will pray . . .

Adoration _____

Confession _____

Thanksgiving _____

Supplication _____

From this meditation today, I will . . .

Think _____

Say _____

Do _____

Vince Lombardi, legendary football coach of the Green Bay Packers, was reprimanding his team for an embarrassing loss. He held the pigskin high and began his remarks with, "Gentlemen, this is a football." The players had apparently forgotten the basics of the game, and Lombardi knew that you never grow beyond certain fundamentals. They form the foundation of success on the field.

It's no different in the Christian life. When the disciples asked Jesus who was the greatest in the kingdom of Heaven, he set a little child before them. Our Lord coached His team to spiritual victory by delivering a "back to basics" message. The qualities of a child, especially a humble, teachable, trusting spirit, form the very foundation of kingdom greatness.

Most football players dream of a Super Bowl victory, or of achieving the ultimate honor—induction into the Football Hall of Fame. But such greatness is reserved only for those who never forgot the basics. Likewise, any disciple of the master must maintain the basic qualities of a little child if he wants to be a champion for Christ.

Thank You, Lord, for making me a part of Your team. Help me maintain those qualities fundamental to lifelong success. In Jesus' name, amen.

SPOTLIGHT
Next Week's Lesson

The children of the kingdom follow the Head of the house as a model of humble service.

September 24

Good, or Best?

There were certain Greeks among them that came up to worship at the feast: the same came therefore to Philip, which was of Bethsaida of Galilee, and desired him, saying, Sir, we would see Jesus (John 12:21, King James Version).

One evening after a church service, revivalist Vance Havner told the song leader, "We had a good service."

This perceptive young man replied, "Too good."

Havner was puzzled. "What do you mean?"

"I know this crowd," the song leader answered bluntly. "They should have been on their faces before God, but everybody settled for a nice, good service."

What a mistake! Sometimes the good is the enemy of the best.

When certain devout Greeks visiting Jerusalem saw the public acclaim Jesus was receiving (see v. 19), they asked Philip if they could see the Lord. There were many religious festivities in progress, all good in themselves. But seeing the Messiah himself was deemed far better! And as Jesus indicated in verses 23-26, enjoying a *celebrated* Christ is good, but serving a *rejected* Christ is best of all.

What did those Gentile seekers learn? Attending public worship is good, but seeing Jesus is better. And a commitment to Christ that is worth dying for . . . is best of all.

Lord, as I spend time with You, help me never to settle for second best. In the name of the Father, the Son, and the Holy Spirit, I pray. Amen.

Scripture: John 12:20-26
Song: *"Teach Me Thy Way, O Lord"*

From this meditation today, I will pray . . .
Adoration _____

Confession _____

Thanksgiving _____

Supplication _____

From this meditation today, I will . . .
Think _____

Say _____

Do _____

SEARCH THE WORD
To see Jesus. To sit in His presence. To hear His gracious words. Pure joy!

September 25

Crawling with Fear

Fear not them which kill the body, but are not able to kill the soul: but rather fear him which is able to destroy both soul and body in hell (Matthew 10:28, *King James Version*).

Scripture: Matthew 10:24-33
Song: *"God, the Omnipotent!"*

From this meditation today, I will pray . . .
Adoration _____
_____
_____

Confession _____
_____
_____

Thanksgiving _____
_____
_____

Supplication _____
_____
_____

From this meditation today, I will . . .
Think _____
_____
_____

Say _____
_____
_____

Do _____
_____
_____
_____

Olga stood quietly against a wooden background in a popular vaudeville show while her partner threw knives and hatchets into the wood around her. All at once, during the act, she let out a scream and promptly fainted. The audience feared the worst. But when she was revived in her dressing room, Olga explained: "I suddenly felt something crawling on my leg and discovered a spider. Oh, I'm *so* afraid of spiders!"

As ridiculous as this performer's phobia in the face of a far greater danger, fearing human beings more than God is even more absurd. That was precisely Jesus' point in today's passage. Without the wrong perspective, we all tend to overreact to persecution.

Jesus reminded His followers to expect ill-treatment (see vv. 24, 25). When it happened, and it would, He told them to remember God's perfect knowledge of the minutest details and His complete control over everything. Finally, Jesus made loyal witness the "make-or-break test" of discipleship (vv. 31, 32). When we remember these things, we will stand firm with nerves of steel.

Heavenly Father, *let me behold You with the eyes of faith until all my fears melt away in Your presence. In Jesus' name I pray. Amen.*

SPOTLIGHT
Next Week's Lesson

Fear inhibits service;
service pushes aside fear.

September 26

No Time Like the Present

The end of all things is at hand: be ye therefore sober, and watch unto prayer (1 Peter 4:7, King James Version).

"This time, like all times, is a very good one, if we but know what to do with it," said Ralph Waldo Emerson. I think the apostle Peter would have agreed. Certainly a bad time is a good time to live for the Lord. To do any less would only make a bad time worse. And if that *bad* time is also the *last* time, then there is even more reason to have a God-focused life.

With the prophetic clock nearing the midnight hour, Peter offers clear instruction regarding the use of time. First, a sober mind and a prayerful heart will preserve our integrity in an evil world (v. 7). Second, we need a fervent love that forgives all wrongs (v. 8). Third, a mutual hospitality and a gracious sharing of God's gifts—be they spiritual or material—will promote healthy relationships (vv. 8-10). And fourth, we need a truth-centered, Spirit-empowered ministry that brings glory to God (v. 11).

Emerson was right. This is a very good time, if we know what to do with it.

Dear Father in Heaven, *help me to live by Your agenda, today and always. May my life be the summary of what I have learned in Your Word, whether I face joyful prospects or painful trials. In the name of Your Son, my Savior, I pray. Amen.*

Scripture: 1 Peter 4:7-11
Song: "This Is the Day"

From this meditation today, I will pray...
Adoration _____
_____
_____

Confession _____
_____
_____

Thanksgiving _____
_____
_____

Supplication _____
_____
_____

From this meditation today, I will...
Think _____
_____
_____

Say _____
_____
_____

Do _____
_____
_____

SEARCH THE WORD
Those who live with the end in mind cannot but pray and maintain a somber mood.

September 27

Your Cash Advance

So when even was come, the lord of the vineyard saith unto his steward, Call the laborers, and give them their hire, beginning from the last unto the first (Matthew 20:8, *King James Version*).

Scripture: Matthew 20:1-16
Song: *"Jesus Paid It All"*

From this meditation today, I will pray...
Adoration _____
_____
_____

Confession _____
_____
_____

Thanksgiving _____
_____
_____

Supplication _____
_____
_____

From this meditation today, I will...
Think _____
_____
_____

Say _____
_____
_____

Do _____
_____
_____
_____

Christian F. Gellert (1715-1769), a German philosopher and author, died at Leipzig where he had been professor of theology at the university. In his final moments, he made this simple request: "Only repeat to me the name of Jesus. Whenever I hear it, or pronounce it myself, I feel myself refreshed with fresh joy. God be praised, only one hour more." All who have served our kind master with a sincere and grateful heart have made similar statements.

Today's parable teaches the prospect of heavenly rewards. And though some will receive more than others, we all have more than we deserve. To be hired at all, that is, chosen to salvation (v. 16), is itself no small compensation. The day we got on His payroll, whether at sunrise or near midnight—or anywhere in between—was the day our lives obtained real value and purpose.

As Gellert learned, just thinking of Jesus is like receiving a generous cash advance before the big payday.

Lord, when I finally stand before You, face to face, I long to hear "Well done, thou good and faithful servant." Thank You for making my life useful in an aimless world. And thank You, as well, for the prospect of the perfect world to come. In Your holy name I pray. Amen.

SPOTLIGHT
Next Week's Lesson

Though not the only nor the primary motivation for service, payment for services done is godly and delightful.

September 28

Back to Work!

Whosoever will be great among you, let him be your minister; and whosoever will be chief among you, let him be your servant (Matthew 20:26, 27, *King James Version*).

Shortly after Jesus told the disciples of His approaching death, the mother of James and John appeared with a special request. She asked the Lord if her two sons could sit on each side of Him in the kingdom. Jesus answered in two parts.

First, He asked whether they could endure the bitter cup of suffering that would precede such an honor. They answered, "We are able." Jesus affirmed their painful destiny, but that alone would not guarantee this position.

The second qualification rested solely with Jesus' heavenly Father (see v. 23). The will of God determines all.

This ambitious mother reminds all parents to beware of wanting more for their children than God intends. To overshoot God's plan is as disastrous as undershooting it. In fact, even attempting to secure an unfair advantage will create a backlash, as it did for James and John (see v. 24) real path to greatness—humble service.

Seeking personal glory just wastes time. Let's get back to work.

Lord, *forgive me when I think more of status than service. The only favor I ask is Your blessing on my humble work. In Jesus' name, amen.*

Scripture: Matthew 20:17-28
Song: *"Work, for the Night Is Coming"*

From this meditation today, I will pray . . .

Adoration _____

Confession _____

Thanksgiving _____

Supplication _____

From this meditation today, I will . . .

Think _____

Say _____

Do _____

SEARCH THE WORD

*Service is glorious.
Selfishness is shameful.
When will we ever learn?*

September 29

Who Was Jesus?

The life appeared; we have seen it and testify to it, and we proclaim to you the eternal life, which was with the Father and has appeared to us (1 John 1:2).

Scripture: 1 John 1:1-4
Song: *"Be Unto Your Name"*

From this meditation today, I will pray...

Adoration _____

Confession _____

Thanksgiving _____

Supplication _____

From this meditation today, I will...

Think _____

Say _____

Do _____

September 29, 30. **Stacey Weeks** *lives in Moose Jaw, Saskatchewan, with her husband and daughter. She writes and also works with children at the local YMCA.*

Is Jesus really God? Was He simply a teacher, a "good man," or an impostor? Movies like *The DaVinci Code* spur heated conversations around the watercooler, in the break room, and the coffeehouse. Who was Jesus?

The search for answers arises in each generation. When the apostle John wrote 1 John around AD 85–90, he was addressing this question. He penned this letter to reassure Christians in their faith and to expose false teachings.

A main problem in the church at this time was conformity to the world's standards and a lack of commitment, much like the challenges we face today. John wanted to put the church back on track as he recapped what he'd witnessed. His eyewitness account is as much a reminder to us as it was to several Gentile congregations in his own day. God, who was from the beginning, came to earth. John heard Him, saw Him, and touched Him. This man Jesus forgave sins, healed the sick, raised the dead. Who else but God in the flesh could do that?

Lord, *may I never forget the depth of Your sacrifice or water down the intensity of Your message. Thank You, in Your precious name. Amen.*

SPOTLIGHT
Next Week's Lesson
Peter would declare it powerfully at Pentecost: "God has made this Jesus . . . both Lord and Christ" (Acts 2:36).

September 30

Victory in Jesus

God raised him from the dead, freeing him from the agony of death, because it was impossible for death to keep its hold on him (Acts 2:24).

One of the last things my Nan said before she died was: "We may not see each other again on earth, but I will be waiting for you in Heaven. Because you believe, our good-bye is not forever."

I find great comfort in that statement. I will see Nan again, because, as she did, I believe in the power of the resurrection and the power in the blood of Christ. There is nothing stronger than it or more important than what you believe regarding it. The power of Jesus' blood has washed me clean and secured my home in Heaven. The resurrection confirms Christ's victory and His control over everything. That belief has changed my life.

In verse 24, Peter began with a statement about the resurrection because it could not be denied. The crowd teemed with people who would verify the event. This enabled Peter to base his message on an unshakable foundation. His audience was witness. They saw it happen. He challenged them to allow it to change their lives. And that is the challenge to all of us to this present hour.

Father, *may I live each day assured of Your victory over death. May I remember that my old life is dead and buried, and I have been resurrected into a new life with Your Son, Jesus. In His name I pray. Amen.*

Scripture: Acts 2:22-35
Song: *"You Are My King"*

From this meditation today, I will pray . . .

Adoration _____

Confession _____

Thanksgiving _____

Supplication _____

From this meditation today, I will . . .

Think _____

Say _____

Do _____

SEARCH THE WORD

Death has strength, but it also has limits. It could not hold Christ; it will not hold the Christian.

—Philippians 2:10

October

GROWTH OF THE NEW COMMUNITY

In him you . . . are being built together to become a dwelling in which God lives by his Spirit.
—Ephesians 2:22

Photo © SW Productions

October 1

The Purpose of Church

They devoted themselves to the apostles' teaching and to the fellowship, to the breaking of bread and to prayer (Acts 2:42).

Scripture: Acts 2:37-47
Song: *"Revive Us Again"*

From this meditation today, I will pray . . .
Adoration _____
_____
_____

Confession _____
_____
_____

Thanksgiving _____
_____
_____

Supplication _____
_____
_____

From this meditation today, I will . . .
Think _____
_____
_____

Say _____
_____
_____

Do _____
_____
_____

I have a friend who is disillusioned by the church. He believes that the cruelest criticism, the juiciest gossip, and the most smug superiority take place on Sunday mornings. He chooses not to follow a God who seemingly prompts this type of response in His children.

It saddens me that this has been his church experience. And it raises a serious question in my mind: What kind of church does God want us to be? According to the apostle Peter, a church gathering should be a place where we are devoted to teaching, fellowship, communion, and prayer. God should be completely free to work within the church, resulting in deep devotion to Him. It should be a gathering where people can find help and comfort. It should be a place where we can worship God without shame.

What a wonderful testimony when seekers see us praising God and enjoying each other's fellowship—and having a good time doing it. When we are truly devoted to God's teaching, we are fulfilling His purposes for the church: reaching the lost, to bring glory to His name.

Lord, *help me take the first steps in personal renewal so that my whole church family can return to Your purposes for us. In Jesus' name, amen.*

SPOTLIGHT
Next Week's Lesson

When the church is on purpose, that purpose is seen to be simple and powerful.

October 1–5. **Stacey Weeks** lives in Moose Jaw, Saskatchewan, with her husband and daughter. She writes and also works with children at the local YMCA.

October 2

The Family Business

Again Jesus said, "Peace be with you! As the Father has sent me, I am sending you" (John 20:21).

I have a friend who owns a chain of veterinarian clinics. His eldest daughter has chosen the field of animal medicine, like her father. She has two sons, and one day she will pass her love and compassion for God's creatures down to them, should they choose to follow in her footsteps. It's a family business.

My husband's uncle is a schoolteacher. His daughter and son are also schoolteachers. He has passed his love of learning and teaching down to his children. It's a family business.

All Christians are part of the family of God, and that family, too, has a business. Jesus says in verse 21, "As the father sent me, I am sending you." The legacy has been passed down to us to fulfill the Spirit-minded mission of our Father.

Just as my friends received special training to learn their family trades, Jesus gives us the Holy Spirit to empower us to reach the lost. We are to preach the good news about Jesus, teach our children to follow in the footsteps of their heavenly Father, and embrace the family business.

Father, *thank You for reminding me that I have a great legacy to pass on to my children. Grant me the boldness, courage, and compassion needed to carry out Your family business. Through Christ I pray. Amen.*

SEARCH THE WORD
Do you feel sent? Where are you going? And why?

Scripture: John 20:19-23
Song: *"Jesus Bids Us Shine"*

From this meditation today, I will pray . . .

Adoration _____

Confession _____

Thanksgiving _____

Supplication _____

From this meditation today, I will . . .

Think _____

Say _____

Do _____

October 3

The Buzz Around Town

So in Christ we who are many form one body, and each member belongs to all the others (Romans 12:5).

Scripture: Romans 12:3-8
Song: *"Make Me a Servant"*

From this meditation today, I will pray . . .
Adoration _____
_____
_____
Confession _____
_____
_____
Thanksgiving _____
_____
_____
Supplication _____
_____
_____

From this meditation today, I will . . .
Think _____
_____
_____
Say _____
_____
_____
Do _____
_____
_____
_____

While I watch a busy bee colony hum, I am awestruck with how God designs nature to speak to us. In a bee colony, the queen bee is in charge of reproducing; she keeps the hive buzzing. Drone bees are companions to the queen. Worker bees collect pollen and nectar and keep the hive cool by fanning their wings.

What would happen if one bee felt superior? The structure of the hive would collapse. Without the queen there is no colony. Without the drones there is no growth in the population. Without the workers, the bees would starve to death. Each function is essential to the health of the whole.

In some ways, the Christian life is like a busy hive. We are all gifted differently, but we need each other for the whole family to function effectively. We should not "think of [ourselves] more highly than [we] ought" (v. 3). We are one body of believers, with individual members, blessed with various gifts. If a bee colony can function as a healthy unit despite vast individual differences, then so can we.

Father, help me to be excited about the gifts with which You have blessed me—and not be jealous of another's. I have something to offer, and I do not need to be ashamed. Keep me faithful, then, in my particular ministry, focusing only on pleasing You. In the name of Christ, amen.

SPOTLIGHT
Next Week's Lesson

Fellowship is sharing
a purpose;
fellowship is sharing the load.

October 4

The Interpreter

All of them were filled with the Holy Spirit and began to speak in other tongues (Acts 2:4).

Raymond G. Gordon, Jr., is the editor of *Ethnologue: Languages of the World*, 15th Edition. This reference book lists 6,912 of the world's known languages. I imagine it is impossible to be fluent in them all! To fill this void, interpreters are employed in multicultural conference situations to translate questions or speeches into the mother tongue of the listening audience.

In the film *The Interpreter*, Nicole Kidman is employed to translate at a United Nations meeting. Imagine her surprise if, when the keynote presenter began to speak, he could miraculously talk in the native tongue of each represented country.

You might think "only in the movies," but you would be wrong. It happened years ago and is recorded in the book of Acts. Amazingly, individuals in an international crowd could recognize their own languages from the mouths of Galilean apostles declaring the wonder of God.

Historically, God has used the spoken word to reach people of all nationalities. In fact, He is speaking to you today. If your heart is open, You will hear the most wonderful things.

Open my ears, Lord. *I want to hear Your declarations of love, Your gentle corrections, and Your wise guidance in my life. In Jesus' name, amen.*

SEARCH THE WORD
Language barriers are no barrier at all to the Lord.

Scripture: Acts 2:1-13
Song: *"Open Our Eyes, Lord"*

From this meditation today, I will pray...
Adoration _____
_____
_____

Confession _____
_____
_____

Thanksgiving _____
_____
_____

Supplication _____
_____
_____

From this meditation today, I will...
Think _____
_____
_____

Say _____
_____
_____

Do _____
_____
_____
_____

October 5

Not Reformed, Reborn

*Then Peter stood up with the Eleven,
raised his voice and addressed the crowd*
(Acts 2:14).

Scripture: Acts 2:14-21
Song: *"Living for Jesus"*

From this meditation today, I will pray . . .
Adoration _____
_____
_____

Confession _____
_____
_____

Thanksgiving _____
_____
_____

Supplication _____
_____
_____

From this meditation today, I will . . .
Think _____
_____
_____

Say _____
_____
_____

Do _____
_____
_____

Peter's audacity while following Jesus could have discredited his entire ministry. He spoke without thinking, he was brazen and hasty, and he denied Jesus three times. What transforms such an impetuous man into one of the pillars of the church?

Peter became a natural leader of the disciples after Jesus ascended into Heaven. He was the first to stand up to the mocking crowd on the Day of Pentecost. This new Peter was forgiven and restored, no longer arrogant and cowardly, but humble and bold. The Holy Spirit gave him a powerful confidence to speak up. He was reborn.

Despite the sins that once entangled us, we too can be reborn. God can take the personality traits that led to our fall and use them to bring Him glory.

God didn't give Peter a personality transplant. He was still bold, daring, and spontaneous. But through the new birth Peter received the indwelling Holy Spirit. Now Peter could use his traits to draw people closer to God, rather than fulfill his own self-centered plans.

Lord, *help me to recognize the personality traits in me that can become either a blessing or a curse. Then, transform these traits into qualities that will bless Your name and draw others closer to You. I pray this prayer in the name of Jesus, my merciful Savior and Lord. Amen.*

SPOTLIGHT
Next Week's Lesson

Church without preaching?
May as well have a refrigerator
with no food.

October 6

Secret Weapon

Then Peter, filled with the Holy Spirit, said to them, "Honorable leaders and elders of our nation"
(Acts 4:8, The Living Bible).

When has someone rained on your parade? We all occasionally face those times when our best efforts seem unappreciated or misunderstood. It happens at home, school, and church—and it happened to the disciples.

It had been an intense time in Jerusalem. The wild series of events following Pentecost were anything but business-as-usual. Healings of body and spirit created joy in some but skepticism, and even hostility, in others.

Peter and John found themselves right in the middle of all the uproar. But notice Peter's attitude. He had been frozen by fear until the fire of God's Spirit transformed him. He and John prayed, and healing happened. How could anyone have a problem with that?

But they did. No matter how sincere our service for the Lord, sooner or later someone or something will try to discourage us. The next time it happens to you, don't try to hang in there by your own strength. The "secret weapon" of the Holy Spirit, so available to Peter and John, is also yours for the asking.

Gracious Father, when I care too much about what others say or think, lift my focus higher, all the way to Your face. In Jesus' name, amen.

Scripture: Acts 4:1-12
Song: *"Holy Spirit, from on High"*

From this meditation today, I will pray...
Adoration _____
_____
_____
Confession _____
_____
_____
Thanksgiving _____
_____
_____
Supplication _____
_____

From this meditation today, I will...
Think _____
_____
_____
Say _____
_____
_____
Do _____
_____
_____

SEARCH THE WORD

Here is Peter's key to success: using God's power to confront and overwhelm human power.

October 6–12. **Shirley Leonard,** from Millville, Pennsylvania, has been a minister's wife for decades. She enjoys reading, painting, and being a church secretary.

October 7

Attitude Adjustment

When the Council saw the boldness of Peter and John, and could see that they were obviously uneducated non-professionals, they were amazed and realized what being with Jesus had done for them!
(Acts 4:13, *The Living Bible*).

Scripture: Acts 4:13-22
Song: *"Breathe on Me, Breath of God"*

From this meditation today, I will pray . . .

Adoration _____
_____
_____

Confession _____
_____
_____

Thanksgiving _____
_____
_____

Supplication _____
_____
_____

From this meditation today, I will . . .

Think _____
_____
_____

Say _____
_____
_____

Do _____
_____
_____
_____

In 1965, a shy girl from a dairy farm in New York was trying to fit in as a freshman at Lycoming College in Williamsport, Pennsylvania. Everybody else seemed more self-confident. How could she ever feel as if she belonged?

I was that girl, and the only way I pulled it off was by staying close to Linda, a friend from home. She was as bubbly and friendly as I was reserved and quiet. Being with her, I dared to smile and relax.

In the face of the unfair accusations of the Sanhedrin, Peter and John could have reacted with either violent anger or cowering fear. They did neither. Peter spoke with respect and confidence. John wasn't cowering, but bold. The Council was impressed. Being with Jesus had made them noticeably different.

Is there an area in your life in which you feel inept and inadequate? Spend some time right now with Jesus and let Him do an attitude adjustment.

Lord, I am too often fearful in my witness to You. Forgive me and transform me. Send your Holy Spirit to perform an extreme makeover in the musty corners of my mind and heart. Through Christ, amen.

SPOTLIGHT
Next Week's Lesson
When leaders are selected and blessed by the Spirit, human inadequacies become God's opportunities.

October 8

To Boldly Go

After this prayer, the building where they were meeting shook and they were all filled with the Holy Spirit and boldly preached God's message (Acts 4:31, *The Living Bible*).

Cuddled together on the couch in front of our television set, my husband and I eagerly awaited the opening line from *Star Trek: Next Generation*. Captain Jean-Luc Picard's deep voice said the words we never tired of hearing regarding the mission of the starship *Enterprise* "to boldly go where no one has gone before." We couldn't wait to see what happened next.

Released from prison, Peter and John joined the rest of the disciples and a crowd of believers in a prayer service. Ho hum? Not on your life! If you look seriously at this passage, you'll find a scene more exciting than any sci-fi fantasy. This was real, and it was full of power. The prayer takes up only a single paragraph, but it changed everything in that situation. Drawing an analogy between current events from Rome to Jerusalem, they invited God to send boldness and healing power to Christ's followers. The answer came in a literal shaking of the building—and a spiritual shaking that would change countless lives.

O Lord God, *I am so grateful for Your Holy Spirit. Thank You for the sweeping difference He makes in my life, replacing confidence for cowardice. Equip me to boldly go where I have seldom been—into lives that need the radical shaking of Your matchless love. In Jesus' name, amen.*

SEARCH THE WORD
If God wants someone's attention, He can get it. Does He have yours?

Scripture: Acts 4:23-31
Song: *"Be Strong and Take Courage"*

From this meditation today, I will pray . . .

Adoration _____

Confession _____

Thanksgiving _____

Supplication _____

From this meditation today, I will . . .

Think _____

Say _____

Do _____

October 9

Radical Righteousness

The property was yours to sell or not, as you wished. And after selling it, it was yours to decide how much to give. How could you do a thing like this? You weren't lying to us, but to God (Acts 5:4, The Living Bible).

Scripture: Acts 5:1-11

Song: *"Truehearted, Wholehearted, Faithful and Loyal"*

From this meditation today, I will pray . . .

Adoration _____

_____

_____

Confession _____

_____

_____

Thanksgiving _____

_____

_____

Supplication _____

_____

_____

From this meditation today, I will . . .

Think _____

_____

_____

Say _____

_____

_____

Do _____

_____

_____

_____

_____

I wish I could just skip over certain passages in the Bible—and this is one of them. A husband and wife sell property but give just part of the money to the early church, claiming it's the full price. Each of them dies instantly after telling that lie.

I try to push away an awful idea. Isn't God overreacting? But I know, way down deep, that God's holiness is as perfect as His justice. I may never really understand this passage, but it teaches me something I need to learn. Ananias and Sapphira wanted to look more pious and generous than they were willing to actually be. The Father who created them and loved them saw right through their phoniness. And clearly, at the very beginning of the church, God's serious intentions must be established—for the good of all the believers at that time and for all who would follow down through the centuries.

Ouch. He sees through my own phoniness! Leaning on His mercy, I dare not underestimate His righteousness.

Search me, Father, and shine light on the hidden places in my heart. Forgive me the times I so easily make excuses for my sin. Teach me to walk in holiness, knowing You alone are holy. In Jesus' name, amen.

SPOTLIGHT
Next Week's Lesson

God's church needs our gifts to bless its growth, but God needs our righteousness even more.

October 10

Get a Grip

My advice is, leave these men alone. If what they teach and do is merely on their own, it will soon be overthrown
(Acts 5:38, *The Living Bible*).

Today a local high school outlawed "hoodies." Those cozy sweatshirts have become a staple in many wardrobes, but it seems they've also become places to hide everything from music to weapons.

"What's the world coming to?" We hear people say that, and we think it ourselves. Reading the daily paper or watching the TV news can be detrimental to our mental health! And sometimes national and world events cause even people of deep faith to get nervous. School violence, political scandals, terrorist threats—it's enough to make you want to crawl back under the covers and hide.

The situation in the early church wasn't much rosier. Danger awaited from the Romans, and sometimes from the Jewish authorities, for any who dared to disagree with them. And yet, here are the disciples, stubbornly refusing to stop speaking about Jesus. Their lives had been so fundamentally changed by the Messiah that they could hardly go about living without sharing what they had experienced of Him. They had been gripped by a force more powerful than fear.

Lord, many things drain my courage and attack my faith. I long to grip Your reality so firmly that all fear must fall away. Through Christ, amen.

Scripture: Acts 5:27-39
Song: *"Be Not Dismayed"*

From this meditation today, I will pray...
Adoration _____
Confession _____
Thanksgiving _____
Supplication _____

From this meditation today, I will...
Think _____
Say _____
Do _____

SEARCH THE WORD

*Truth conquers a lie.
To think a lie is winning or will win is to believe Satan's lie.*

October 11

Gossiping the Gospel

But the believers who had fled Jerusalem went everywhere preaching the Good News about Jesus!
(Acts 8:4, *The Living Bible*).

Scripture: Acts 8:1-8
Song: *"Tell It Out with Gladness"*

From this meditation today, I will pray . . .
Adoration _____

Confession _____

Thanksgiving _____

Supplication _____

From this meditation today, I will . . .
Think _____

Say _____

Do _____

In study hall, my friend Linda and I passed notes to each other written in French. We had two reasons. We needed the practice and somehow, we thought, if we were caught, the teachers on duty wouldn't know what we were saying. It never occurred to us that even the shop or drivers' ed teachers might have taken French at some point in their academic careers. And the threat of detention couldn't squelch our need to share our lives with each other.

After Stephen's murder, the believers scattered in many directions. So would they keep quiet about their beliefs after seeing what happened to him? Talking about the Nazarene could be hazardous to their health, so why borrow trouble?

But the Bible paints a vivid picture of men whose need to tell the Christ story was stronger than their fear. Like Linda and me, they were compelled to share their journey. As teenagers, we wrote about our parents, our boyfriends, and our dreams. The disciples talked about a person who had changed their souls. No comparison.

Lord, it is all too tempting to gossip about trivial things. Help me to talk instead about what matters—to talk about You. In Christ's name, amen.

SPOTLIGHT
Next Week's Lesson

God's plan is simple: believers go everywhere with the good news.

October 12

Ripples of Redemption

God's message was preached in ever-widening circles, and the number of disciples increased vastly in Jerusalem; and many of the Jewish priests were converted too (Acts 6:7, The Living Bible).

From the warm security of the dining room window, I watched the breeze kick up ripples on the pond. The movement was beautiful, as if God were creating a unique choreography for the falling leaves, a performance just for me. My spirits lifted out of the doldrums I'd been experiencing. I nestled in His presence, soaking up the wonder of the scene.

A phone call jarred me back to earth. When I returned to the window, the wind had died down, and the glorious dance was over. Then came the splash. A frog had jumped into the water, creating a series of ripples that spread halfway across the pond. The frog wasn't very big, but the effects were far-reaching.

The persecution of the early believers could have ended the work of Christ. Logically, it should have. But in God's economy, the subtraction of freedom resulted in the multiplication of ministry. Like ripples in a pond, the glory spread in expanding circles—reaching down through time, even to you and to me.

God, I am grateful for those who've gone before me, spreading Your truth. Help me carry on their work in some way today. In Jesus' name, amen.

Scripture: Acts 6
Song: *"People Need the Lord"*

From this meditation today, I will pray . . .
Adoration _____

Confession _____

Thanksgiving _____

Supplication _____

From this meditation today, I will . . .
Think _____

Say _____

Do _____

SEARCH THE WORD
Wherever we live, we should help to send out the ripples of God's redemption.

October 13

I Didn't Make It Up

The gospel I preached is not something that man made up (Galatians 1:11).

Scripture: Galatians 1:11-17
Song: *"Stand by the Bible"*

From this meditation today, I will pray . . .
Adoration _____
_____
_____

Confession _____
_____
_____

Thanksgiving _____
_____
_____

Supplication _____
_____
_____

From this meditation today, I will . . .
Think _____
_____
_____

Say _____
_____
_____

Do _____
_____
_____

In Bible college I learned that some time back in the AD 300s, when a church council met in Carthage to discuss which books had been received as genuine Scripture, they applied four tests to each document considered. Those tests involved analyzing apostolicity, universality, content, and inspiration.

Each document had to come from an apostle or a close associate of an apostle. It had to have been widely accepted and used by the churches down through the years. The subject matter had to conform with the established *regula fidei* (the "rule of faith") and finally, the document would show evidence of divine inspiration.

Paul had once been a persecutor of Christians, thinking he was doing God's work by ridding the world of people who believed in Jesus. However, as he turned his life over to the Lord, he recognized that, without a doubt, men did not make up the gospel of Jesus Christ. For him, truth rang out as the gospel came straight from the throne of God. We can be sure of that too. We can trust our Bible.

Father, *I'm so grateful for the written Word of God, the Bible, that You have given us. Keep me reading it every day! In Jesus' name, amen.*

October 13–19. **Dell Smith Klein,** *of Yarnell, Arizona, is a writer, singer, and storyteller who travels throughout the West sharing the gospel of Jesus.*

SPOTLIGHT
Next Week's Lesson
Witnessed and revealed—that was Paul's experience with the gospel from the dusty Damascus road to evangelistic success in Rome.

October 14

It's Not a Lie!

I assure you before God that what I am writing you is no lie. . . . "The man who formerly persecuted us is now preaching the faith he once tried to destroy" (Galatians 1:20, 23).

When Dale applied for ministerial credentials, those in charge requested that he write out his testimony. Dale's strong relationship with God may have been evident to those closest to him, but church leaders needed to examine the evidence of his life before they presented him with those important credentials. Dale wrote several pages that began, "I was saved by faith, through the blood of Jesus Christ." He wrote about attending college and seminary, and about various retreats he'd attended.

In our Bible reading today, Paul longed for his associates to be assured that he was telling the truth. He wanted all around him to know of his relationship with the Lord. People knew he was the one who had persecuted the church, but they began to see him in a new light. Their previous enemy had suddenly met Jesus on the road to Damascus. As Paul told his skeptics these truths, their hearts opened to him. In fact, they began to praise God heartily because of him.

Dear Heavenly Father, *I long to be an asset to the church and not a hindrance. Thank You for helping me to maintain the truth in my relationships with others. I can be that asset only as I share, honestly and fairly, with others. In the name of Jesus, my Savior, I pray. Amen.*

Scripture: Galatians 1:18-24
Song: *"I've Found a Friend"*

From this meditation today, I will pray . . .
Adoration _____

Confession _____

Thanksgiving _____

Supplication _____

From this meditation today, I will . . .
Think _____

Say _____

Do _____

SEARCH THE WORD
A transformed life is irrefutable. What about yours?

October 15

You Want Me to Give Up What?

Whatever was to my profit I now consider loss for the sake of Christ
(Philippians 3:7).

Scripture: Philippians 3:2-11
Song: *"Bless His Holy Name"*

From this meditation today, I will pray . . .
Adoration _____
_____
_____

Confession _____
_____
_____

Thanksgiving _____
_____
_____

Supplication _____
_____
_____

From this meditation today, I will . . .
Think _____
_____
_____

Say _____
_____
_____

Do _____
_____
_____
_____

My husband and I decided to downsize. We held a yard sale and took some items to a charity thrift store. When we moved into a one-bedroom cottage, I needed to downsize a bit more. Yet we found that we spent more time traveling from place to place in our little travel trailer then we did in our cottage.

Still, I clung to some of the things I had accumulated over the years. I especially wanted to keep my grandmother's gravy boat, the doll house my husband and I built during our first year as a married couple, and a trunk full of photo slides. I wasn't so willing to give those things up.

Paul talked about things he *willingly* gave up for Christ. As I read today's passage in the Bible, I found myself becoming more willing to let "things" go. I took grandma's gravy boat to the antique store. The church nursery could use that sturdy doll house. And my daughters are dividing the slides among them. I can see now that none of those things are as important as serving the Lord.

Dear Heavenly Father, *because of Your provision over the years, I have all that I need. Thank You. Keep me in Your will as I seek to serve You. And may I always hold my belongings with open hands, knowing they are "on loan" from You. In the name of Your Son, my Savior, I pray. Amen.*

SPOTLIGHT
Next Week's Lesson

Paul was a respected, trusted Jewish scholar. He had much to give up, but he willingly did.

October 16

Wild Woman for God

The church . . . was strengthened; and encouraged by the Holy Spirit, it grew in numbers, living in the fear of the Lord (Acts 9:31).

Linda was such a wild woman that I wondered how she ended up attending our conservative church. She had no concept of church manners. She hugged people and kissed them on the mouth. In the middle of the sermon, she'd call out a question. Our minister would respond to her questions and go on teaching.

Not long after she began attending church, Linda had a stroke. She could hardly talk, and her right side was completely paralyzed. As she began to recover, she learned to write with her left hand so she could fill in the blanks in a women's Bible study workbook.

Linda was baptized that spring. Two more strokes followed, but her infirmity never dampened her enthusiasm for life or for the Lord. She volunteered to help with Vacation Bible School and made pizza for the youth group. This wild woman for God passed away in September. Her encouragement and enthusiasm for life continues to spur us on.

Dear Heavenly Father, *it is with people like Linda on my mind that I come to You today. They may not know all the rules, yet they encourage and bless me as vessels of the Holy Spirit. I lift a thankful heart for them. In the holy name of Jesus, my Lord and Savior, I pray. Amen.*

Scripture: Acts 9:22-31
Song: *"Jesus, Lover of My Soul"*

From this meditation today, I will pray . . .
Adoration _____

Confession _____

Thanksgiving _____

Supplication _____

From this meditation today, I will . . .
Think _____

Say _____

Do _____

SEARCH THE WORD

"Wild living" can be God-directed instead of hell-bent.

October 17

Grape Bubble Gum

My God will meet all your needs according to his glorious riches in Christ Jesus (Philippians 4:19).

Scripture: Philippians 4:10-20
Song: *"Jesus Loves the Little Children"*

From this meditation today, I will pray . . .
Adoration _____
_____
_____

Confession _____
_____
_____

Thanksgiving _____
_____
_____

Supplication _____
_____
_____

From this meditation today, I will . . .
Think _____
_____
_____

Say _____
_____
_____

Do _____
_____
_____
_____

Jobless and near the end of his savings, Brad prayed for his family's needs. One day, in the grocery store, his 6-year-old begged for grape bubble gum. Brad hated to refuse, but even that small purchase wasn't in the budget. Brad could hardly see through his tears as he drove home. When he pulled into the driveway, he noticed brown bags sitting beside the front door. Inside he found groceries and . . . grape bubble gum! That small gift encouraged him to remember that God meets needs—and even throws in extra blessings from time to time.

Paul poured out his heart concerning the Philippians' spiritual need before expressing his gratitude for the gifts the church had sent with Epaphroditus. When he used the words "God will meet all your needs according to his glorious riches in Christ Jesus," he was making sure his readers understood that it was not to them, or to himself, but to God that their gratitude belonged. It is a joy to know that God meets our needs. And He meets them far beyond our expectations.

Almighty and everlasting Father, *thank You for meeting my needs, and thank You for the abundance with which You meet them. Like Paul, I recognize that You supply all things according to Your riches in Christ Jesus. In His precious name I pray. Amen.*

SPOTLIGHT
Next Week's Lesson

Up until his encounter with Christ, Paul depended on himself. Later he knew, "God's grace is sufficient."

October 18

Drums? O, No!

"Who are you, Lord?" Saul asked. "I am Jesus whom you are persecuting" (Acts 9:5, 6).

Saul thought he was doing a good work for God. Instead, it was the Lord himself he was persecuting.

On Wednesday nights our church music is upbeat and joyful. So, one night a 15-year-old brought his drums and set them up on the platform so he could participate with the worship team.

The following Sunday morning, a church member insisted that the drums be removed. I explained that the boy wasn't planning to play drums on Sunday morning. And I also shared my concern that if the church rejected the boy's music he might himself feel rejected by the church. As the worship team sang that morning, the complainer sat with folded arms and an angry face.

Sometime during the service, though, the Lord spoke to her heart. Afterwards, she apologized to the minister and to the worship team. The woman thought she was upholding the integrity of the church. Instead, her attitude was hurtful. Like Saul, she had it wrong. But also like Saul, she set it right.

Heavenly Father, help me not to look down on those who are new to the faith. Help me to recognize that I might discourage and defeat others with negative words and actions. May I always remain positive and encouraging. Through Christ I pray. Amen.

SEARCH THE WORD

It is always possible to be sincerely wrong. Wisdom trumps sincerity.

Scripture: Acts 9:1-9
Song: *"He's the Lord of Glory"*

From this meditation today, I will pray . . .

Adoration _____

Confession _____

Thanksgiving _____

Supplication _____

From this meditation today, I will . . .

Think _____

Say _____

Do _____

October 19

Just As I Am

The Lord said to Ananias, "Go! This man is my chosen instrument to carry my name before the Gentiles and their kings and before the people of Israel" (Acts 9:15).

Scripture: Acts 9:10-21
Song: *"Just As I Am"*

From this meditation today, I will pray . . .
Adoration _____
_____
_____
Confession _____
_____
_____
Thanksgiving _____
_____
_____
Supplication _____
_____
_____

From this meditation today, I will . . .
Think _____
_____
_____
Say _____
_____
_____
Do _____
_____
_____
_____

New in town, I went to the bank to set up an account. A teller with tattoos and a nose ring waited on me. In my desire to witness my faith to her, I asked if she'd lived in town long. "Only a few months," she said. "My husband is the minister of one of the town's churches."

I hoped my face didn't register my thorough surprise. As I walked away, I thought of an old song we used to sing, "Just as I Am." I wondered how often I looked at a person and failed to see the heart.

Saul was a man who wanted to do God's bidding. He thought those who believed in Jesus were a cult that needed to be destroyed. He sought out believers to throw them in jail and beat them.

And I imagine Ananias may have felt a bit like I did when I first met that tattooed bank teller. But I learned that because of her background and interests, the teller-minister's wife could reach people I might never even have the opportunity to meet. That was their ministry in town, and it was a good one.

Heavenly Father, *thank You for loving me just as I am. With a transparent heart I come to You and I ask that You look inside and change anything that does not line up with Your purposes. Through Christ my Lord, amen.*

SPOTLIGHT
Next Week's Lesson

Ananias "didn't want to,"
but he realized God's will is more
important than our wants.

October 20

Seeing with Jesus' Eyes

Lord, you know everyone's heart
(Acts 1:24).

Scripture: Acts 1:15-26
Song: *"Be Thou My Vision"*

This month I've been challenged repeatedly to serve as a minister of reconciliation. It's been difficult to be a peacemaker among those unwilling to forgive or admit mistakes. The hardest part has been trying to decipher the truth amidst so many differing versions of the same event. It's been an impossible task for me, but God's Word has been a lamp unto my feet.

As I sought direction in Scripture, my role became clear. Only God knows the heart. Only God knows the wounds and motivations behind people's perceptions and actions in life. My task was not to reconstruct every detail of what happened, but to love those who had been hurt while holding everyone accountable for their behaviors. As I focused on each individual involved, I resolved to help them come closer to God *through* their hurt rather than *around* it. It worked.

In 2 Corinthians 5:16, Paul exhorts us to "regard no one from a worldly point of view." When we view each other's weaknesses through the mind of Christ, we are better able to edify, to strengthen, to love.

Lord, *thank You for cleansing my heart with Christ's precious blood. Help me to see others through His eyes, with compassion. In His name, amen.*

From this meditation today, I will pray...
Adoration _____
_____
_____
Confession _____
_____
_____
Thanksgiving _____
_____
_____
Supplication _____
_____
_____

From this meditation today, I will...
Think _____
_____
_____
Say _____
_____
_____
Do _____
_____
_____

SEARCH THE WORD
No one can fool God. Everyone's heart tells the truth.

October 20–26. **Amaryllis Sanchez Wohlever** *is a medical doctor, wife of a seminarian, and mother of three fun-loving children. She enjoys dancing with them.*

October 21

Blessed Through Giving

Freely you have received, freely give
(Matthew 10:8).

Scripture: Matthew 10:1-15

Song: *"Praise God from Whom All Blessings Flow"*

From this meditation today, I will pray . . .
Adoration _____
_____
_____

Confession _____
_____
_____

Thanksgiving _____
_____
_____

Supplication _____
_____
_____

From this meditation today, I will . . .
Think _____
_____
_____

Say _____
_____
_____

Do _____
_____
_____

Giving and receiving are kingdom concepts. "We love because he first loved us" (1 John 4:19), and "God loves a cheerful giver" (2 Corinthians 9:7). All good things come from God and return to Him, from the very love that led to the whole creation, to our particular material possessions. God is maker, keeper, sustainer. In fact, Colossians 1:17 tells us that in Jesus "all things hold together." Indeed, "by him all things were created" (Colossians 1:16).

I have learned much about receiving and giving in the past two years. After working full-time for 10 years as a medical doctor, God called me to leave the exam room and follow my husband to seminary. We have received financial gifts and prayer support through many people who believe in our calling. At times, God's provision has been overwhelming, moving me to tears. As a result of the generosity showered upon us, I have become a more cheerful giver. I now live each day actively looking for opportunities to give.

By sharing with thankful hearts, we bless the giver from whom all blessings flow. Thanks be to God!

Father, *as I seek Your kingdom and Your righteousness, You faithfully meet all my needs. You are a God of blessing who sustains, who gives, who loves. Help me to give out of love as well. Through Christ, amen.*

SPOTLIGHT
Next Week's Lesson
Who in the church at Antioch imagined the scope of their decision? Then and now such decisions have unimaginable consequences.

October 22

All for His Sake

On my account you will be brought before governors and kings as witnesses to them and to the Gentiles (Matthew 10:18).

This passage reminds me of the reality and prominence of God's plan. When we interpret our earthly circumstances through worldly eyes, it is easy to despair. Sometimes things don't look so good for believers, do they? But when we perceive through the Spirit, we remember God's sovereignty and can trust that He is still in control.

After Saul's conversion, he was persecuted every day of his life. Jesus' words recorded by Matthew came true for Paul and for all the disciples. They were sent out "like sheep among wolves" (v. 16), but their persecution served to spread the gospel message throughout the world. There was a purpose in everything that the disciples had to endure, and the same is true for us.

God's rules have not changed, and "Jesus Christ is the same yesterday and today and forever" (Hebrews 13:8). In all things, God still "works for the good of those who love him, who have been called according to his purpose" (Romans 8:28).

Beloved, that includes you and me. He holds us in the palm of His hand. Hallelujah!

Lord, *thank You that my suffering is not in vain when I suffer with You and for You. Your grace is sufficient for me. In Jesus' name, amen.*

Scripture: Matthew 10:16-25
Song: *"He Has Promised"*

From this meditation today, I will pray...
Adoration _____
Confession _____
Thanksgiving _____
Supplication _____

From this meditation today, I will...
Think _____
Say _____
Do _____

SEARCH THE WORD
Whether to governors or kings or to neighbors and "nobodies," witness!

October 23

Sharpening Our Sword

I did not come to bring peace, but a sword
(Matthew 10:34).

Scripture: Matthew 10:32-39
Song: *"I Call on Thee, Lord Jesus Christ"*

From this meditation today, I will pray . . .

Adoration _____
_____
_____

Confession _____
_____
_____

Thanksgiving _____
_____
_____

Supplication _____
_____
_____

From this meditation today, I will . . .

Think _____
_____
_____

Say _____
_____
_____

Do _____
_____
_____

Three years ago I had a dream of Heaven. As I climbed up a ladder along with countless angels, my surroundings became progressively more colorful. There were rainbows, bubbles, waterfalls, and a blinding brilliance that filled me with joy.

Suddenly, I was taken to a place of despair and darkness. There were shrieks and gnashing of teeth, and I was desperate to leave. Then God's Word came to me, and I started repeating, "Greater is He who is in me than he who is in the world" (see 1 John 4:4). With each uttered word, I was moved farther from Hell and closer to glory. Finally, I was back in Heaven, and I woke up.

God's Word is powerful. When Jesus was tempted in the desert, He defeated the devil through the Word, the sword of the Spirit. God's Word is "living and active" (Hebrews 4:12). As we sharpen our Sword through use, we are rescued, healed, restored, renewed. The Word gives us victory.

The fact is, Jesus brought us a sword. He wants us to use it that we might live victoriously, just like Him.

Lord, *the words You speak are spirit and they are life. Stir up a hunger in my heart for the Word, that I may be transformed in my mind, having victory over all my foes. In the name of the Father, the Son, and the Holy Spirit, I pray. Amen.*

SPOTLIGHT
Next Week's Lesson

Paul's call was not to mend fences but to break them. The sword of the Spirit could do it.

October 24

Running After the Mystery

Have nothing to do with godless myths and old wives' tales; rather, train yourself to be godly (1 Timothy 4:7).

Today's passage warns us against distractions, especially verbal debates about doctrinal differences that lead nowhere. Rather than waste our time on such discussions, we should train ourselves in godliness. So what should this training look like?

In 1 Timothy 3:16, Paul says, "Beyond all question, the mystery of godliness is great: He appeared in a body, was vindicated by the Spirit, was seen by angels, was preached among the nations, was believed on in the world, was taken up in glory." Paul defines the mystery of godliness as the life, death, and resurrection of Jesus. As we train ourselves to be godly, we enter into the very life of Christ. Growing in godliness is all about becoming like Him by the power of the Spirit.

My intense training program in godliness took off when I started meditating on Scripture and applying its truth in my daily life. In Romans 12:1, 2, Paul exhorts us: "to offer your bodies as living sacrifices," choosing to be "transformed by the renewing of your mind."

God's Word is the treadmill of the spiritual life.

Father, as Your spoken Word brought forth the whole creation, speak life into me through Your written Word. Renew my mind, that I may be fully equipped for every good work. Through Christ I pray. Amen.

SEARCH THE WORD

Myths and tales or the "mystery of godliness"— which occupies your time?

Scripture: 1 Timothy 4:6-16
Song: *"So Let Our Lips and Lives Express"*

From this meditation today, I will pray...

Adoration _____

Confession _____

Thanksgiving _____

Supplication _____

From this meditation today, I will...

Think _____

Say _____

Do _____

October 25

How's Your Heart?

For this people's heart has become calloused; they hardly hear with their ears, and they have closed their eyes (Acts 28:27).

Scripture: Acts 28:25-31

Song: *"Purer in Heart, O God"*

From this meditation today, I will pray . . .

Adoration _____

_____

_____

Confession _____

_____

_____

Thanksgiving _____

_____

_____

Supplication _____

_____

_____

From this meditation today, I will . . .

Think _____

_____

_____

Say _____

_____

_____

Do _____

_____

_____

_____

A hard heart is far from God. It is unyielding, judgmental, uncaring, self-centered, and stubborn. A hard heart hates; it is unforgiving and exudes death. Conversely, a soft heart yields. It gives the benefit of the doubt. It considers the needs of others. It cares. It loves. A soft heart provides rich soil for a fruitful walk with God and one another.

Once God's love was poured into his heart, Paul lived yielded to the Holy Spirit. God's love transformed him. He received a new heart that was soft and eager to share Christ "boldly and without hindrance" (v. 31).

We, too, were given new hearts when we were baptized. Still, do you agree that our tendency to develop a hard heart is not completely gone? I am so thankful for the Holy Spirit's conviction; because He lives in me, I cannot keep a calloused heart for very long. Hardness of heart is uncomfortable within me now. Praise God!

The more we yield to the Holy Spirit, the softer our hearts become, open to receive and give the love of Christ, who is our life.

Lord, *I cannot live abundantly apart from You. Help me to yield to the Holy Spirit daily, that I may live in love each day. I pray this prayer in the precious name of Jesus my Savior. Amen.*

SPOTLIGHT
Next Week's Lesson

Calloused hearts are hard to soften. Paul would find that out daily.

October 26

Feeding on Him

While they were worshiping the Lord and fasting, the Holy Spirit said, . . . (Acts 13:2).

The more I yield to the Holy Spirit, the more I hear God's voice. I remember one of the first times this happened. It was 1998, shortly after I attended a retreat that changed my life. During the second night there, Jesus' love overwhelmed me; He ministered to the depths of my being.

Soon I started reading the Bible regularly. I was working as a family doctor at Hurlburt Field Air Force Base in Fort Walton Beach, Florida. I read the Bible during lunch and between patients. I learned to live in God's presence by abiding in His Word.

One afternoon, after several challenging patients, I needed a break. I headed to the snack bar when suddenly God spoke to my heart, saying, "Why not feed on Me instead?" Without missing a beat I headed back to my office, where the Lord fed my soul through His Word.

Jesus said, "My sheep listen to my voice; I know them, and they follow me" (John 10:27). Yes, Lord, You are my shepherd. I know Your voice, and I want to follow You.

Lord, *You said to Your disciples, "I have food to eat that you know nothing about" (John 4:32). Yes, Lord, I know. I've tasted it. There is no food like the sound of Your voice. Speak to me, Lord; open my ears to hear You and my heart to obey You. In Your name I pray. Amen.*

Scripture: Acts 13:1-12

Song: *"Speak, O Lord, Thy Servant Heareth"*

From this meditation today, I will pray . . .

Adoration

Confession

Thanksgiving

Supplication

From this meditation today, I will . . .

Think

Say

Do

SEARCH THE WORD
The one caught up in worship opens himself to the Spirit, for he's ready to listen.

October 27

Following in the Dark

Simon himself believed and was baptized. And he followed Philip everywhere, astonished by the great signs and miracles he saw
(Acts 8:13).

Scripture: Acts 8:12-25

Song: *"Where He Leads Me I Will Follow"*

From this meditation today, I will pray...

Adoration _____
_____
_____

Confession _____
_____
_____

Thanksgiving _____
_____
_____

Supplication _____
_____
_____

From this meditation today, I will...

Think _____
_____
_____

Say _____
_____
_____

Do _____
_____
_____

"Pastor, I think he exited here," I said attempting to keep our mini-mission team together as our two vans zoomed down the super highway. Following someone at night challenged everyone to stay alert. It took us about two minutes to realize I was wrong.

Although we started out following a trustworthy friend, the further we traveled the more difficult it was to distinguish his van from the rest. Our minister noted the frame around the license plate and focused on that. But I inadvertently misled him because I had no focal point.

Similarly, Simon started the Christian walk following his trustworthy friend, Philip. But Simon had his eyes on the wrong focal point. Even though Scripture says he believed, he continued traveling in spiritual darkness because he had not repented of his sins.

Often we wander off the straight and narrow path due to ignored sins. Repentance turns us around and steers us safely to our eternal destination.

Father, *thank You for the light of the world. I ask for Your guidance and strength to overcome the temptations of darkness. In Christ's name, amen.*

October 27-31. **Brenda K. Hendricks** *is a prolific writer from Freeburg, Pennsylvania. She grooms dogs in her spare time to support her writing habit.*

SPOTLIGHT
Next Week's Lesson
The Christians of the first century resemble those of the twenty-first: incomplete and flawed, in need of correction.

October 28

Desert Drive

Now an angel of the Lord said to Philip, "Go south to the road—the desert road—that goes down from Jerusalem to Gaza" (Acts 8:26).

"Why now? I thought my job was secure," Joyce cried when God redirected her course. Going back to school after the age of 50 shook her from her comfort zone and threw her onto a "desert road." On graduation day, every one of her classmates told her they never would have made it through the course without her friendship and encouragement. After Joyce's "desert" experience, God rewarded her with a job far better than she'd imagined.

When God redirected his course, Philip obeyed without complaint and traveled the designated desert road. Before long, he met a man sincerely searching for the truth. Philip then realized God's purpose in taking him from a successful ministry in Jerusalem. Placing him on the desert road involved encouraging others along the way.

Life is unpredictable. Jobs are terminated. Plans change. However, God is in control of all things and has a purpose for sending us out on the next desert road. When we are obedient, He opens Heaven's gates and pours blessings on us—and on each person we meet in Christ's name.

Omniscient Father, *You know the plans You hold for me, which may include a "desert road." Grant me wisdom cheerfully to encourage others along the way. In Jesus' name I pray. Amen.*

SEARCH THE WORD
There is no unlikely place for a gospel encounter, so go where God says.

Scripture: Acts 8:26-38
Song: *"God Leads Us Along"*

From this meditation today, I will pray . . .

Adoration _____

Confession _____

Thanksgiving _____

Supplication _____

From this meditation today, I will . . .

Think _____

Say _____

Do _____

October 29

Zealous for God

I was thoroughly trained in the law of our fathers and was just as zealous for God as any of you are today
(Acts 22:3).

Scripture: Acts 22:3-16

Song: *"There Is Power in the Blood"*

From this meditation today, I will pray . . .

Adoration _____

_____

_____

Confession _____

_____

_____

Thanksgiving _____

_____

_____

Supplication _____

_____

_____

From this meditation today, I will . . .

Think _____

_____

_____

Say _____

_____

_____

Do _____

_____

_____

_____

On August 14, 2003, a glitch in the nation's power grid stranded commuters in New York City, Detroit, and Toronto. Hordes of people groped their way in the darkness to surface from subways and swarmed around docks waiting for ferries to take them home.

Thousands of people, who lived within walking distance, plodded through the streets on that hot and muggy afternoon. Amazingly, most remained calm and eager to show the world they could persevere until they arrived home. Some walked over eight miles to their destinations—only to find that they couldn't enter the buildings. Although their zeal carried them to the door, they lacked the power that their electronic keys demanded for entry.

Before his conversion, Paul was much like those walkers. He knew where he wanted to go. He was willing to go the distance. However, had he continued on the course, he would have been extremely disappointed when he reached Heaven's gates. All the zeal he could muster would have lacked the power to gain entry.

There is only one source of power that unlocks the gates of Heaven: the blood of Jesus Christ.

O God, ignite in me the zeal to do good works empowered by Your Son's precious blood. In Jesus' name I pray. Amen.

SPOTLIGHT
Next Week's Lesson

Zeal can be directed or misdirected. Truth is the difference, as Paul's letters challenge.

October 30

Unlikely Recipients

Some of them . . . began to speak to Greeks also, telling them the good news about the Lord Jesus. . . . and a great number of people believed and turned to the Lord (Acts 11:20, 21).

Equipped with coupons for frozen treats redeemable at a local restaurant, I distributed goodwill to the obvious—parents with small children. Broadening my mission, I shared the coupons with department store cashiers and bank tellers. Sour faces softened into pleasant smiles. Wrinkles seemed to vanish from elderly faces as they thanked me for an unexpected favor. However, handing coupons to burly men seemed ridiculous because the coupon awarded a meager four-ounce serving of ice cream. Amazingly, even they received it with as much enthusiasm as the children.

Equipped with the good news of a risen Savior, first-century Christians traveled into distant cities sharing with the obvious—other Jews searching for the Messiah. Courageously, they broadened their mission by opening the gospel to unlikely recipients. Through God's mercy and grace, Greeks believed with as much enthusiasm as the children of Israel.

Sovereign God, *You know the ones who need to hear the good news of Jesus Christ. Equip me with enthusiasm and courage that I might share the hope that is in me with someone today. I pray this prayer in the name of Jesus, my merciful Savior and Lord. Amen.*

Scripture: Acts 11:19-26

Song: *"Tell Out the Wonderful Story"*

From this meditation today, I will pray . . .

Adoration _____

Confession _____

Thanksgiving _____

Supplication _____

From this meditation today, I will . . .

Think _____

Say _____

Do _____

SEARCH THE WORD

History demonstrates one evangelism tenet: there are no unlikely recipients.

October 31

Entrapment

God did this so that men would seek him and perhaps reach out for him and find him, though he is not far from each one of us (Acts 17:27).

Scripture: Acts 17:22-28

Song: *"Lead Them to Thee"*

From this meditation today, I will pray...
Adoration _____
_____
_____

Confession _____
_____
_____

Thanksgiving _____
_____
_____

Supplication _____
_____
_____

From this meditation today, I will...
Think _____
_____
_____

Say _____
_____
_____

Do _____
_____
_____
_____

A scrawny, odd-looking creature staggered onto the road in front of us. At second glance, we realized it was a tiny kitten with its head stuck in a bag. Parking the car, my husband picked up the pathetic creature, removed the bag, and sat it on the path that led home. When Gene returned to the car, he said the bag was a single-serving, cat-food pouch. In an effort to consume every last morsel of food, the kitten trapped herself in darkness.

With an earnest desire to delve into religion, the Athenians surrounded themselves with as much philosophy and religious myth as available, trapping themselves in spiritual darkness. God sent Paul to "pull the bag of deceit" off their heads and expose them to the light of Jesus Christ.

Many false doctrines infiltrate the church in the guise of tolerance. God gave us His written Word to help us seek Him and find Him through the sacrifice of Jesus Christ. He beckons us to expose others to the Light and set their feet on the only path that leads to Heaven.

Creator and sustainer of my soul, thank You for setting my feet on the path that leads to Your door. Help me to expose others to the light of Jesus Christ. In His name, I pray. Amen.

SPOTLIGHT
Next Week's Lesson

How far away is God?
Only as far
as we have walked away.

November

CHALLENGES IN THE NEW COMMUNITY

*You are the body of Christ,
and each one of you is a part of it.*
—1 Corinthians 12:27

Photo © SW Productions

November 1

Bind Us Together, Lord

There is one body and one Spirit—just as you were called to one hope when you were called—one Lord, one faith, one baptism; one God and Father of all (Ephesians 4:4-6).

Scripture: Ephesians 4:1-6
Song: *"The Church's One Foundation"*

From this meditation today, I will pray . . .
Adoration _____
_____
_____

Confession _____
_____
_____

Thanksgiving _____
_____
_____

Supplication _____
_____
_____

From this meditation today, I will . . .
Think _____
_____
_____

Say _____
_____
_____

Do _____
_____
_____

November 1, 2. **Brenda K. Hendricks** *is a prolific writer from Freeburg, Pennsylvania. She grooms dogs in her spare time to support her writing habit.*

After assembling a 1500-piece puzzle, I felt it was a shame to dismantle it and stuff it back into the box with the intent of some day reassembling it. The picture of the lighthouse was too beautiful—and the task too tedious—to start all over again another day. However, moving the puzzle proved impossible. No matter how tightly joined those pieces appeared to be, the picture crumbled at the slightest movement. The perfect solution—apply adhesive in order to bind the pieces together permanently. Glued to a snack stand, that puzzle continues to showcase our diligence with its beauty.

In assembling the body of Christ, God designed each believer with a specific purpose and placement within the church. Even though we seem intricately connected, God realized how easily we would crumble under the shifting currents of worldly pressures. His perfect solution?—the gift of the Holy Spirit applied to the hearts of all believers. He permanently binds us in the bond of unity and love.

Father, *I'm thankful that You've placed us in the world to show forth one hope, one Lord, one faith, one baptism, and one God. Amen.*

SPOTLIGHT
Next Week's Lesson

One, one, one, one, one, one, one, one—the whole number for the church.

November 2

Making a Memorial

Until we all reach unity in the faith and in the knowledge of the Son of God and become mature, attaining to the whole measure of the fullness of Christ (Ephesians 4:13).

Already 60 years in the making, a monument honoring the Native American hero, Crazy Horse, stands high in the mountains of South Dakota. But only the face is completed. Since the death of the original sculptor, Korczak Ziolkowski, in 1982, the work continues under the talented hands of seven of his ten children. Considering the meticulous procedure, it is doubtful that Ziolkowski's children will live to complete the project. In that event, the organization will assign others the task.

God assigns prophets, evangelists, ministers, and teachers to sculpt Christians into memorials honoring Jesus. The procedure takes a lifetime of meticulous work. When necessary, others pick up the project where the first had to leave off. Even this devotional was designed by our Lord to chisel a little here or polish a bit there. The author is honored to be used by Him to impart His truths to fellow believers. Through the discipline it took to write this devotion, she too has been chiseled and polished. In this way, we, His precious monuments, build up one another to reflect the fullness of Christ.

Divine Creator, *bless those You have chosen to sculpt me into the likeness of Your Son, Jesus Christ. In His name I pray. Amen.*

Scripture: Ephesians 4:7-16
Song: *"Lead Me to Calvary"*

From this meditation today, I will pray . . .
Adoration _____
Confession _____
Thanksgiving _____
Supplication _____

From this meditation today, I will . . .
Think _____
Say _____
Do _____

SEARCH THE WORD
Unity, faith, knowledge equals mature fullness. A worthy goal, a demanding process.

November 3

What's the Big Deal?

[They] argued forcefully and at length. Finally, Paul and Barnabas were sent to Jerusalem, accompanied by some local believers, to talk to the apostles and elders about this question (Acts 15:2, *New Living Translation*).

Scripture: Acts 15:1-5
Song: *"By Grace I'm Saved"*

From this meditation today, I will pray . . .
Adoration _____
_____
_____

Confession _____
_____
_____

Thanksgiving _____
_____
_____

Supplication _____
_____
_____

From this meditation today, I will . . .
Think _____
_____
_____

Say _____
_____
_____

Do _____
_____
_____

When I was a teen, I asked my friend, Sarah, if she wanted to come to church with me. Her father looked at me, puzzled, and said, "But she can't go. She doesn't have a hat and gloves." Such accessories were common when he was growing up; he assumed it was still a requirement. (Apparently, he hadn't been to church recently.)

We all have certain preconceived notions about worship, don't we? Often, these ideas have little scriptural basis. In the early church, some Pharisees became Christians and brought their religious traditions with them. They insisted that Gentiles must first become converts to Judaism if they were to be eligible for salvation through Christ. It became a blistering dispute in the early church.

Paul knew that the very essence of the gospel message hinged on this debate: What did Jesus Christ do for me on the cross? This was the crux of the dispute. It is still the most important question you will ever answer.

Heavenly Father, *when You sent Your Son to the cross, He did all that was necessary to win my salvation. Thank You, in Jesus' name. Amen.*

SPOTLIGHT
Next Week's Lesson

In Christianity there is room for opinion, but no room for conflict on "what is written."

November 3-9. **Suzanne Woods Fisher** lives in the San Francisco area with her husband and four kids. She is a contributing editor for Christian Parenting Today.

November 4

Adding Layers?

We believe that we shall be saved through the grace of the Lord Jesus, just as they will (Acts 15:11, *Revised Standard Version*).

Scripture: Acts 15:6-11
Song: *"Jesus Opened Up the Way"*

In our day and age, it's hard to believe that the early church was divided over an issue like circumcision. More specifically, church leaders argued about whether Gentiles needed to be circumcised before they could receive salvation through Christ. To modern sensibilities, circumcision is just an elective medical procedure. But to the early church in the first century, it represented much more. It symbolized the covenant God had made with Abraham. It meant obedience to the Law.

And now Paul traveled all the way to Jerusalem to meet with the church elders and apostles about this question. He insisted that newly converted Gentiles did not require circumcision to be in right relationship with God. Jesus Christ's death and resurrection was the fulfilled promise. The law could still act as a moral guide for believers, but salvation could only come through grace alone. No further layer need be added to this plan from God.

Are you struggling with a divisive issue in your church? If so, consider: Does Scripture clearly and consistently support your own position? It's important to know.

Father, *thank You that I don't need to add layers to the "system" to be accepted by You. Your system is grace, freely bestowed. So reshape my thinking about any legalisms I may still cherish. Through Christ, amen.*

From this meditation today, I will pray...
Adoration _____
Confession _____
Thanksgiving _____
Supplication _____

From this meditation today, I will...
Think _____
Say _____
Do _____

SEARCH THE WORD

Salvation rests on one bedrock layer: God's grace.

November 5

Listen!

That the remnant of men may seek the Lord, and all the Gentiles who bear my name, says the Lord (Acts 15:17).

Scripture: Acts 15:12-21
Song: *"Able to Save"*

From this meditation today, I will pray . . .
Adoration _____
_____
_____

Confession _____
_____
_____

Thanksgiving _____
_____
_____

Supplication _____
_____
_____

From this meditation today, I will . . .
Think _____
_____
_____

Say _____
_____
_____

Do _____
_____
_____
_____

While at the Jerusalem conference, Paul and Barnabas spoke to a hushed crowd, sharing the signs and wonders God had performed for the believing Gentiles. Then James, a prominent leader of the church in Jerusalem, affirmed Paul's assertion that Gentiles should not be put under the Mosaic system. No circumcision required! With keen awareness, James quoted from the book of Amos, confirming God's intent to save all who are lost.

Many believe that Gentile Christians outnumbered Jewish Christians at this critical juncture in the early church's history. What might have happened had this fledgling church split apart? Thankfully, we don't have to wonder. The assembly listened to the guiding wisdom of God, transmitted through the mouth of Paul, and ended up protecting and preserving the early movement. The conference ended with the apostles, the elders, and all of the church in agreement about this important debate. The question was settled once and for all: All believers were saved by grace alone. And God was glorified through this powerful display of unity.

Heavenly Father, help me to learn from Paul's crisis-management skills. He listened to You and sought Your wisdom. May Your truth become so much a part of me, too, that I can't be led astray. In Jesus' name, amen.

SPOTLIGHT
Next Week's Lesson
Being Christian does not depend on heritage or tradition; it depends entirely on God's grace and our free will.

November 6

The Offending Cross

If you confess with your mouth, "Jesus is Lord," and believe in your heart that God raised him from the dead, you will be saved (Romans 10:9).

A friend of mine often objects to what he calls the narrow-mindedness of Christianity. "There are many paths leading up the mountain of faith," he insists. "Who is to say that Jesus is the only way?" Well, Jesus said it, for one: "I am the way and the truth and the life. No one comes to the Father except through me" (John 14:6).

Paul affirmed it too: "If you confess with your mouth, 'Jesus is Lord,' and believe in your heart that God raised him from the dead, you will be saved" (Romans 10:9). It sounds so gracious and loving, doesn't it? Confess and believe, and you will be saved. Yet it's a statement that leaves many, like my friend, offended.

The cross does offend people. It leads to that thorny and unpopular premise that *there is only one way to God.* Yet if it were possible that humans could be saved any other way, the cross would not have been necessary. It really is simple. God has established a way to salvation through His own self-sacrifice by His Son, Jesus. Do I accept His offer? Do I confess and believe?

My Redeemer, *thank You for providing a way back to You so that I will spend eternity in Your Holy presence. Teach me to revel in Your presence, even now, until the day I see You, face to face. In Your name, amen.*

SEARCH THE WORD
Narrow-minded thinkers reject God's open arms, when they decide His arms should be wider still.

Scripture: Romans 10:5-9
Song: *"O Be Saved"*

From this meditation today, I will pray...

Adoration _____

Confession _____

Thanksgiving _____

Supplication _____

From this meditation today, I will...

Think _____

Say _____

Do _____

November 7

How Else Will They Hear?

*How, then, can they call on the one they have not believed in?
And how can they believe in the one of whom they have not heard?
And how can they hear without someone preaching to them?
And how can they preach unless they are sent?* (Romans 10:14, 15).

Scripture: Romans 10:10-17
Song: *"Disciples of All Nations"*

From this meditation today, I will pray . . .

Adoration _____
_____
_____

Confession _____
_____
_____

Thanksgiving _____
_____
_____

Supplication _____
_____
_____

From this meditation today, I will . . .

Think _____
_____
_____

Say _____
_____
_____

Do _____
_____
_____
_____

A brilliant debater, Paul used a sequence of rhetorical questions with his audience to stress the importance of preaching the gospel. He was building up to his main point: the need to send preachers to the mission field.

God could have chosen another means, rather than humans, to spread the message, of course. Angels would have been quite convincing, for example. But perhaps human beings are the best at reaching other humans.

God doesn't want anyone to miss the opportunity to be saved. Christ's very last words, right before He ascended, were: "Therefore go and make disciples of all nations, baptizing them in the name of the Father and of the Son and of the Holy Spirit, and teaching them to obey everything I have commanded you" (Matthew 28:19, 20). We Christians must share the message of salvation. How wrong it would be to keep others from enjoying the love and forgiveness of our heavenly Father!

Dear Lord, *open my eyes to those in my own mission field who haven't heard of You. Help me to overcome any shyness or reluctance as I seek to share my faith. I pray in Jesus' holy name. Amen.*

SPOTLIGHT
Next Week's Lesson

"How?" is a core question for living one's life. "How can I be saved?" is the right question for wrongdoers.

November 8

Holy and Wholly!

They saw that I had been entrusted with the task of preaching the gospel to the Gentiles, just as Peter had been to the Jews (Galatians 2:7).

For the last six years, I have been raising puppies for Guide Dogs for the Blind in San Rafael, California. An eight-week-old puppy is entrusted to me from the GDB kennels, and for the next 16 months I will love, train, and socialize that puppy. After formal training from instructors, the dog will be partnered with a blind individual. Together, they will become a team.

But not all of the puppies become guides. A Guide Dog is one that seems to take to its entrusted task with a natural intuition.

It was clear to the leaders of the early church that God had entrusted Peter with the task of preaching the gospel to the Jews, and Paul to the Gentiles. Not exclusively, of course. When Paul entered a town, he went first to the temple. And we know Peter ate with Gentiles. But each man knew his principal calling. God had entrusted them according to their passions.

Do you know what your calling is? Where are your passions? God has given you that interest for a purpose.

Lord, *You made me with a purpose, but what did You have in mind? Lead me clearly to uncover and develop those interests and abilities. Make the work of my hands today count for eternity. I pray in Jesus' name. Amen.*

SEARCH THE WORD

Being "entrusted" always involves responsibility; it always involves tasks.

Scripture: Galatians 2:1-10
Song: *"Amazing Love"*

From this meditation today, I will pray . . .

Adoration _____

Confession _____

Thanksgiving _____

Supplication _____

From this meditation today, I will . . .

Think _____

Say _____

Do _____

November 9

Gravity's Pull

When Peter came to Antioch, I opposed him to his face, because he was clearly in the wrong (Galatians 2:11).

Scripture: Galatians 2:11-21
Song: *"Grace and Truth Shall Mark the Way"*

From this meditation today, I will pray . . .
Adoration _____

Confession _____

Thanksgiving _____

Supplication _____

From this meditation today, I will . . .
Think _____

Say _____

Do _____

Those were strong words from Paul. He called Peter a hypocrite! What had he done? Peter had come up to visit Paul in Antioch and had comfortably eaten with the Gentiles. Then certain Jewish legalists arrived to join him, and he buckled—he went back to his old, legalistic eating pattern. He even influenced Barnabas—Paul's faithful sidekick—to follow his lead!

This wasn't just about food preferences, of course. It came back to the question, settled long ago, of whether circumcision (or any other legalism) was necessary for salvation. With characteristic bluster, Peter acted first and thought about it later. He turned from liberty in Christ back to bondage under law.

I have a little bit of Peter's personality in me, and I suspect that most of us can relate to him to some degree. Our old habits can be like gravity, pulling us back to a rather sad but comfortable way of living. Peter had spent three years shadowing Christ, yet he still battled with his sinful nature. Thankfully, Paul's divinely inspired guidance pulled him back.

Dear God, *I know that unless I stay in steady communication with Your Spirit within me, sin will pull me down. Give me the eyes to see my sins, confess them to You—and turn away from them! In Christ's name, amen.*

SPOTLIGHT
Next Week's Lesson

No one—not even an apostle— is free to set restrictions on the gospel.

November 10

Who's Afraid?

*God is within her, she will not fall;
God will help her at break of day* (Psalm 46:5).

The girl's breath came in frightened gasps. Night after night, she faced the gloomy gauntlet. Trees loomed like bony witches as she hurried along between deep roadside ditches, sure that some toothy thing would clamber out and chase her down. She chastised herself for entertaining such silly fears. But every night she arrived home in a cold sweat, heart racing with the effort it took not to run.

One day, she came across a tattered bookmark that she'd been given long ago in Sunday school. The shepherd pictured on the bookmark seemed wise and kind, but the stout staff in his hand made it clear that He knew how to deal with bandits and wolves. She held the picture in mind as she headed home that night. And she whispered the psalm that went with it: "The Lord is my Shepherd."

She could almost feel Him beside her, strong and fearless, the moment she called. Years later, after she'd met the shepherd personally, she realized that He really had been there. Now she knew His promise, too, never to leave.

Lord, help me to remember that You are my powerful and loving Shepherd. Thanks for Your promise never to leave me alone. In Jesus' name, amen.

SEARCH THE WORD

If the Lord is my shepherd, I will have no reason to fear.

Scripture: Psalm 46
Song: *"All Through the Night"*

From this meditation today, I will pray . . .

Adoration _____

Confession _____

Thanksgiving _____

Supplication _____

From this meditation today, I will . . .

Think _____

Say _____

Do _____

November 10–16. **Ronda Brunea,** of Cherry Creek, New York, is a single mother of four. She loves to read and collect amusing and fairly useless pets, like sheep.

November 11

Diabolical Distraction

He who began a good work in you will carry it on to completion until the day of Christ Jesus (Philippians 1:6).

Scripture: Philippians 1:3-11
Song: *"The Heart of Worship"*

From this meditation today, I will pray . . .
Adoration _____
_____
_____

Confession _____
_____
_____

Thanksgiving _____
_____
_____

Supplication _____
_____
_____

From this meditation today, I will . . .
Think _____
_____
_____

Say _____
_____
_____

Do _____
_____
_____
_____

Our setting: the unseen world surrounding human activity. A demonic professor instructs a student in the art of distraction. "So, encouraging him to focus on how wonderfully he's serving the Enemy wasn't effective, eh?"

"No, your nastiness."

"Then try offering him wormy thoughts about what a disappointment he must be to that One he serves. You can grind him into the dust by making him think only of himself. Don't let him think about other humans at all. And make sure his thoughts of his God produce guilt; this will entice him to avoid that miserable idea of . . . *grace*."

Both demons shudder. "The really beautiful thing is, he'll mistake these thoughts for humility and think he's doing a good thing to reflect upon his wickedness. Really, he's simply enjoying self-centeredness at its opposite extreme! 'It's all about me' is the thing to remember—good me or bad me makes no difference. Just keep the focus on 'me,' and you will successfully distract him from accomplishing the Enemy's purposes."

Good Master, *You knew what You were getting when You chose me. I make mistakes, but please don't let me spend too much time thinking about either my accomplishments or my failures. It's all about You, Lord, and what You began in me You will complete. Thanks, in Jesus' name. Amen.*

SPOTLIGHT
Next Week's Lesson

Philippians is the Spirit's "joy" letter.
It deserves a regular reading;
it offers a marvelous boost.

November 12

The Mess Becomes Beautiful

Now I want you to know, brothers, that what has happened to me has really served to advance the gospel (Philippians 1:12).

Her world has been smashed, her dreams cruelly shattered. There is someone to blame, the one who performed the offending deed. She could choose hatred. She could snarl bitterly every time someone spoke his name. She might even spend the rest of her life indulging in a continuous tirade against that perpetrator. And she knows people who live that way. They're ugly in spirit, and when she's around them, she feels as though their poison might seep into her skin through their breath.

There is another choice, but she knows it will not be easy. She can choose to obey God—the more difficult path because it means forgiving and letting go of the anger. But then comes the fun part, where she will stand back and watch Him turn the devil's plan on its head. She'll have her sweet "revenge" by choosing purposeful, obedient action rather than allowing another's actions to dictate her response. She will choose peace, which is more valuable than everything she lost. She will trust her Lord to fashion the mess into a beautiful, holy thing.

O Lord, help me to remember that my real enemy is the evil one and that my salvation comes in loving You. Help me to trust and obey, even when I can't see how You might possibly use it for good. Waste nothing, Lord. Use every crumb of my pain to advance Your work! In Jesus' name, amen.

Scripture: Philippians 1:12-18
Song: *"Beauty for Ashes"*

From this meditation today, I will pray . . .
Adoration _____
Confession _____
Thanksgiving _____
Supplication _____

From this meditation today, I will . . .
Think _____
Say _____
Do _____

SEARCH THE WORD
God will work all things together for good for those who love Him
(see Romans 8:28).

November 13

I Have Decided

I eagerly expect and hope that I will in no way be ashamed, but will have sufficient courage so that now as always Christ will be exalted in my body, whether by life or by death (Philippians 1:20).

Scripture: Philippians 1:19-26
Song: *"I Have Decided to Follow Jesus"*

From this meditation today, I will pray...
Adoration _____
_____
_____

Confession _____
_____
_____

Thanksgiving _____
_____
_____

Supplication _____
_____
_____

From this meditation today, I will...
Think _____
_____
_____

Say _____
_____
_____

Do _____
_____
_____
_____

Those who hate the gospel have killed the young minister. His wife is left alone amidst a village full of hostile and dangerous people. The government will not help her. There are no other believers nearby, but she is strengthened, knowing that many brothers and sisters around the world are praying for her.

She remembers the day she confided in her husband, "I am not certain that I will have sufficient courage, if death should be required of me."

Her husband had comforted her, wiping away her tears of shame. "None of us has that faith in ourselves. We must have that faith in God. He will provide the strength when we need it. Whatever happens, Dear, He will give us the courage that we need to be faithful. Only decide in your heart that you will never turn back, and the most difficult question has been answered." The young widow looks out her window and considers a village full of helpless, imprisoned souls. She straightens, brushes the wrinkles from her gown, and goes out to minister among them.

Lord, *You know how often I am afraid of the things You ask me to do—and the things You might ask of me! Help me, in Christ's name. Amen.*

SPOTLIGHT
Next Week's Lesson

Hope leads to joy;
joy leads to hope—a beautiful circle
Paul draws for all Christians.

November 14

Royalty in Disguise

Whatever happens, conduct yourselves in a manner worthy of the gospel of Christ (Philippians 1:27).

An exiled king wanders his domain in disguise. Unknown and unappreciated, he guards his people against terrors that would overwhelm and destroy them if he should abandon his charge. Rather than appreciate his work, however, the people regard him with suspicion.

And yet, there is something about this man that makes them shrink into themselves should he look their way. They seem to well up with unaccountable guilt when he regards them with a loving glance, as he so often does. He possesses a certain regality that cannot be veiled by the travel-worn clothing. He stands erect; his stride is confidant, his voice kind or stern as needed.

People get the disturbing feeling that he knows exactly who he is and what he is meant to be doing. Some are jealous and hate him because of it. But every so often, one will edge closer, cloaked by darkness, and ask this strange man what it is that makes him so different. Soon they are conducting themselves in the same worthy manner as their ever-so-worthy mentor.

O God, strengthen my inner person so that, no matter what my circumstances may be, I will conduct myself in a way that reveals my true identity. Whether I have support from others or find myself abandoned and alone, I ask one thing: Let me be faithful to You. In Jesus' name, amen.

SEARCH THE WORD
Many parents say it to their children: "Remember who you are." Christian parents add, "Remember Whose you are."

Scripture: Philippians 1:27-30
Song: *"The Great Adventure"*

From this meditation today, I will pray . . .

Adoration _____

Confession _____

Thanksgiving _____

Supplication _____

From this meditation today, I will . . .

Think _____

Say _____

Do _____

November 15

Aliens and Strangers

Our citizenship is in heaven
(Philippians 3:20).

Scripture: Philippians 3:17–4:1
Song: *"This World Is Not My Home"*

From this meditation today, I will pray . . .
Adoration _____

Confession _____

Thanksgiving _____

Supplication _____

From this meditation today, I will . . .
Think _____

Say _____

Do _____

"Man, do you ever feel as if being in this world just hurts too much—like you can't stand it anymore?" The second young man glanced at his friend and then back to the gang of kids clustered outside the school. "Yeah. I mean, look at them! I try to tell them they're headed for real trouble. I want to point them in the right direction, but they look at me like I'm nuts. It's like being in a lifeboat watching the *Titanic* go down, and the people on board won't believe the ship's sinking. I feel so helpless sometimes, not to mention feeling like the biggest misfit in the universe!"

His friend smiled. "Why does it surprise us that we don't fit in? Hey, this isn't our permanent address."

The young man thought for a moment. "Yeah, you're right. It's not our home. We're just here on assignment for awhile, right?"

"You know, we can't save the whole world, buddy. But we have an assignment while we're here. And we're not supposed to let it drag us down."

"How?"

"Come on, let's pray. It'll help them and us."

Abba Father, *this world is not my home. Show me what You want me to do here, and strengthen me to obey. When it seems like too much, remind me of that beautiful, restful place ahead. Through Christ I pray. Amen.*

SPOTLIGHT
Next Week's Lesson
Earthly citizenship can bring pride or shame. Heavenly citizenship brings joy and never causes disgrace.

November 16

Crazy Peace

The peace of God, which transcends all understanding, will guard your hearts and your minds in Christ Jesus (Philippians 4:7).

"Pam, I just heard what's happened. You must be so upset! Is there anything I can do?"

"Thanks, Judy, but there's really nothing anyone can do."

"It's weird; you look so calm."

Pam laughed. "I can't say I'm completely calm, at least not inside, but I'm working on it. What I do have is a peace that I can't explain, except to say that it's supernatural. It's not coming from me, that's for sure."

"How can you possibly have peace at a time like this?"

"It's because I know the one who's in charge of all things. He's promised not to give me more than I can bear. I know He's got everything under control, even though it sure doesn't look that way for now. And I believe He'll use all of this somehow for the good, if I trust Him with it. I just keep asking Him to help me to believe and be faithful."

"You are nuts." Judy looked wistful. "But I kind of wish I was your kind of crazy."

Jehovah Shalom, *You are the God of peace. I give You my heart. Help me feel and believe that You love me in all situations. Through Christ, amen.*

Scripture: Philippians 4:2-9
Song: *"It Is Well with My Soul"*

From this meditation today, I will pray . . .

Adoration _____
_____
_____

Confession _____
_____
_____

Thanksgiving _____
_____
_____

Supplication _____
_____
_____

From this meditation today, I will . . .

Think _____
_____
_____

Say _____
_____
_____

Do _____
_____
_____
_____

SEARCH THE WORD
*Jesus said,
"Peace I leave with you;
my peace I give you"*
(John 14:27).

November 17

A Time to Go Forth

God did not give us a spirit of timidity, but a spirit of power, of love, and of self-discipline (2 Timothy 1:7).

Scripture: 2 Timothy 1:3-7
Song: *"A Charge to Keep I Have"*

From this meditation today, I will pray . . .
Adoration _____
_____
_____

Confession _____
_____
_____

Thanksgiving _____
_____
_____

Supplication _____
_____
_____

From this meditation today, I will . . .
Think _____
_____
_____

Say _____
_____
_____

Do _____
_____
_____

"O Lord, what have I done? Why didn't you stop me?" I had assisted in planning Christian events with established groups before. This time I was sponsoring my first, all on my own. It was a dinner theater for single Christians. Tickets were dispersed to their locations for sales. Newspapers, TV, and radio announcements were airing promising skits, comedy, door prizes, and more. Paralyzed with fear, I knew there was no turning back. I fretted about everything. "What if nobody comes? What if everyone hates it? What if . . . ?"

In due season the dormant potential in our lives demands to flow, while circumstances conspire to build dams of fear. Armed with a team of prayerful people, who were generous with encouragement, I saw this dam demolished. We enjoyed success, thanks be to God.

God has given each of us spiritual gifts to use in His service. The great challenge is to venture forth and use them in His power. Fear must flee in the face of His marvelous power.

Dear God, *help me to proceed with the plans You've laid on my heart, in spite of my fears. In Christ's precious name I pray. Amen.*

SPOTLIGHT
Next Week's Lesson

We must see these qualities in church leaders: boldness, power, love, self-discipline.

November 17–23. **Jeri Darby** is an author and conference speaker who lives and works in Bay City, Michigan.

November 18

A Real Friend

I am not ashamed, because I know whom I have believed, and am convinced that he is able to guard what I have entrusted to him for that day (2 Timothy 1:12).

"Who are you talking to?" I'd ask, with a questioning frown.

"My friend," my 4-year-old daughter would answer emphatically. Only no one was there. Yet, lively conversation streamed from her bedroom, and she insisted her "friend" was real.

I became a bit concerned, but I soon learned that young children often entertain imaginary friends. (Who knows, I probably had one as a child.)

Do skeptics view Christians like this—as we continue to insist that Jesus is our companion and friend, that we walk and talk with Him daily? I can't *see* His presence, yet I *know* His presence; He is no imaginary friend. All who are indwelt by His Spirit know a real and abiding fellowship with this Savior.

Thankfully, as we continue to nurture our friendship with Jesus and boldly proclaim Him Lord, onlookers will glimpse His reality in the way we live. In fact, our lives can be the bridge for others to connect with a real friend.

Dear God, *help me to experience deeper realities of Your presence, day by day. And let that presence shape my life into a glowing witness to Your reality. In the holy name of Jesus, my Lord and Savior, I pray. Amen.*

Scripture: 2 Timothy 1:8-14
Song: *"My Jesus, I Love Thee"*

From this meditation today, I will pray . . .

Adoration _____

Confession _____

Thanksgiving _____

Supplication _____

From this meditation today, I will . . .

Think _____

Say _____

Do _____

SEARCH THE WORD
Conviction knows no shame. It knows only trust and obedience.

November 19

You're Included

I am obligated both to Greeks and non-Greeks, both to the wise and the foolish (Romans 1:14).

Scripture: Romans 1:8-17
Song: *"Tell the Whole Wide World"*

"I was on the summit with a Muslim, a Jew, and an atheist," the speaker said, sharing a story from his recent mountain-climbing venture. "While there, God gave me a special love for those people," she continued, going on to describe the special bond that formed among them.

Paul, steeped in Judaism, paved the way for salvation among the Gentiles. Like him, we are called to minister to the nations.

Thankfully, living in the United States makes it possible for us to meet and befriend folks from all over the world—without ever treading foreign soil. What a broad representation of diverse cultures exists in almost every neighborhood!

I'm thankful that when Jesus surrendered to the cross, He did so for all humanity. The blessings and promises of the Bible are inclusive: "Whosoever will, may come." Regardless of ethnicity, intelligence, financial status—Jesus died for everyone. So, to each lovely and unique heart, let us be ready with the invitation to eternal life.

Father, give me the wisdom to witness to cultures different from mine. Like the great apostle Paul, fill me with a genuine eagerness to share the good news with every person I meet, manifesting Your love in the most practical ways. In the name of Jesus, Lord and Savior of all, I pray. Amen.

From this meditation today, I will pray . . .
Adoration _____
Confession _____
Thanksgiving _____
Supplication _____

From this meditation today, I will . . .
Think _____
Say _____
Do _____

SPOTLIGHT
Next Week's Lesson

Leaders who have no driving sense of obligation have little motivation for true service.

November 20

Let's Not Forget

Remember Jesus Christ, raised from the dead, descended from David. This is my gospel (2 Timothy 2:8).

Stress had numbed my mind, and I was barely able to function from day to day. What a situation I faced! I could choose to walk forward in faith or in fear. Actually, I mostly teetered between the two. Internalizing my pain, I felt as if my head would implode, and I could barely manage to utter a prayer.

Then God began to draw my focus back to the Scriptures. Today's Scripture begins, "Remember Jesus Christ." My sufferings in this life shrink down to size when placed alongside what Jesus endured on the cross for me.

When life bombards us with tough situations that seem unfair and unmanageable, let us simply remember our beloved Savior. God's power was sufficient to raise Jesus from the dead, and this same power is able to resurrect courage, determination, and strength within us. In Him, we can overcome every challenge. As a wise and experienced missionary once told a group of young people: "The hand that *points* the way is the same hand that *provides* the way."

Father, *thank You that as I recall the cross, I am reminded of Your sacrifice of love and of Your resurrecting power. Help me to remember, too, that You are always with me, supplying abundant grace and power for all that confronts me, today and always. In Jesus' name I pray. Amen.*

Scripture: 2 Timothy 2:8-13
Song: *"Alas! and Did My Savior Bleed?"*

From this meditation today, I will pray . . .

Adoration _____

Confession _____

Thanksgiving _____

Supplication _____

From this meditation today, I will . . .

Think _____

Say _____

Do _____

SEARCH THE WORD

The more we know about Jesus and experience His presence, the easier it is to remember Him daily.

November 21

Friendly Reminders

Keep reminding them of these things. Warn them before God against quarreling about words; it is of no value, and only ruins those who listen (2 Timothy 2:14).

Scripture: 2 Timothy 2:14-19
Song: *"Jesus, the Very Thought of Thee"*

From this meditation today, I will pray...

Adoration _____
_____
_____

Confession _____
_____
_____

Thanksgiving _____
_____
_____

Supplication _____
_____
_____

From this meditation today, I will...

Think _____
_____
_____

Say _____
_____
_____

Do _____
_____
_____
_____

I distinctly remember telling my son to wash his face, comb his hair, and change his shirt before we leave. "Are you ready?" I yell before getting into the car.

"Yeah, Mom." He climbs into the passenger seat as I gawk in disbelief. "You haven't done one thing I asked!"

I impatiently insist he go back and try again. "Why didn't you...?" my questions follow behind him as he re-enters the house. ("Oh, I forgot," is his usual response.)

Weary with the repeated scenario, I threaten to make him a cassette recording titled, "My Instructions before Leaving Home." He could review it before ever getting into the car.

God quickly jolts my memory with how often I "forget" to live in ways that honor Him. And I instantly feel more compassion for my son.

Have you noticed that God's Word abounds in repetitious reminders? No doubt He knows how easily we can forget His goodness, and that all of His reminders have only our best at heart.

Father, *forgive me when I hear Your wise guidance but so quickly forget. Bring Your Word once again to the forefront of my mind when I allow myself to become preoccupied with my own agenda. In Jesus' name, amen.*

SPOTLIGHT
Next Week's Lesson

Leaders too often speak expectations rather than reminders. Paul reminds Timothy he is, first of all, one who reminds.

November 22

Time to Stop the Tape?

Continue in what you have learned and have become convinced of, because you know those from whom you learned it
(2 Timothy 3:14).

I love listening to nonfiction books on tape. But I try to be careful about what I choose. Recently I checked out an audio book at the library and found that the author had some excellent insights about the spiritual life. As I continued listening, though, she began veering down the path of New Age reasoning. Time to stop the tape!

We live in exciting times when new information can circle the globe with little effort—whether it be fact or fiction. The subtleties here are myriad, and so often dubious teachings can come wrapped in seemingly scriptural principles. Beware!

God wants us to continue to grow in the knowledge of Him. We are to learn and teach others the unsullied doctrines that have stood the test of time down through the ages in the church. In other words, healthy spiritual growth depends upon our ability to avoid heretical innovations. Straying down paths that merely mimic the Bible can only lead us into spiritual deception.

Father, *there are so many teachings becoming popular and being embraced by many these days. Illuminate my mind only by the truth of Your Word that I will not be misled. And as I learn from You, give me the will and wisdom to teach others. Through Christ my Lord, amen.*

Scripture: 2 Timothy 3:14-17
Song: *"Lord, Speak to Me"*

From this meditation today, I will pray...
Adoration _____

Confession _____

Thanksgiving _____

Supplication _____

From this meditation today, I will...
Think _____

Say _____

Do _____

SEARCH THE WORD
If you are convinced, continue; trust apostolic doctrine to see you through.

November 23

Endure the Hardship

But you, keep your head in all situations, endure hardship, do the work of an evangelist, discharge all the duties of your ministry (2 Timothy 4:5).

Scripture: 2 Timothy 2:1-3; 4:1-5
Song: *"Ye Servants of God, Your Master Proclaim"*

From this meditation today, I will pray . . .
Adoration _____
_____
_____

Confession _____
_____
_____

Thanksgiving _____
_____
_____

Supplication _____
_____
_____

From this meditation today, I will . . .
Think _____
_____
_____

Say _____
_____
_____

Do _____
_____
_____
_____

Picking it up from the pay phone, one of the security guards said in disgust, "Someone must have just left it here! Let's see if they are doing it outside." The two guards scanned the halls frantically and then darted out the doors.

I was strolling through the mall, but the urgency of their actions caused me concern. "Someone must have done something dangerous," I surmised. Later, I learned the officers were in hot pursuit of . . . a Christian who was passing out tracts explaining the gospel.

Society sometimes puzzles me. During this time of my life, I was struggling with difficulties and had wandered away from the church. I felt alienated from God and could have used any reminder of His faithfulness. Yet these Christians were being pursued by well-meaning citizens as if they were vicious criminals. True, the mall likely had some guidelines about distributing literature. But my point is simply this: However we seek to share the gospel, we will no doubt face some stiff opposition. Don't be surprised by it; determine to endure in God's strength.

Lord, *You commanded me to "go." Give me courage to open up the gospel in a world that tries so hard to shut it out. In Jesus' name, amen.*

SPOTLIGHT
Next Week's Lesson

Leaders always have the choice: lose your cool or keep your head. Which is the godly choice?

November 24

Lost

*I came from the Father and entered the world;
now I am leaving the world and going back to the Father*
(John 16:28).

I'd entered unfamiliar territory. The further I drove, the more uneasy I grew. Finally, I had to admit I was lost. When I stopped at a gas station to ask for directions, the clerk was thoroughly unclear about how I ought to proceed.

A person standing at the counter overheard my dilemma, however, and interrupted: "Oh, I know where that is. In fact, I'm going that way myself. Just follow me."

When we drew near to my destination, he honked and pointed to the parking lot I needed. I was so grateful, and having a guide to direct me, I enjoyed the trip.

I don't know the literal "route" to Heaven, but I do know that my Lord Jesus Christ dwelled there from eternity, came to earth, and then went back again. I can trust Him to take me to Heaven, and I can trust Him to be my guide today and every day along all the pathways I'll travel while on this earth. All I have to do is ask for His wise and clear direction.

Father, *thank You for Your most excellent guide in Your Son, Jesus. Thank You for making the way to You so clear: through the cross of Christ, I have forgiveness of sins and adoption into Your family. In His name, amen.*

Scripture: John 16:25-33

Song: *"Jesus, Like a Shepherd Lead Us"*

From this meditation today, I will pray . . .

Adoration _____

Confession _____

Thanksgiving _____

Supplication _____

From this meditation today, I will . . .

Think _____

Say _____

Do _____

SEARCH THE WORD

Jesus has been there. He knows the way. What better guide could you have?

November 24–30. **Sally Jadlow** serves the greater Kansas City area as a chaplain to corporations. She is the author of an historical novel, *The Late Sooner*.

November 25

No Garbled Message Here!

We also thank God continually because, when you received the word of God, which you heard from us, you accepted it not as the word of men, but as it actually is, the word of God, which is at work in you who believe
(1 Thessalonians 2:13).

Scripture: 1 Thessalonians 2:13-16
Song: *"Tell the Blessed News"*

From this meditation today, I will pray . . .
Adoration _____
_____
_____

Confession _____
_____
_____

Thanksgiving _____
_____
_____

Supplication _____
_____
_____

From this meditation today, I will . . .
Think _____
_____
_____

Say _____
_____
_____

Do _____
_____
_____
_____

As children, we played a game called "Telephone." All players sat in a circle. The first person whispered a phrase to the one on her right. The next person whispered the same phrase to the next. Around the circle it went until the last person spoke it aloud. Then the first person verbalized the original phrase—which was usually entirely different from the final version!

It's not so different now, over 50 years later. Usually, by the time a story goes around a few times, it's nothing like the original. The "facts" tend to become distorted.

There is something very comforting in knowing that the good news Paul preached about Jesus is the same message now as it was in the first century. The essential facts of His eternal deity, blessed incarnation, atoning death, glorious resurrection, ascension, and second advent remain at the heart of our faith, unchanged.

And the message hasn't lost any of its original power, either. It still changes lives today, just as it did when Paul first preached it.

Father, *thank You that Your Word is clear and trustworthy, no matter how many times it is told and retold. In the name of Jesus, amen.*

SPOTLIGHT
Next Week's Lesson

Weakness? insults? hardships? persecutions? difficulties? Paul had them all . . . but he had grace!

November 26

Many Adoptions

Not only so, but we ourselves, who have the firstfruits of the Spirit, groan inwardly as we wait eagerly for our adoption as sons, the redemption of our bodies (Romans 8:23).

One of our sons-in-law has been adopted four times so far in his 34 years. No, he's not an incorrigible youth that had to be handed off repeatedly to new families. His first adoption occurred when his birth-mother gave him to his adoptive parents. Scott's adoptive father died when he was only a year and a half old. In the years following, his adoptive mother remarried. His new stepfather adopted him when Scott was three years old.

His third adoption occurred when Scott, as a young man, was baptized and adopted as a son into God's own family. Several years later, when he married our daughter, we "adopted" him as our own son.

Even though he's been adopted these many times, he still looks forward to the manifestation of his ultimate adoption: when he will receive his glorified body as God has promised. Until that day, all of us believers "groan inwardly," as Paul says. As we await our full redemption, let us face our daily tasks with joy—and a powerful witness to the one who makes every aspect of our glorious future possible, our Lord Jesus Christ.

Father God, *thanks for my heavenly destination, which is far beyond anything I could ever imagine. In Christ's name, amen.*

SEARCH THE WORD

Adoption is a good thing in the physical realm; in the spiritual realm, it is a marvelous state.

Scripture: Romans 8:18-25
Song: *"Adopted"*

From this meditation today, I will pray . . .

Adoration _____

Confession _____

Thanksgiving _____

Supplication _____

From this meditation today, I will . . .

Think _____

Say _____

Do _____

November 27

In the Hard Places

Paul and Barnabas appointed elders for them in each church and, with prayer and fasting, committed them to the Lord, in whom they had put their trust (Acts 14:23).

Scripture: Acts 14:21-23
Song: *"Trust and Obey"*

From this meditation today, I will pray . . .

Adoration _____
_____
_____

Confession _____
_____
_____

Thanksgiving _____
_____
_____

Supplication _____
_____
_____

From this meditation today, I will . . .

Think _____
_____
_____

Say _____
_____
_____

Do _____
_____
_____
_____

"What seems to be the problem?" I asked.

"He's just impossible," she said. "Sneaks out of the house in the night. Skips school. Poor grades. Just don't know what I'm going to do with him."

"Do you think you've worried enough to change him?"

"What do you mean?"

"Well, obviously, all your worry hasn't changed his behavior, has it?"

"No. Probably won't either," she said, as she dabbed at her eyes with a tissue.

"Then let's do what God's Word says to do. Suppose we pray together, and fast, and commit him to the Lord?"

"Think it will work?"

"It sure beats worrying. I used to fret and stew over everything, until I realized that when I let God be in charge, He takes care of things better than I ever could."

"My worry is telling God I don't trust Him enough to let Him handle it, isn't it?"

And that was the day Millie let Jesus begin to operate in her son's life.

Lord, *help me to trust You a little bit more in every situation I face. It's a growth process for me; help me along! In Jesus' name, amen.*

SPOTLIGHT
Next Week's Lesson

Grace does not exclude authoritative leadership. The church needs both.

November 28

Crises for the "Christ Ones"

*If you suffer as a Christian, do not be ashamed,
but praise God that you bear that name
(1 Peter 4:16).*

In one of those terrible times in my life when the walls were caving in around me—and everything I perceived to be solid, shook and trembled—I sat in prayer with my journal on my lap and wrote this:

> My Child,
> I do no permit trials to strangle
>   but to strengthen.
> I do not allow heartache to hurt
>   but to heal.
> I do not send pain to punish
>   but to increase perseverance.
> Receive all I have to give
>   that you may become all
>   I see you to be.

Pausing to look at things from God's perspective will give us a whole new clarity in our lives. He sees our struggles in the context of the whole journey, our destination being the moment we stand face to face in His presence. Until then, we can be thankful to bear the name, "Christ one."

Father God, *help me to get Your take on a situation before I go into a tailspin that leads nowhere. In the name of Christ my Lord, amen.*

Scripture: 1 Peter 4:12-19

Song: *"Leaning on the Everlasting Arms"*

From this meditation today, I will pray . . .

Adoration _____

Confession _____

Thanksgiving _____

Supplication _____

From this meditation today, I will . . .

Think _____

Say _____

Do _____

SEARCH THE WORD
Many children learn to dislike their names. No child of God dislikes the name He gives: "Christ One."

November 29

Already Loved!

Rise up and help us; redeem us because of your unfailing love (Psalm 44:26).

Scripture: Psalm 44:17-26
Song: "What Wondrous Love Is This?"

From this meditation today, I will pray . . .
Adoration _____
_____
_____

Confession _____
_____
_____

Thanksgiving _____
_____
_____

Supplication _____
_____
_____

From this meditation today, I will . . .
Think _____
_____
_____

Say _____
_____
_____

Do _____
_____
_____
_____

While taking a class in world religions, I was struck with a wonderful insight. Nowhere in any religion in the world, with the exception of Christianity, is God revealed as a loving Father who redeems us by grace alone.

I was stumped by the word *redeem* for a long time. Then one day I stumbled across an explanation of the Bible's original Greek word: It means to "buy back" a slave from the market. I suddenly saw the implication: I was a slave held by Satan. When I accepted Christ and entered the waters of baptism, I was released from that bondage. No longer Satan's property, I didn't have to do his bidding. I received a new master.

Let's face it. There is no reason in the world God would purchase me (I'm not that cute). The only reason He bought me back from the slave market is because of His unconditional love. And His offer isn't just extended to me but to everyone. All are invited to receive His priceless gift of salvation, purchased with His Son's blood.

Religions tell us to earn God's love by serving Him. Christianity calls us to show our gratitude, in loving service, for the love we already have.

God, *thank You for Your love that is greater than I can know. But help me to grasp it a little more deeply with each new day. In Jesus' name, amen.*

SPOTLIGHT
Next Week's Lesson

God's design for His church is perfect. The people in it aren't . . . yet.

November 30

Strength in Weakness

For Christ's sake, I delight in weaknesses, in insults, in hardships, in persecutions, in difficulties. For when I am weak, then I am strong (2 Corinthians 12:10).

Recently, while struggling through a "down day," I read an account of Fannie Crosby, the famous hymn writer who wrote over 8,000 gospel song texts. She authored songs like "Blessed Assurance" and "I Am Thine, O Lord." She was born in 1820 and lost her eyesight when she was only six weeks old.

Once a well-intentioned minister remarked to her, "I think it is a great pity that the master, when He showered so many gifts upon you, did not give you sight."

She replied, "Do you know that if at birth I had been able to make one petition to my creator, it would have been that I should be born blind?"

"Why?" asked the surprised minister.

"Because when I get to Heaven, the first face that shall ever gladden my sight will be that of my Savior."

Oh, that I might be delivered from distractions and hunger for Heaven as Fannie did! Her weaknesses could have made her bitter; instead, they made her better-fit for her glorious home.

Lord God, hone me for Heaven through each day, in every way. May the ultimate goal—to see You face to face—remain in the center of my vision through every circumstance, trial, and heartache. In Christ's name, amen.

SEARCH THE WORD

God expects His children to find strength in weakness, and He will provide it.

Scripture: 2 Corinthians 11:16-18, 21-30; 12:9, 10

Song: "Open My Eyes, That I May See"

From this meditation today, I will pray . . .

Adoration _____

Confession _____

Thanksgiving _____

Supplication _____

From this meditation today, I will . . .

Think _____

Say _____

Do _____

*For the foolishness of God
is wiser than man's wisdom,
and the weakness of God
is stronger than man's strength.*

1 Corinthians 1:25

December

COMMITMENT TO THE MESSIAH

"There is no Rock like our God."
—1 Samuel 2:2c

Photo © Lidquid Library

December 1

The Waiting Rock

*There is no one holy like the L*ORD*;
there is no one besides you; there is no Rock like our God*
(1 Samuel 2:2).

Scripture: 1 Samuel 2:1-10
Song: *"My Hope Is Built"*

From this meditation today, I will pray . . .

Adoration _____

Confession _____

Thanksgiving _____

Supplication _____

From this meditation today, I will . . .

Think _____

Say _____

Do _____

December 1–7. **Judyann Grant** *serves the Lord in her local church as secretary and children's mission's director. She lives in Mannsville, New York.*

A dozen yards up from the road, a heart-shaped rock is embedded in our dirt and stone driveway. Dubbed "the waiting rock," it's the perfect size and shape for little feet to stand upon and wait.

You see, when our eldest granddaughter was 4, she caught the preschool bus at our home. At 8:15 each weekday morning, Grampy and Bailey walked hand-in-hand down the driveway to await the big yellow bus. As Bailey stood with her feet planted firmly on the rock, she and Grampy talked, sang, or told stories.

In Hannah's story, we learn about the rewards of waiting patiently. While longing for her prayer for a child to be fulfilled, Hannah planted her future firmly on God, the solid Rock. Her confidence lay in God's ability to bring her painful wait to a happy conclusion. And when He did, her heart overflowed with thanksgiving and praise.

At times when God seems unresponsive, I too plant my feet on the "waiting rock"—trusting the Rock of Ages to hear my prayer and do what He knows is best for me.

Father, *teach me to wait patiently on the Solid Rock until Your answer comes. In Jesus' precious name I pray. Amen.*

SPOTLIGHT
Next Week's Lesson

Stand firmly, wait patiently for God's good timing.

December 2

The Family Tree

In the sixth month, God sent the angel Gabriel to Nazareth, a town in Galilee, to a virgin pledged to be married to a man named Joseph, a descendant of David (Luke 1:26, 27).

When I said "Yes" to my future husband's proposal, I didn't know he had famous ancestors. How exciting to learn that his relatives were descendants of a U.S. President, Ulysses S. Grant! I apparently had at least some claim to an impressive historical figure.

After we wed, Don gave me two heirlooms that had been in his family for years: Grandmother Ruth's 1898 Singer sewing machine cabinet and Aunt Mabel's Larkin secretary desk. One day, we'll pass them to our children.

When Mary agreed to marry Joseph, I wonder whether she was aware that King David's bloodline ran through the young carpenter's family tree? Perhaps she was excited to become part of a respected family. Then, what a blessing to be chosen as the mother of God's Son—through whom would come salvation for all. How that news must have sent Mary's heart soaring! The angel certainly promised an awesome legacy for the newborn: The babe would inherit the throne of King David as His birthright. He would reign over the house of Jacob forever.

O Lord, *thank You that, through Your Son, I am counted among the branches of Your family tree—and have become heir to all the riches of Heaven. In Christ's blessed name I pray. Amen.*

SEARCH THE WORD

How wonderful to be part of a royal family!

Scripture: Luke 1:26-33
Song: *"Blest Be the Tie That Binds"*

From this meditation today, I will pray . . .

Adoration _____

Confession _____

Thanksgiving _____

Supplication _____

From this meditation today, I will . . .

Think _____

Say _____

Do _____

December 3

Momentous Moment

The Holy Spirit will come upon you, and the power of the Most High will overshadow you. So the holy one to be born will be called the Son of God (Luke 1:35).

Scripture: Luke 1:34-38

Song: *"All to Jesus I Surrender"*

From this meditation today, I will pray . . .

Adoration _____

Confession _____

Thanksgiving _____

Supplication _____

From this meditation today, I will . . .

Think _____

Say _____

Do _____

I vividly recall my husband's reaction when I announced he was going to be a first-time father. Getting home from work a few minutes before he did, I stuffed a small, round pillow under my blouse. When he came in the door, instead of rushing to greet him, I kept my back to him. Immediately sensing something askew, Don came behind me and encircled my waist with his arms. He jumped when he felt the bump in my middle. I whirled around and exclaimed, "You're going to be a father!" My method, though corny, was effective. "Hooray!" he shouted, jumping for joy.

The virgin Mary may have lacked confidence in telling Joseph of her impending motherhood. Since they were not yet married, she no doubt feared his reaction. Yet, despite her fears, Mary said, "May it be to me as you have said," (v. 38). Unreservedly, she submitted herself to God as His chosen vessel, placing herself, her baby, and their future in God's hands. In the end, Joseph—just like my husband—accepted the joyous news as a gift from God.

Heavenly Father, *when the future seems uncertain, help me confidently place my life—and the lives of my loved ones—in Your capable, loving hands. In the name of Jesus I pray. Amen.*

SPOTLIGHT
Next Week's Lesson

The reward for obedience is worth whatever it costs us.

December 4

A Godly Heritage

Moved by the Spirit, he went into the temple courts. When the parents brought in the child Jesus to do for him what the custom of the Law required, Simeon took him in his arms. (Luke 2:27).

Scripture: Luke 2:25-35
Song: *"Children of the Heavenly Father"*

We presented each of our daughters at a very young age to be dedicated to God and to receive His blessing. The ceremony offered us time to draw aside from the immediate demands of parenting and look forward to their future. As we held each girl in our arms, we knew that the dedication ceremony gave no guarantee of future joy, nor was it a guarantee against future heartache. (As they grew from childhood to adulthood, we experienced equal measures of both.)

Yet, we reminded ourselves that our children were in the Lord's hands. We trusted Him to fulfill His purpose for each of their lives, and we endeavored to live in ways worthy to be imitated. Now that our girls have children of their own, we continue to trust Him to work in their lives and help them to be good parents.

Joseph and Mary brought Jesus to the temple that day to fulfill the Law. Their act, too, was a way of offering His life into the hands of the Father. And how excellently Jesus would please His parents—the earthly ones and the heavenly one!

Lord, as I influence the children around me, help me to submit to Your transforming influence in my own life. Through Christ my Lord, amen.

From this meditation today, I will pray . . .

Adoration _____

Confession _____

Thanksgiving _____

Supplication _____

From this meditation today, I will . . .

Think _____

Say _____

Do _____

SEARCH THE WORD

Present back to God the present He's given to you: your child.

December 5

A Glimpse of Glory

On the third day a wedding took place at Cana in Galilee. Jesus' mother was there (John 2:1).

Scripture: John 2:1-11
Song: *"The Glorious Gates of Righteousness"*

From this meditation today, I will pray . . .
Adoration _____
_____
_____

Confession _____
_____
_____

Thanksgiving _____
_____
_____

Supplication _____
_____
_____

From this meditation today, I will . . .
Think _____
_____
_____

Say _____
_____
_____

Do _____
_____
_____
_____

Weddings vary as much as the brides who plan them. Our eldest daughter chose a traditional church wedding with a pianist, candles, aisle-runner, cushioned pews, and florist bouquets. The bride posed confidently in a beautiful gown, the groom in a tuxedo. A professional photographer captured each moment.

Our youngest daughter was married in a tree-lined park nestled on the shores of a lake. Balloons, streamers, and wildflowers fluttered in the breeze. The casually-dressed bride walked down a grassy "aisle" to join her khaki-dressed groom. Guests, with their own cameras, captured the day on film. If there had been a problem at either wedding, I'm sure, as the mother of the bride, I would have been called upon to "fix it."

Mary, a hands-on mom, became aware of a problem at the wedding she and her Son were attending. She turned to Jesus to "fix" the beverage shortage, and Jesus granted her request. After all, He cared about weddings. His future ministry would demonstrate how the love of a man for a woman so aptly symbolizes God's love for His bride, the church.

Heavenly Father, *may each wedding or anniversary celebration remind me of Your precious love for Your Church. In Jesus' name I pray. Amen.*

SPOTLIGHT
Next Week's Lesson

Mary's own wedding was humble and quiet, yet she helped someone else have a happy one.

December 6

When Appearances Deceive

So when they met together, they asked him, "Lord, are you at this time going to restore the kingdom to Israel?" (Acts 1:6).

Daddy took his 3-year-old daughter fishing. Wanting to shield her from the unpleasantness of baiting the hook, he did it out of her sight. Then . . . *plunk!* He dropped the line in the water and handed Kaylee the pole.

At the slightest movement of the bobber, Kaylee begged, "I wanna see the fish!" Her impatience grew each time she drew in the line and found only a wiggly worm. Finally, exasperated, she scolded her father: "Daddy! Stop catching *worms!*"

Kaylee's confusion came from her misinterpretation of the facts. "Confused" may describe how the disciples felt as they watched Jesus ascend into the clouds. Through-out Jesus' ministry, the disciples thought they knew how His story would end. They had seen Jesus honored and scorned, crucified and resurrected. Now, perhaps, He would claim His kingdom on earth. Their shortsightedness caused them to jump to the wrong conclusion.

Jesus worked behind the scenes to fulfill His Father's plan. Only after the disciples spent time praying and growing in the Spirit would they understand—Jesus' kingdom was not of this world.

God, *forgive me when I jump to the wrong conclusions about Your plans. Help me trust You, even when I don't understand. Through Christ, amen.*

SEARCH THE WORD

Jesus changed the confused and cowardly into the calm and courageous.

Scripture: Acts 1:6-14
Song: *"Give to the Winds Thy Fears"*

From this meditation today, I will pray . . .

Adoration _____

Confession _____

Thanksgiving _____

Supplication _____

From this meditation today, I will . . .

Think _____

Say _____

Do _____

December 7

The Promise to Come

Mary said: "My soul glorifies the Lord and my spirit rejoices in God my Savior" (Luke 1:46, 47).

Scripture: Luke 1:46-55
Song: *"To God Be the Glory"*

From this meditation today, I will pray . . .
Adoration _____
_____
_____

Confession _____
_____
_____

Thanksgiving _____
_____
_____

Supplication _____
_____
_____

From this meditation today, I will . . .
Think _____
_____
_____

Say _____
_____
_____

Do _____
_____
_____
_____

In the middle of a typical 1950s December, my mother's due date approached. I would be born any day! Winters then were what we now call "old-fashioned." Snow fell thick and deep early in the season and lingered until late spring. Not an ideal time to live in an isolated farmhouse, on an unpaved road, with a baby due!

With my birth imminent, my 9 and 10-year-old sisters bundled up in heavy coats and trudged a mile to use the neighbor's phone. From there they could summon the country doctor. Thankfully, the doctor arrived before I did. My mother praised the Lord for the safe, home delivery of her early Christmas gift.

Growing up, I was teased about having a birthday so close to Christmas. Did I feel shortchanged because my presents came wrapped in Christmas paper? Not at all. There were songs and celebrations, star-filled skies, and miracles waiting to unfold at each birthday. It is an honor to celebrate my birthday so close to that of my Lord's. With Mary, my soul rejoices in the promised gift of God.

My Lord God, *thank You for the gift of Your Son and for a mother who taught me how much You love me. May I be faithful in passing on what I have learned of Your goodness and grace. In the name of the Father, the Son, and the Holy Spirit, I pray. Amen.*

SPOTLIGHT
Next Week's Lesson

"It is good to praise the LORD and make music to your name, O Most High" (Psalm 92:1).

December 8

Heavenly Visitors

Abraham hurried into the tent
(Genesis 18:6).

While Abraham meditated on the Lord, he realized that heavenly visitors had arrived. He asked his wife, Sarah, to make cakes. Then he ran to fetch a calf for a meal, since he was anxious to extend generous hospitality.

In my younger years, I thought I had to make a homemade dessert and serve several dishes when we had friends over for a visit. But after working outside the home for several years, I've learned to prepare more simple dishes. We can still offer wonderful hospitality to a few friends. But there are limits to how often we can entertain—and the amount of preparation I can do. Yet the fellowship is always worth the effort.

Abraham's visitors had a message for him that would change his life. As we have opened our home to missionaries, ministers, and other visitors, my perspective on life has broadened too. My life is richer because of these friends who have shared a cup of coffee or a meal. In fact, we've sometimes wondered if a few of them weren't also heavenly visitors.

Lord, *as I spend time before You in prayer, remind me that I can bless and be blessed by my fellowship with other believers. And may our fellowship always take precedence over the details of the meal! In Jesus' name, amen.*

SEARCH THE WORD

Hospitality that waits for perfection rarely happens.

Scripture: Genesis 18:1-8
Song: *"Approved in Every Way"*

From this meditation today, I will pray...

Adoration _____

Confession _____

Thanksgiving _____

Supplication _____

From this meditation today, I will...

Think _____

Say _____

Do _____

December 8–14. **Phyllis Qualls Freeman** and her husband, of Hixson, Tennessee, love to see their grandchildren participating in church, school, and sports.

December 9

At the Appointed Time

Is anything too hard for the LORD? I will return to you at the appointed time next year (Genesis 18:14).

Scripture: Genesis 18:9-14
Song: *"Mighty Lord, Extend Thy Kingdom"*

From this meditation today, I will pray . . .
Adoration _____
_____
_____

Confession _____
_____
_____

Thanksgiving _____
_____
_____

Supplication _____
_____
_____

From this meditation today, I will . . .
Think _____
_____
_____

Say _____
_____
_____

Do _____
_____
_____
_____

The Lord said He would return "at the appointed time." And the Lord did visit Sarah as He said, and He did unto Sarah as He had spoken: she had a son, Isaac. God fulfills His promises at His pre-appointed time.

My sister, Dot, says that God sometimes waits until her prayer seems beyond the hope of an answer. Then He so often brings an *unexpected* answer. She also taught me about God's perfect timing when she shared her concept of how God sees our circumstances. Dot calls it His "panoramic vision." From a panoramic X-ray, a dentist can determine whether wisdom teeth are forming and if any of them will need to be extracted. He can also see decay that might be hidden from the natural eye.

We usually trust the dentist's wisdom regarding the timing of any needed dental surgery. So perhaps I could learn to trust God's evaluation of what He sees coming my way. Then I could more fully trust His timing for the answer to each prayer—whether it's "yes," "no," or "wait"—instead of clinging so tightly to my own expectations.

All-seeing God, *help me trust Your timing for bringing Your promises to pass. You know best when I need something, because You have a good plan for my entire life! Thank You, in Jesus' name. Amen.*

SPOTLIGHT
Next Week's Lesson
Even to the elderly and barren, God can give a child.

December 10

While We Obey

And it came to pass, that, while he executed the priest's office before God . . . (Luke 1:8, *King James Version*).

Everyone knew about, but no one mentioned, the large round lump on Mrs. Robbin's cheek. It was slightly smaller than a tennis ball, but her doctors would not try to remove it because the tumor's roots spread into her ear.

For years she asked for prayer that God would heal this condition, but nothing happened. So she went about raising her large family, teaching Sunday school, and being a faithful Christian.

One Wednesday night we noticed a large, flat patch over the place where Robbie's lump had been. Robbie said that two days before, she saw a bit of fluid leaking from the site. Then, for days, the place seeped what appeared to be tissue and the roots of the tumor.

Her children had never seen their mom without the lump on her cheek. Everyone rejoiced because of the change. We also noted that this miracle didn't happen because Robbie did, or did not do, a certain thing. It didn't seem to happen as a result of a certain person's faith. But as Robbie continued to be faithful, God was at work in her life.

Gracious Heavenly Father, *when I wonder whether You have heard my prayers, remind me that You are constantly working in me. As I stay faithful in my own calling, You are faithful as well. In Jesus' name, amen.*

SEARCH THE WORD

God loves to surprise us with answers to our prayers.

Scripture: Luke 1:5-11
Song: *"I Am the God That Healeth Thee"*

From this meditation today, I will pray . . .

Adoration _____

Confession _____

Thanksgiving _____

Supplication _____

From this meditation today, I will . . .

Think _____

Say _____

Do _____

December 11

Expectation of Joy

Thou shalt have joy and gladness; and many shall rejoice at his birth
(Luke 1:14, *King James Version*).

Scripture: Luke 1:12-20
Song: *"Joy Unspeakable"*

From this meditation today, I will pray . . .
Adoration _____
_____
_____

Confession _____
_____
_____

Thanksgiving _____
_____
_____

Supplication _____
_____
_____

From this meditation today, I will . . .
Think _____
_____
_____

Say _____
_____
_____

Do _____
_____
_____
_____

When we first moved to Ohio, my husband (who grew up in Minnesota) routinely watched the weather forecast in the wintertime. We were at the home of friends one evening when he looked out and saw it snowing. He grew very serious and said, "We'd better head for home."

I was raised in Michigan—familiar with driving in snow and ice—so I did not understand his constant expectation that the weather would make the roads impassable. His experience with Minnesota blizzards and snow drifts six feet high caused him to expect and prepare for the worst.

Our expectations often flow from our past experiences. Perhaps this is why some people have difficulty expecting blessings from God; they just aren't used to seeing things turn out for the good.

We, who know the promises of God's Word, can choose to believe for the best and blessed outcome. Why? Because God is faithful. He loves to bring joy and gladness to us. His plan for us is a good plan. Look for, and expect, joy.

Faithful God in Heaven, *forgive me for anticipating less than You desire for me. Raise the level of my expectations. And help me to know Your joy, in the good times and in the times of trial. I pray this prayer in the name of Jesus, my merciful Savior and Lord. Amen.*

SPOTLIGHT
Next Week's Lesson

Never expect less than the best from the Giver of all good gifts.

December 12

He Looks upon Me

He looked on me, to take away my reproach among men
(Luke 1:25, *King James Version*).

A mother brought her 14-year-old daughter before a TV "judge," stating that the daughter intentionally dressed in a way that would cause men to lust for her. The judge wisely sent the girl to a couple of women who would serve as role models. They'd show her how she could dress more modestly (and thus become more truly attractive as a young lady). After this encounter, the teenager actually changed her attitude. And she instantly began to enjoy more self-respect.

I grew up in a day when dressing modestly was highly valued. Yet, I have come to realize that even though my outer appearance does reflect my inner person to some degree, God looks deeper. He sees my heart.

God sees me individually, viewing even my stresses and temptations, my dreams and longings. Yes, He sees my faults and failures, but the Holy One delights in giving me a deeper measure of abundant life. If only I will open my heart to Him, day by day, I need never suffer any form of reproach.

All-seeing God, *help me to live my life in a way that brings You pleasure when You see me. Then help me to keep the intent of my heart pure so that others can see beyond my weaknesses and failures to the glory of Your presence within me. In the name of Your Son, my Savior, I pray. Amen.*

Scripture: Luke 1:21-25
Song: *"He Looked Beyond My Fault"*

From this meditation today, I will pray...

Adoration _____

Confession _____

Thanksgiving _____

Supplication _____

From this meditation today, I will...

Think _____

Say _____

Do _____

SEARCH THE WORD

"Let the beauty of Jesus be seen in me."
—Albert Orsborn

December 13

Believing the Unexplainable

Blessed is she that believed: for there shall be a performance of those things which were told her from the Lord (Luke 1:45, *King James Version*).

Scripture: Luke 1:39-45
Song: *"Mary, Did You Know?"*

From this meditation today, I will pray . . .
Adoration _____
_____
_____

Confession _____
_____
_____

Thanksgiving _____
_____
_____

Supplication _____
_____
_____

From this meditation today, I will . . .
Think _____
_____
_____

Say _____
_____
_____

Do _____
_____
_____
_____
_____

Did Mary fully comprehend the prophesy Elisabeth proclaimed? She may not have understood it with her mind; however, she believed it in her heart.

As we neared retirement, my husband and I knew we couldn't continue to maintain the home we enjoyed. Then our older son shared with us that he and his wife wanted us to live near them; thus, they could help whenever we needed some assistance. We thought they'd get a larger home with property where we might put a small trailer-home for us. But God had a bigger idea.

The beginning of a new chapter in our lives started as we moved into a large home with a suite of two rooms and bath just for the two of us. We share the rest of the house with my son's family, and I even share an upstairs office with my grandson, Joshua.

We know there's a purpose here. Far beyond our comfort and enjoyment, we feel that God has more in mind than we imagined. Already God is bringing in visitors whose lives need to be touched by His love through us.

God of abundance, *thank You for provision that seemed unbelievable. Help me continually believe You for blessings—that we might pass on the overflow to those whose lives need refreshing. In Jesus' name, amen.*

SPOTLIGHT
Next Week's Lesson
Elizabeth was blessed by God beyond her wildest dreams.

December 14

Rejoice with Your Neighbor

And her neighbors and her cousins heard how the Lord had showed great mercy upon her; and they rejoiced with her (Luke 1:58, *King James Version*).

Scripture: Luke 1:57-63
Song: "Always Something New in Jesus"

My little puppy, Poco, had to do a lot of adjusting when we moved in with my son's family and his two cats. Poco handled it all fairly well, but every time she began to eat from her dog dish, Mattie Cat would pounce at her. Even though there were different food dishes and plenty of food, Mattie seemed to begrudge any intruder in her home.

Sometimes people are like that. Though God's mercies and blessings are abundant, some want it all for themselves. Don't we know there is plenty for everyone?

I once felt jealous about a great blessing someone else received. But the Lord seemed to remind me: maybe that person *needed* the small miracle—and the Lord had trusted me to be faithful *without* a miracle. I think about it often and am humbled by God's goodness toward me.

Can we rejoice when our brothers and sisters are blessed? Can we enjoy watching others receive good things? God has allowed the blessings. Let us rejoice with those who receive such goodness from His hand.

God, when You abundantly bless another, help me enjoy Your generosity to them. Whether or not I receive the same good thing, grow me into a maturity that allows heartfelt celebration with them. In Jesus' name, amen.

From this meditation today, I will pray . . .
Adoration _____
Confession _____
Thanksgiving _____
Supplication _____

From this meditation today, I will . . .
Think _____
Say _____
Do _____

SEARCH THE WORD

Be as happy for others as you would have them be happy for you.

December 15

What Lies Ahead?

Declaring the end from the beginning, And from ancient times things which have not been done, Saying, "My purpose will be established, And I will accomplish all My good pleasure"
(Isaiah 46:10, New American Standard Bible).

Scripture: Isaiah 46:8-13
Song: "Take My Life and Let it Be"

From this meditation today, I will pray . . .
Adoration _____
_____
_____

Confession _____
_____
_____

Thanksgiving _____
_____
_____

Supplication _____
_____
_____

From this meditation today, I will . . .
Think _____
_____
_____

Say _____
_____
_____

Do _____
_____
_____

My wife and I have lived in eight states since we were married in 1950, and even lived twice in Minnesota. Why did we move so much? I changed jobs, even careers, and attended three different universities in three states, earning graduate degrees in two of them.

Yes, we moved constantly, and enjoyed every place where we landed. Yet I believe the Lord has orchestrated all of our life experiences ultimately for *His* pleasure. For example, in our last move we left jobs in Missouri in order to attend a church in Oklahoma, where we have lived for over 20 years.

God knows the end from the beginning, but can we depend on Him to lead us in the most practical daily decisions of our lives? He directs us for His pleasure; therefore, let us enjoy bringing a smile to His face through all our words and deeds. And as we consider our next move, may we ask first how it might bring Him glory.

Heavenly Father, *I thank You that You have led me in paths for Your pleasure. In the name of Christ I pray. Amen.*

December 15-21. **Richard Rundell** *of Haskell, Oklahoma, is a freelance writer and author of several Christian books and numerous Christian articles.*

SPOTLIGHT
Next Week's Lesson

It pleased God to send simple shepherds to announce the Savior's birth.

December 16

The Lord's Beauty

*The earth is the L*ORD*'s, and all its fullness,*
The world and those who dwell therein. For He has founded
it upon the seas, And established it upon the waters
(Psalm 24:1, 2, New King James Version).

In July of 1963 my wife and I traveled to Wisconsin to visit relatives. Even though I had lived there several years before, this time I especially noticed the beauty of the strip cropping in southwest Wisconsin. I saw the golden yellow of the oats, alternating with the corn and alfalfa, each revealing its own distinctive shade of green.

Yes, when we farmed in Wisconsin, we planted the crops but the Lord, through His provision of rain, sun, seasons, and soil made them grow. And the earth, the crops, livestock, trees, and grass—all proclaim His power and glory. Looking at His works we can discern, at least to some degree, the character of our Almighty Lord.

But in order to appreciate the handiwork of God, we often need to step back from our own busyness. To appreciate the beauty of the earth, it's time to look around a bit! And to appreciate the beauty of the persons whom the Lord has placed in our world—"those who dwell therein"—we may well need to stop and make a friend.

Great God of Creation, *I thank You that You have made a beautiful earth for me to enjoy—and for my eyes to behold. When I look, let me truly see! In the holy name of Jesus, my Lord and Savior, I pray. Amen.*

SEARCH THE WORD

Do you see what I see?
—God's glorious world!

Scripture: Psalm 24
Song: *"For the Beauty of the Earth"*

From this meditation today, I will pray . . .

Adoration _____
_____
_____

Confession _____
_____
_____

Thanksgiving _____
_____
_____

Supplication _____
_____
_____

From this meditation today, I will . . .

Think _____
_____
_____

Say _____
_____
_____

Do _____
_____
_____

December 17

From Rags to Riches

He raises the poor out of the dust, And lifts the needy out of the ash heap (Psalm 113:7, New King James Version).

Scripture: Psalm 113
Song: *"Lift Up Your Hearts"*

From this meditation today, I will pray . . .
Adoration _____

Confession _____

Thanksgiving _____

Supplication _____

From this meditation today, I will . . .
Think _____

Say _____

Do _____

I was born and raised on a dairy and hog farm in southern Wisconsin during the depression. As a family, by many standards, we were poor. But we never considered ourselves in that light.

The depression of the 1930s forced my dad and other farmers to hang on tightly to their farms. So we always had milk, eggs, chicken, pork, and a big garden to sustain us. And on Saturday nights we went to town to "trade" our eggs for many of our groceries.

For seven years, I attended a one-room country school. Then because of my father's poor health, we moved to a small city. I was too young to even dream of getting a graduate degree. But years later I was blessed with the opportunity to attend college, eventually earning a PhD.

Who would guess a product of a country school would earn a doctorate from Michigan State? Yet it all unfolded, step by step, by God's gracious, lifting hand. And isn't that the way it is with all things in our lives, even our salvation? As an old offertory sentence says: "All things come of thee, O Lord, and of Thine own have we given thee."

God who lifts me up, *I praise You that by Your grace I can look forward to daily blessings under Your care. In the precious name of Jesus, amen.*

SPOTLIGHT
Next Week's Lesson

"Humble yourselves before the Lord, and he will lift you up"
(James 4:10).

December 18

Let It Rain

Fire and hail, snow and clouds; Stormy wind, fulfilling His word (Psalm 148:8, *New American Standard Bible*).

Oh, those rainy days of June in Wisconsin! Why did it seem to rain so often when we finally had our hay cut and raked? Could we discern the coming weather to time our haying between the rains? Well, sometimes. Yet all the crops needed the rain. The snow, hail, and clouds with rain all came at the appointed time under the sovereignty of God.

I have gardened most of the years of my life, even planted gardens in seven states. And sometimes, just when I planned to work in the garden, God would send His rain.

But let us praise the Lord for rain to water the gardens and the grass. It falls according to the great cycles of weather that He set in motion from the beginning of creation. The rain and snow fall under His watchful eye.

Of course, He knows what we need better than we do, in order for us to live lives pleasing to Him. He looks for an open-hearted servant, in all kinds of weather, who will drink in His blessings and go forth to do His will.

Lord, *I have grown in my appreciation for Your creation, with its weather patterns that work for my good. Help me also to grow in my desire to serve You. You have sprinkled into my life the spiritual gifts to carry out Your work; give me the will to follow through! In Jesus' name, amen.*

SEARCH THE WORD
Whatever the weather, let's labor together.

Scripture: Psalm 148
Song: *"Father, Who on Man Dost Shower"*

From this meditation today, I will pray . . .

Adoration _____

Confession _____

Thanksgiving _____

Supplication _____

From this meditation today, I will . . .

Think _____

Say _____

Do _____

December 19

Dwell in This Reality!

Now is manifested, and by the Scriptures of the prophets, according to the commandment of the eternal God, has been made known to all the nations, leading to obedience of faith
(Romans 16:26, *New American Standard Bible*).

Scripture: Romans 16:25-27
Song: *"He Lives"*

From this meditation today, I will pray . . .

Adoration _____
_____
_____

Confession _____
_____
_____

Thanksgiving _____
_____
_____

Supplication _____
_____
_____

From this meditation today, I will . . .

Think _____
_____
_____

Say _____
_____
_____

Do _____
_____
_____
_____

The well-known hymn "He Lives" ends with the words, "You ask me how I know He Lives—He lives within my heart."

We'd sung it many times in the churches we had attended up to this point in our lives. We had again sung this song in our local church in Minnesota. Then, in 1974, my wife and I came to Christ in this church.

In a few weeks, we sang the song again. But this time the old hymn came alive to me as it never had before. It no longer meant just a pretty song but a reality in my heart. I now knew Jesus did, indeed, live in my heart. Moreover, the Bible now came alive to me.

Before Jesus' earthly ministry, many believed in a coming Messiah—but to them it meant waiting for a time well into the future. After Pentecost, though, He became a constant reality in the hearts of the believers. Moreover, the apostle Paul wrote of that mystery now manifested, "Christ in you, the hope of glory" (Colossians 1:27). Don't we all seek to dwell in that reality?

Dear Lord, *thank You for sending Your Holy Spirit to dwell within me. May He lead me into fruiful service today! In Christ I pray. Amen.*

SPOTLIGHT
Next Week's Lesson

The waiting is over.
The Messiah is here!

December 20

The Miracle of Birth

*She brought forth her firstborn son,
and wrapped him in swaddling clothes, and laid him in a manger;
because there was no room for them in the inn*
(Luke 2:7, King James Version).

While operating our livestock farm in Wisconsin, I helped with the births of dairy calves, pigs, and lambs. I also witnessed the miracle of birth with foals, puppies, chicks, and goslings. I often marveled at the providence of God in all these births. The mammals brought forth their newborn in similar ways, but with the chicks and goslings, God appointed them to peck their ways to life out of their shells.

The Bible tells us of no midwife or relative or other people present at the birth of Jesus, except for the shepherds who visited after His birth. But Jesus was born at the appointed time, the appointed place, the appointed way, of the appointed person.

No birth has ever compared to the Incarnation—the awesome miracle of God himself taking on human flesh to save the world from sin. There wasn't a quite room for Him in the local hotels of Bethlehem. But I am so thankful that we can make room for Him in our hearts at a moment's notice. It is as simple as turning our eyes to meet His loving gaze upon us.

Father, *the birth of Your Son transformed the cosmos. May it also powerfully affect my words and deeds this day. Through Christ my Lord, amen.*

SEARCH THE WORD
*A virgin gives birth
and everything changes.*

Scripture: Luke 2:1-7
Song: *"What Child Is This?"*

From this meditation today, I will pray . . .

Adoration _____

Confession _____

Thanksgiving _____

Supplication _____

From this meditation today, I will . . .

Think _____

Say _____

Do _____

December 21

God's Peace

Glory to God in the highest, and on earth peace, good will toward men (Luke 2:14, *King James Version*).

Scripture: Luke 2:8-20
Song: *"Let There Be Peace on Earth"*

From this meditation today, I will pray . . .
Adoration _____
_____
_____

Confession _____
_____
_____

Thanksgiving _____
_____
_____

Supplication _____
_____
_____

From this meditation today, I will . . .
Think _____
_____
_____

Say _____
_____
_____

Do _____
_____
_____
_____

Living in Farmington, Minnesota, and seeking employment, I sent my résumé to a company in Cedar Falls, Iowa. Soon they asked me to come for an interview.

When I arrived in the city, I stopped in a convenience store to ask directions. The lady at the counter told me the company was in the exporting business. I wondered, "What could I do at such a company? Would it even interest me?"

But the Lord gave me peace during the daylong interview. And the job prospect excited me. Furthermore, the Lord gave me peace about accepting the position.

That work as an agricultural commodity market analyst turned out to be the most interesting and rewarding job of my career. I could fully integrate my farm background with my education to accomplish important work.

God's peace comes to our earth, our very being, in the midst of our everyday living. Through it, we can extend good will to all with whom we work and live. It is a commodity in short supply these days—yet God offers it in abundance.

Dear Father in Heaven, *help me actively pursue Your peace for my life as You make it available. Help me to pass Your peace on to my family and friends. In the name of Jesus, Lord and Savior of all, I pray. Amen.*

SPOTLIGHT
Next Week's Lesson

Into our ordinary days God inserts the extraordinary.

December 22

Dressed the Part

What did you go out to see? A man dressed in fine clothes?
(Luke 7:25).

Of all the people who stepped off the small plane onto the tarmac, he was the last man I thought to be our guest. With his face half-covered by a shaggy beard and dressed in jeans, T-shirt, a worn cowboy hat, and boots, he walked forward with an extended hand and a big smile. This was our church's missionary speaker for the week? (And did I mention his earring?)

When John the Baptist came as a herald announcing the ministry of the Lord Jesus Christ, he didn't look anything like people expected. He showed up dressed in "clothing made of camel's hair" (Mark 1:6). He didn't *act* in accord with their expectations either. He wasn't a "reed swayed by the wind" (v. 24), but a man who spoke the truth plainly. And Jesus commended him for it.

Will the Lord someday commend me as one who fulfilled His expectations? Will He joyfully declare I lived in accord with His will? Will He one day say to me, "Well done, good and faithful servant" (Matthew 25:21)?

Lord, help me to act, dress, and speak as one who lives in daily obedience to You. I pray that I'll not do or say anything today that brings shame to Your name or pain to Your heart. In Jesus' name, amen.

Scripture: Luke 7:24-29
Song: *"Live Out Thy Life Within Me"*

From this meditation today, I will pray . . .
Adoration _____
Confession _____
Thanksgiving _____
Supplication _____

From this meditation today, I will . . .
Think _____
Say _____
Do _____

SEARCH THE WORD
Focus on fulfilling Jesus' expectations; forget about other people fulfilling yours.

December 22–28. **Katherine Douglas** is a published author, speaker, and neonatal respiratory therapist who resides in Berkey, Ohio.

December 23

Simulated Sunlight

He himself was not the light; he came only as a witness to the light (John 1:8).

Scripture: John 1:6-9
Song: *"Shine, Jesus, Shine"*

From this meditation today, I will pray . . .
Adoration _____
Confession _____
Thanksgiving _____
Supplication _____

From this meditation today, I will . . .
Think _____
Say _____
Do _____

When Doug built a room-within-a-room in his basement, he didn't want the finished product to feel or look like a windowless dungeon. So he constructed "windows" of opaque acrylic on one wall. He hung attractive window shades and suspended lights behind the faux windows. Now, with the flick of a switch, he has the illusion of sunlight blazing through from just outside his below-ground sanctuary.

John the Baptist didn't appear haphazardly on the scene before Jesus began His earthly ministry. He "was sent from God" (v. 6) and came as a witness to the true light. John the Baptist and the apostle John, who wrote this Gospel, both affirmed that only Jesus is "the true light that gives light to every man" (v. 9). This was no illusion or simulation. As predicted, the "sun of righteousness" (Malachi 4:2) had come at last.

For those days when we're in the dark—when we don't understand what's happening around us—we can still know that our source of light and love is with us. Our shining, everlasting Savior is the real thing.

God of light, *thank You for sending Jesus, my greatest source of light, love, and life. Let me be a clear window through which He shines brightly. In His name I pray. Amen.*

SPOTLIGHT
Next Week's Lesson

John the Baptist shone a spotlight on the sins of the people.

December 24

Humble Pie

He is the one who comes after me, the thongs of whose sandals I am not worthy to untie (John 1:27).

As a self-assured young man, Dick lived his life recklessly. Then he lost his left arm in a car accident.

Recovering in the hospital, he told his doctor, "I'll be OK; I'll manage." His doctor barely looked up from his chart. "Is that so? Wait until you try to tie your shoes for the first time."

Dick quickly learned humility. He wears slip-on shoes or shoes with self-adhesive straps. Because of his humbling accident, Dick isn't able to tie his—or anyone else's—shoes.

In humble honesty, John the Baptist said he would never presume to even untie the sandals of Jesus. He recognized Jesus as the one and only God-man. And the Baptist admitted he was only "the voice"; Jesus was the Lord of all (v. 23).

I've not had a humbling experience as painful and life-changing as Dick has suffered—nor do I want one. When I read about John the Baptist, I realize I wouldn't be worthy to untie *his* sandals! But I want to learn from John's example and live a life of humble service.

Lord over all, teach me to live a life of service and humility. To regard others as better than myself. To be honest about who I am and who You are. In the powerful name of Jesus I pray. Amen.

SEARCH THE WORD
"Really great men have a curious feeling that the greatness is not of them, but through them."—John Ruskin

Scripture: John 1:19-28
Song: *"Pass Me Not, O Gentle Savior"*

From this meditation today, I will pray . . .
Adoration _____

Confession _____

Thanksgiving _____

Supplication _____

From this meditation today, I will . . .
Think _____

Say _____

Do _____

December 25

He's Here!

The next day John saw Jesus coming toward him and said, "Look, the Lamb of God, who takes away the sin of the world!" (John 1:29).

Scripture: John 1:29-34
Song: *"Good Christian Men, Rejoice"*

From this meditation today, I will pray...

Adoration _____

Confession _____

Thanksgiving _____

Supplication _____

From this meditation today, I will...

Think _____

Say _____

Do _____

Their daughter, an Air Force nurse, wouldn't be home for Christmas. At first she couldn't get leave. When she did, there were no flights.

But the nurse's sister had a plan. "See if you can get a flight into Detroit. It would only be an hour's drive for us—and a great surprise for Mom and Dad." When nurse Nancy surprised her parents on Christmas, their happy cry rang out: "She's here!"

To the shepherds, the angel announced the arrival of "a Savior . . . Christ the Lord" (Luke 2:11). Some 30 years later, John the Baptist declared this Savior had come and was starting His ministry. Jesus was "the Lamb of God and "the Son of God" (vv. 29, 34). Just as the angels had proclaimed to the shepherds, so John announced to his hearers: "He's here!"

We too may anticipate our Savior's coming. We can look forward to the day when "the Lord himself will come down from heaven" (1 Thessalonians 4:16). That will be a coming like no other.

Almighty and everlasting Father, I praise You for coming to earth on that first Christmas in the person of Jesus. Thank You that someday He will return as promised. Come, Lord Jesus, I pray! Amen.

SPOTLIGHT
Next Week's Lesson

"O come, let us adore him,
Christ the Lord."
—John F. Wade

December 26

Tell the Truth

You have sent to John and he has testified to the truth (John 5:33).

Not long ago a woman in our community called 9-1-1. She told the police she had been kidnapped, but escaped. She was now alone in the park. Could the police come and rescue her?

The police rescued her . . . but they also investigated her story. No one could validate the alleged victim's account, because it never happened. She made up the story.

Jesus always told the truth. He claimed to *be* the Truth (John 14:6), and He said there were two others to testify to the truth of what He said. One was His Father; the other was John the Baptist (see John 5:37 and the verse above).

Christ knew that the people He spoke to esteemed John. So He cited John's truthful testimony about Him.

When others look at my life, I want it to give testimony to the truth of who Jesus is. I don't need to make up stories for attention. Jesus Christ has given me a life worth living, and I am happy to share about it. Like the old hymn says, this is my story—and I want to praise my Savior all day long.

God of all truth, *help me be a person who always tells the truth. Help me to be honest in my work and in my relationships. Let my life be a reflection of the truth that is in your Son, the one who loves me and lives within me. I pray in His precious name, amen.*

SEARCH THE WORD

Let our lives reflect the truth of our testimonies about Jesus.

Scripture: John 5:30-35
Song: *"Blessed Assurance"*

From this meditation today, I will pray . . .

Adoration _____

Confession _____

Thanksgiving _____

Supplication _____

From this meditation today, I will . . .

Think _____

Say _____

Do _____

December 27

Friend of the Groom

The friend who attends the bridegroom waits and listens for him, and is full of joy when he hears the bridegroom's voice. That joy is mine, and it is now complete (John 3:29).

Scripture: John 3:22-30
Song: *"Friend of Sinners, Lord of Glory"*

From this meditation today, I will pray . . .

Adoration _____

Confession _____

Thanksgiving _____

Supplication _____

From this meditation today, I will . . .

Think _____

Say _____

Do _____

Their friendship began when they were both cadets at the US Naval Academy. Now the best man raised his soda bottle to toast his friend and his new bride. He was obviously proud and happy for the newlyweds at the table with him.

"To the happy couple," he began, "on this day I thought would never come!" (And the parents of the beautiful, 30-something bride couldn't have agreed more!)

In today's Scripture reading, the ministry of John the Baptist is coming to a close. His disciples whine that Jesus is baptizing and seems to be drawing everyone over to Him. Yet John shows no regret or sorrow. He tells his disciples that his joy was now complete. He'll now be content to fade into obscurity while the Christ rises to prominence.

We too can be like John. Others can see our lives, our encouraging words and good works, and rejoice in our Savior. It's a privilege like no other to witness to Christ's excellence with our own lives. Just like being the best man at a long-awaited wedding.

Dearest Lord, *thank You for my special relationship with You. I praise Your Son, Jesus, because He's both bridegroom and friend. Thank You that I can share all my joys with Him. I pray in His precious name, amen.*

SPOTLIGHT
Next Week's Lesson

As the forerunner of Christ, John delivered his message, and then faded into the background.

December 28

Does the Walk Match the Talk?

Produce fruit in keeping with repentance. And do not begin to say to yourselves, "We have Abraham as our father." For I tell you that out of these stones God can raise up children for Abraham (Luke 3:8).

When Mark was a boy, he got together with his friends for some destructive "fun." With rocks in hand, they broke a number of windows in their school building. They never got caught and never "ratted" on each other. But when Mark became a Christian years later, he knew he should make amends.

Imagine the surprise when he went to the board of education, confessed to his boyhood vandalism, and insisted on paying for the windows he had broken! The board accepted payment 20 years after the fact.

God cares that we show the genuineness of our repentance in measurable, observable acts of restitution. He cares little if we're royals or commoners. The Lord says we can't rest on our bloodline or ancestry to impress Him. If He wants, He can make people from stones.

If we have plenty, we're to be generous. If we're soldiers, we're to be content with our pay. If we're CPAs, we're to be honest in business. And if we've broken windows, we're to pay for them.

Father, *I've not always done right. Help me demonstrate the genuineness of my faith by righting my wrongs when I can. In Christ's name, amen.*

Scripture: Luke 3:7-18
Song: *"Channels Only"*

From this meditation today, I will pray...

Adoration _____

Confession _____

Thanksgiving _____

Supplication _____

From this meditation today, I will...

Think _____

Say _____

Do _____

SEARCH THE WORD

What wrong do you need to make right?

December 29

Mistaken Blame

*He that backbiteth not with his tongue, . . .
nor taketh up a reproach against his neighbor*
(Psalm 15:3, *King James Version*).

Scripture: Psalm 15
Song: *"I Want to Be Like Jesus"*

From this meditation today, I will pray . . .
Adoration _____
_____
_____

Confession _____
_____
_____

Thanksgiving _____
_____
_____

Supplication _____
_____
_____

From this meditation today, I will . . .
Think _____
_____
_____

Say _____
_____
_____

Do _____
_____
_____

December 29–31. **Carol Russell,** *of Fort Scott, Kansas, has written articles and stories in Christian magazines, as well as take-home papers for children and adults.*

"I think she's guilty," I said, with an emphases on guilty. She was the new girl in the dorm, and now we were missing various small items. To me, all evidence pointed to Beth. We didn't have a problem before she moved in, so I concluded it must be her. I slandered Beth with harsh words and spoke against her reputation.

I was wrong, of course, but it was too late to take back my accusations. Beth eventually forgave me, but the damage caused many tears.

Jesus said we are to love our neighbors as ourselves. We are not to speak evil or defame them. God wants us to think the best of our fellow Christians and encourage, uplift, and enlighten with our words.

We are not perfect, nor can we be. Thankfully, God sent His Son to the cross to pay for our imperfections. However, should we not examine ourselves to see whether we truly love our neighbor as Jesus commanded?

Heavenly Father, *thank You for loving and forgiving me. As You have loved me, teach me to love others. I love You, Lord, and want others to see You through me. Give me grace to love my neighbor, to understand, and not be judgmental of others. In His holy name. Amen.*

SPOTLIGHT
Next Week's Lesson

"May the words of my mouth . . .
be pleasing in your sight, O Lord"
(Psalm 19:14).

December 30

I Can Do This

The Lord is my light and my salvation; whom shall I fear? The Lord is the strength of my life; of whom shall I be afraid? (Psalm 27:1, *King James Version*).

Aunt Neil smiled at me. "Don't worry. God and I can do this." Because of a childhood accident, my aunt was blind. Since the age of 9, she had depended heavily on others. Now, she wanted a guide dog and independence. But she would have to fly to Columbus, Ohio, without family, to train with her dog for six weeks.

When she returned with her dog, she said: "See, I told you God and I could do this." Her faith demonstrated that God was in control of her life.

Doubt comes to all Christians at one time or another. I worried about Aunt Neil traveling, but she knew she would not be alone. God would be with her. He heard her prayer, and she was certain she was in His care. Her trust was complete.

Paul learned to be content in whatever circumstance he faced. He was stoned, shipwrecked, imprisoned, and starved; still, he trusted in the Lord.

I would love to follow his example. Wouldn't you?

Dear Lord, *I pray that the eyes of my heart may see as clearly as Aunt Neil's could see. Let me not be blinded by the things I see, but let me see by faith. Thank You that I can always trust Your promises. I pray this prayer in the name of Jesus, my merciful Savior and Lord. Amen.*

SEARCH THE WORD

Faith conquers fear every time.

Scripture: Psalm 27:1-6
Song: *"Trusting Jesus"*

From this meditation today, I will pray . . .

Adoration _____

Confession _____

Thanksgiving _____

Supplication _____

From this meditation today, I will . . .

Think _____

Say _____

Do _____

December 31

The Shepherd's Care

*He maketh me to lie down in green pastures:
he leadeth me beside the still waters* (Psalm 23:2, *King James Version*).

Scripture: Psalm 23
Song: *"Savior, Who Thy Flock Art Feeding"*

From this meditation today, I will pray . . .
Adoration _____

Confession _____

Thanksgiving _____

Supplication _____

From this meditation today, I will . . .
Think _____

Say _____

Do _____

Did you know that sheep fear swiftly moving waters? They require quiet waters or streams, because if their wool becomes wet it will pull them under—and they can't swim! Also, they must change pastures often because they eat the grass so close to the root that it needs a chance to grow again.

And sheep require constant care relying heavily on the shepherd. As long as the sheep follow their shepherd, they will have their needs met. He is an expert and knows the best places for food and water. The shepherd carries olive oil as a remedy for the injured or scratched lambs.

The Lord, our Shepherd, cares for us in the way a shepherd cares for his sheep. He sees that we have our basic needs met and often blesses abundantly above them.

Sometimes we focus only on our wants instead of our needs. Our Shepherd isn't holding things back from us. But just as sheep can overeat and suffer illnesses or death, so we often desire things that will hurt us.

The Shepherd gave His life for His sheep; we can trust Him for our needs.

Father God, *thank You for the green pastures and still waters in my life. I trust You for my care and protection. Please, help me always recognize the difference between my wants and my needs. In Jesus' name, amen.*

SPOTLIGHT
Next Week's Lesson
Shepherds who care for sheep and midwives who protect baby boys illustrate God's love.

January

OLD TESTAMENT PEOPLE OF COMMITMENT

*Commit to the L*ORD *whatever you do,
and your plans will succeed.*
—Proverbs 16:3

Gary Allen, Editor

January 1

Tasting God's Word

O taste and see that the Lord *is good: blessed is the man that trusteth in him* (Psalm 34:8, King James Version).

Scripture: Psalm 34:4-14

Song: *"Come and Dine"*

From this meditation today, I will pray . . .

Adoration _____

_____

_____

Confession _____

_____

_____

Thanksgiving _____

_____

_____

Supplication _____

_____

_____

From this meditation today, I will . . .

Think _____

_____

_____

Say _____

_____

_____

Do _____

_____

_____

"I don't like that." Many times I heard this when I placed new foods on our dinner table. I realized that children are reluctant to try new foods; mine were no exception. Because of this, we adopted a rule in our home. Each person was to taste *at least one spoonful* of everything on the table. It was amazing how foods they supposedly "didn't like" became favorites after the first taste.

Sometimes folks are quick to say, "I can't read that." They believe that reading the Bible is difficult, even though they have never given it a good try. But after that first taste, so many begin to love partaking of the Word as a regular mode of living.

My husband told the children, "If your mother went to all the trouble to fix this for you, then you can go to all the trouble to taste it." It's difficult to imagine all the goodness of God unless we first taste it ourselves. And, for further encouragement, the psalmist tells us the words of Scripture are sweet to the taste, even sweeter than honey.

Heavenly Father, *You have given me words to live by, words that will comfort and encourage me. I pray that You would guide me as I read and study them this day. I pray in the name of Your Son, Jesus. Amen.*

SPOTLIGHT
Next Week's Lesson

Become strong enough to face down a pharaoh by feeding on the Word of God.

January 1–4. **Carol Russell,** *of Fort Scott, Kansas, has written articles and stories in Christian magazines, as well as take-home papers for children and adults.*

January 2

The Way He Chooses

What man is he that feareth the Lord? Him shall he teach in the way that he shall choose (Psalm 25:12, *King James Version*).

Me? You want me to have a speaking ministry? These were the thoughts rolling around in my head. I never before considered a speaking ministry, but the more I prayed and listened for God's answer, the more I knew He was leading me into another avenue for service. I'd taught Sunday school and Bible studies for many years. Now it appeared that God was revealing a new direction for me.

The Scriptures inform us that God will lead us in the way He has chosen. And, thankfully, He will never ask us to do anything He has not equipped us to do. He will give us the tools—the spiritual gifts, strength, and wisdom—for the task, no matter what the ministry may be.

The Bible offers countless examples of the ways He prepares people for His work: David had a sling, Dorcas had a needle, Samson had a jawbone. Similarly, God called Moses for a special mission. This great shepherd of God's people initially had great doubts, but he followed the way that God chose for him. With doubts, I began a speaking ministry, but the doubts soon faded. What way has God chosen for you?

Dear Lord, *I thank You for showing me the pathways to tread. In your strength, may I be an effective servant for you. In Jesus' name, amen.*

SEARCH THE WORD

What is that in your hand? Use it in the Lord's service.

Scripture: Psalm 25:12-22
Song: *"Follow On"*

From this meditation today, I will pray . . .

Adoration _____

Confession _____

Thanksgiving _____

Supplication _____

From this meditation today, I will . . .

Think _____

Say _____

Do _____

January 3

Standing in Awe

Let all the earth fear the LORD:
let all the inhabitants of the world stand in awe of him
(Psalm 33:8, *King James Version*).

Scripture: Psalm 33:8-18
Song: *"America the Beautiful"*

From this meditation today, I will pray . . .
Adoration _____

Confession _____

Thanksgiving _____

Supplication _____

From this meditation today, I will . . .
Think _____

Say _____

Do _____

"Wow, there really are stars!" At the age of 10, after I received my new glasses, I saw the stars for the first time. What an awesome sight. Such beauty and majesty to behold!

Because of my poor eyesight, I had been unable to see the multitude of those twinkling lights in the night sky. I thought people were making up stories about stars and airplanes. I would usually respond with something like "Sure" or "Yes, of course" whenever someone mentioned something I could not see.

A kind of spiritual blindness sometimes hinders us from seeing the beauty of God. Other times, we fail to notice the wonders of creation because we're just too wrapped up in our own lives. We fail to see and stand in awe of His beauty and goodness toward us.

Mother cried when she realized I'd never seen the stars. How it must hurt God when His children gloss over the beauty of His world, along with the care and love He has for each of us. Why not stop for a moment today to really see the beauty of God's creation—and savor the wonders of His gracious blessings in Your life?

Heavenly Father, *help me to see not only the beauty of this world, but also the glory of Your plan of salvation for me. Through Christ I pray. Amen.*

SPOTLIGHT
Next Week's Lesson

Awe and amazement
fill our hearts as the beauty
of God's plan unfolds.

January 4

Obeying God

The midwives feared God, and did not as the king of Egypt commanded them, but saved the men children alive (Exodus 1:17, *King James Version*).

Scripture: Exodus 1:8-21
Song: *"I Will Pilot Thee"*

The manager put the report back on my desk and gave me this instruction: "Just change the inventory a little. Show we sold more of the promotional suits and drop some of the other sales."

I knew he wanted to look good in the company supervisor's eyes, but this was wrong. "I'm sorry, Mr. Smith. My ethics just won't let me do as you ask." Although he was displeased with me, he did allow me to give an accurate report to the supervisor.

When Pharaoh told the midwives in Egypt to kill all the baby boys, they had a problem. They knew they were responsible to God and that His was a higher authority. However, what would Pharaoh do if they disobeyed?

While our superiors may condone certain behaviors, it is God's law we are to obey. Today, employment relationships can bring us many problems, especially when supervisors ask us to do something we know is wrong.

Just as the midwives must choose Pharaoh or God, we frequently face similar choices. Whom do we obey?

Lord, thank You for Your laws and guidance. Help me always remember that I am accountable for my actions, that I must sometimes say "No," even at great personal cost. I pray through my deliverer, Jesus. Amen.

From this meditation today, I will pray . . .

Adoration _____

Confession _____

Thanksgiving _____

Supplication _____

From this meditation today, I will . . .

Think _____

Say _____

Do _____

SEARCH THE WORD

Remember Who you work for.

January 5

Somebody Has to Follow

*Just as we fully obeyed Moses, so we will obey you.
Only may the Lord your God be with you as he was with Moses
(Joshua 1:17).*

Scripture: Joshua 1:10-18
Song: *"Follow Me, the Master Said"*

From this meditation today, I will pray . . .

Adoration _____
_____
_____

Confession _____
_____
_____

Thanksgiving _____
_____
_____

Supplication _____
_____
_____

From this meditation today, I will . . .

Think _____
_____
_____

Say _____
_____
_____

Do _____
_____
_____

The Israelites didn't exactly obey Moses in all things . . . but they should have. Somebody has to follow. After all, there can't be leaders without followers. The Bible everywhere tells us that. Take, for example, those who followed David, both in exile and on the throne. Or consider the men and women who went where Jesus went, all over Galilee and then up to Jerusalem. In our Scripture passage today, we read of those who pledged Joshua obedience upon entering the land of promise. Somebody has to follow.

A dean at a woman's college sent a questionnaire to parents of prospective students. "Is your daughter a good leader?" one of the questions asked. After the responses came in, the dean wrote to the parents of a particular applicant: "Thanks for sending your daughter to be a member of our first-year class. Inasmuch as the class numbers 325, and we've already been assured of 324 leaders, we are delighted your daughter is coming along to be a follower."

Dear God, *as a disciple of Jesus, may I follow Him where He goes in that part of the world where I live. In His name I pray. Amen.*

January 5-11. **Phillip H. Barnhart** *ministered in eight churches in three states for over 45 years. He has written 14 books and lives on Perdido Bay, Florida.*

SPOTLIGHT
Next Week's Lesson

Are you ready
to follow wherever
Jesus leads?

January 6

Faith Gets the Job Done

It was by faith that the people of Israel marched around Jericho seven days, and the walls came crashing down (Hebrews 11:30, *New Living Translation*).

Read the 11th chapter of Hebrews and you come away feeling you can do just about anything—if you have faith. "By faith . . . by faith . . . by faith . . ." the cadence goes on and on. Sacrifice offered, blessing given, deliverance managed, exodus accomplished, victory achieved—all by faith.

By faith mountains are moved, Jesus said. Faith is best understood as *response*, our response to God's faithfulness. Who God is, what God does, comes first. Faith responds to the character and action of God, both of which are revealed and, ultimately, experienced as trustworthy.

We are led to faith by the evidence of God's grace and power. We lift the sails because we've seen God send the wind. As someone has put it: "Sorrow looks back, worry looks around, faith looks up." And the uplook of faith produces the outlook of confidence.

Faith as response is why Jeremiah could buy a field in Anathoth, Elijah could see rain in a cloud the size of a man's hand, and two midwives could refuse to obey the wicked command of a powerful pharaoh.

Dear God, by faith I go forward each day. Faith takes fear out of my challenges, puts love in my relationships, brings hope to my plans, and gives power to my walk. Thanks be to You, through Christ my Lord! Amen.

SEARCH THE WORD

*Fear says, "Play it safe!"
Faith says, "Let's roll!"*

Scripture: Hebrews 11:23-31
Song: *"My Faith Looks Up to Thee"*

From this meditation today, I will pray . . .

Adoration _____

Confession _____

Thanksgiving _____

Supplication _____

From this meditation today, I will . . .

Think _____

Say _____

Do _____

January 7

Word Gets Around

*We have heard how the L*ORD *dried up the Red Sea when you came out of Egypt* (Joshua 2:10, New Century Version).

Scripture: Joshua 2:8-11
Song: *"Tell Me the Story of Jesus"*

From this meditation today, I will pray . . .

Adoration _____
_____
_____

Confession _____
_____
_____

Thanksgiving _____
_____
_____

Supplication _____
_____
_____

From this meditation today, I will . . .

Think _____
_____
_____

Say _____
_____
_____

Do _____
_____
_____
_____

Rahab became Israel's ally because she had heard what God had done. God's reputation preceded Him. Drying up a sea, eliminating a couple of formidable kings, ruling Heaven and earth—all this God had done. All this Rahab had heard. And hearing stories about God's greatness made Rahab a believer.

Dr. Peter Joshua, renowned minister and evangelist, was won to Christ by the witness of one girl. An unemployed actor, he slept in alleys at night and accepted handouts by day. One evening, in London's Hyde Park, he saw a Salvation Army girl standing up to speak. Wanting to give her support, he found himself her only audience. Instead of speaking, she began singing a hymn about the worthlessness of the world compared to the glories and goodness of Christ.

Looking Joshua in the eye, she quoted several Bible verses, turned, and went her way. Peter Joshua received Christ. Word got around to him. Word gets around to us.

Dear God, *thank You for those who told me the story of Jesus. I stand on the shoulders of their witness, looking into the face of Your glory. Their testimony is my creed, their words my life. What they told to me, I tell to others. In the holy name of Jesus, my Lord and Savior, amen.*

SPOTLIGHT
Next Week's Lesson

Everything you've heard about
God's power is true—
and much, much more!

January 8

Helping People on Their Way

So she let them down by a rope through the window, for the house she lived in was part of the city wall (Joshua 2:15).

Rahab believed, then she acted. Rahab was a helper. Acknowledging what God had done, she made a deal with the two spies and helped them on their way.

Long-stemmed flax, like what had hidden the spies on Rahab's roof, had been spun and braided into a strong rope. Down that rope the spies shinnied to safety and returned to tell Joshua that it was time to enter the land of promise.

There's a story of an old man who carried a little can of oil with him everywhere he went. If he passed through a door that squeaked, he poured a little oil on the hinges. If a gate was hard to open, he oiled the latch. Basically, he passed through life making it easier for those who came after him.

Some misunderstood the old man and called him odd. But he went steadily on, refilling his can when it went empty, oiling all the hard places he found.

For me, his example means simply this: I should be an equal opportunity Christian, helping everyone I can.

Dear Father, *may I see each day the people You give me to help. May I love them as You love them and give myself to them as You give yourself to me. May I put them on the strength of my heart and carry them into Your presence. In the name of Your Son, my Savior, I pray. Amen.*

SEARCH THE WORD

Lend a hand where you can.

Scripture: Joshua 2:15-21
Song: *"Help Somebody Today"*

From this meditation today, I will pray...

Adoration _____

Confession _____

Thanksgiving _____

Supplication _____

From this meditation today, I will...

Think _____

Say _____

Do _____

January 9

Saved . . . to Do Good

Likewise also was not Rahab the harlot justified by works, when she had received the messengers, and had sent them out another way?
(James 2:25, *King James Verson*).

Scripture: James 2:21-26
Song: *"A Charge to Keep I Have"*

From this meditation today, I will pray . . .
Adoration _____
_____
_____
Confession _____
_____
_____
Thanksgiving _____
_____
_____
Supplication _____
_____
_____

From this meditation today, I will . . .
Think _____
_____
_____
Say _____
_____
_____
Do _____
_____
_____
_____

We are not saved *by* works, but we are saved *for* works. The conflict some see between Paul and James on this subject misunderstands both of these great biblical writers. Paul argues against a false doctrine that keeping the law, apart from faith, will accomplish salvation. James does not see faith alone as deficient, but argues that a genuine faith will always result in good deeds.

They both agree that if saved people produce no works, they probably aren't saved in the first place. Similarly, Jesus said we will know people are saved when they bear fruit in the kingdom.

In the courtyard of a quaint little church in a French village stood a beautiful marble statue of Jesus with His hands outstretched. During World War II, a bomb struck and dismembered the statue. Later, the villagers gathered up the statue's fragments to reconstruct it . . . but could not find the hands. They planned to have a new statue built until one of them came up with an alternate idea. They attached a plaque at the base of the statue that read, "I have no hands but your hands."

God, *lead me from belief to behavior, from doctrine to duty, from creeds to deeds. And may it all be done in Your strength. Through Christ, amen.*

SPOTLIGHT
Next Week's Lesson

A battle is coming; make sure you're on the winning side.

January 10

How Did They Get There?

. . . and Salmon the father of Boaz by Rahab . . .
(Matthew 1:5, *Revised Standard Version*).

Rahab ran a successful little establishment in the red-light district of Jericho. Yet there she is in the genealogy of Jesus Christ. Tamar duped her father-in-law into having sex with her, got pregnant, and gave birth to twins. Yet there she is in the genealogy of Jesus Christ. Bathsheba committed adultery with David, became pregnant, and allowed her husband's murder to confuse paternity. Yet there she is in the genealogy of Jesus Christ.

How did they get there? They got there by the grace of God. The list of names in Matthew's first chapter is a genealogy of God's grace, the undeserved favor that always has room for the unlikely, the unlovely, the uncredentialed. God's grace exists for those who don't have a very good record, and it is lightning fast on its feet of forgiveness.

Did Rahab deserve God's grace? Did Tamar deserve God's grace? Did Bathsheba deserve God's grace? To deserve grace nullifies its definition. Grace is what we *don't* deserve but get anyway. Grace happens.

Lord, *thank You for the grace I need when I've done something I shouldn't have and can't get over it. Thank you for the grace I need when my mind is confused, when my heart is confounded, when there is conflict in my soul. Thank You so much, in the name of Jesus. Amen.*

Scripture: Matthew 1:1-6
Song: *"Amazing Grace"*

From this meditation today, I will pray . . .
Adoration _____

Confession _____

Thanksgiving _____

Supplication _____

From this meditation today, I will . . .
Think _____

Say _____

Do _____

SEARCH THE WORD

None of us deserves the gift of God's grace.

January 11

Promises: Made for Keeping

Joshua said to the two men who had spied out the land, "Go into the prostitute's house and bring her out and all who belong to her, in accordance with your oath to her" (Joshua 6:22).

Scripture: Joshua 2:1-4, 11-14; 6:22-25
Song: *"Standing on the Promises"*

From this meditation today, I will pray...
Adoration _____

Confession _____

Thanksgiving _____

Supplication _____

From this meditation today, I will...
Think _____

Say _____

Do _____

Joshua insisted the promise made to Rahab would be kept. She and her family would be rescued from Jericho, just as she was told they would be.

Promises are made for keeping. Hudson Taylor, pioneer missionary in China, firmly believed God knew his needs and would meet them. On one occasion, when Taylor's assets were down to 87 cents, he wrote a friend, "We have this amount—and all the promises of God."

A promise is a pledge that proclaims a reality not yet present. There are thousands of promises in the Bible about what we can expect from God. Those promises are not subject to review. He keeps them.

With every call of God comes the promise to provide what is necessary to carry out that call. When God puts us on the road, He shows up to walk with us, just as He promised He would. As Dwight L. Moody once said, "God never made a promise that was too good to be true."

No matter how dark things get, **Dear God**, *I hold on to the promise of light. No matter how lost I am, dear God, I hold on to the promise of rescue. No matter how rough the passage is, I hold on to the promise of a safe landing. In Jesus' precious name, amen.*

SPOTLIGHT
Next Week's Lesson
Rahab risked her life; Joshua kept his promise.

January 12–18. **Maxine E. Holder** *founded a Christian writer organization in Texas that has now grown to seven chapters.*

January 12

Stay Strong

Aaron and Hur held his hands up—one on one side, one on the other . . . Moses built an altar and called it The Lord *is my Banner* (Exodus 17:12, 15).

Scripture: Exodus 17:8-16
Song: *"There Is a Fountain"*

There are times when my grandchildren, ages 13 through 25, come to me and tell me their woes. Listening closely makes them know they are very important to me and their granddad. We assure them as we pray for them—and they know that Jesus cares as well.

Encouragement is just what they hope to receive. A tender touch, a warm smile, and agreement with their good choices keeps them headed in the right direction.

Have you noticed how encouragement seems to strengthen the ones we love? And what encouragement Aaron and Hur offered Moses! They stood strong by his side as they held up his arms to ensure victory.

When Moses said, "The Lord is my Banner," these men knew where their strength came from. Through all of our battles, the Lord God is with us. He is our ever-present strength, and we can proclaim that strength to all we meet, as a blessed word of encouragement.

Father, *I come to You, knowing You are my all and all, the strength I need for each day. Your mercy and grace bring me through each decision I make. Thank You, in Jesus' name. Amen.*

From this meditation today, I will pray . . .
Adoration _____
_____
_____
Confession _____
_____
_____
Thanksgiving _____
_____
_____
Supplication _____
_____
_____

From this meditation today, I will . . .
Think _____
_____
_____
Say _____
_____
_____
Do _____
_____
_____
_____

SEARCH THE WORD

A listening ear and a loving touch lift the spirits.

January 13

He Renews Our Strength

If the Lord *is pleased with us, he will lead us into that land. . . . Only do not rebel against the* Lord *. . . Their protection is gone, but the* Lord *is with us*
(Numbers 14:8, 9).

Scripture: Numbers 14:6-10
Song: *"The Love of God"*

From this meditation today, I will pray . . .

Adoration _____
_____
_____

Confession _____
_____
_____

Thanksgiving _____
_____
_____

Supplication _____
_____
_____

From this meditation today, I will . . .

Think _____
_____
_____

Say _____
_____
_____

Do _____
_____
_____
_____

Since committing my life to the Lord, I've prayed for eyes to see what He expects of me. And I trust Him to unfold His will for me, even though sometimes the answer is "no" or "wait."

After I suffered a long, nine-year bout with painful injuries following an automobile accident, my doctors found a way to ease my pain. And, thankfully, I was able to avoid living in a wheelchair. Through that time I came to the end of myself and learned to trust God deeply.

The Lord was with me through every difficult day, hour, and moment. Some believers thought I should be instantly healed, but I knew from studying His Word that He would heal me when, and if, He chose to do so. In any case, I simply determined to enjoy His constant presence.

In biblical days, those two wise men, Joshua and Caleb, lived with deep sorrow—until Joshua realized that the people had finally rejected their advice. Still, these men continued to depend on God. And, as He promises to do for us, He renewed their strength.

Heavenly Father, *how I praise You for Your indwelling Spirit! Help me to depend on Your strength every day as You lead me into paths of kingdom service. In the name of Jesus, my Savior, I pray. Amen.*

SPOTLIGHT
Next Week's Lesson

As Joshua said,
"If God is with us, no giant can harm us."

January 14

Finish the Job

May the Lord*, the God of the spirits of all mankind, appoint a man over this community . . . one who will lead them out and bring them in, so the* Lord*'s people will not be like sheep without a shepherd* (Numbers 27:16, 17).

Scripture: Numbers 27:12-23
Song: *"Savior, Like a Shepherd Lead Us"*

Moses didn't want to leave his leadership position without making sure someone was fully trained to lead in his place. He first asked God to help him find that certain person, and that person was Joshua. Eventually, Moses guaranteed his people that Joshua was qualified. Confidence in this new leader helped make the transition.

Years ago I founded a Christian writer's organization that has now grown to seven chapters throughout Texas. Part of my job was to make sure our leaders realized our purpose: *ministry*. This requires leadership that is trained and accountable.

I'm so encouraged when I see Moses laying his hands on Joshua as the Lord instructed. Like Moses, we writers set up a formula for raising up leaders among us: pray, select, develop, and commission. It's a process we can apply in almost any form of ministry. After all, the Great Commission is always before us; let us continue to finish the job.

Dear Heavenly Father, *I know that You hold me accountable to use my spiritual gifts in service to You and Your people. Give me the grace and strength to do so, day by day. I pray in Jesus' name. Amen.*

From this meditation today, I will pray . . .

Adoration _____

Confession _____

Thanksgiving _____

Supplication _____

From this meditation today, I will . . .

Think _____

Say _____

Do _____

SEARCH THE WORD

A leader's last job: find a godly replacement.

January 15

Strong in Him

Be strong and courageous. Do not be afraid or terrified because of them, for the Lord your God goes with you; he will never leave you nor forsake you"
(Deuteronomy 31:6).

Scripture: Deuteronomy 31:1-8
Song: *"Fear Not, O Little Flock"*

From this meditation today, I will pray . . .
Adoration _____
_____
_____

Confession _____
_____
_____

Thanksgiving _____
_____
_____

Supplication _____
_____
_____

From this meditation today, I will . . .
Think _____
_____
_____

Say _____
_____
_____

Do _____
_____
_____
_____

There was a war going on, and Joshua was to inherit the leadership position from Moses. For Moses realized he was about to die.

Moses also knew that the people must learn to depend on God for their future. Therefore, he showed them how to shake off their fears and forge ahead. God himself would go before them. In His strength, they could face any challenge.

There were times when I dreaded taking a test in school or facing someone who laughed at me for my faith. Do you know what helped the most? Repeating God's Word in my heart. That simple act seemed to renew my strength and keep me strong.

Life is often a giant challenge for us human beings. But my attitude is: Better to go to my knees and draw on God's mighty resources than to wallow in fear or despair. Then I do not face my fears alone; I can "be strong and courageous," depending solely on the Almighty Lord of all. He created and controls all things. And He lives within my heart.

Lord, *how good to know You are ever near! You lift me up when I am down and bring renewed faith when I ask. Thank You, in Jesus' name. Amen.*

SPOTLIGHT
Next Week's Lesson

"Courage is fear that has said its prayers."
—Dorothy Bernard

January 16

He Redeems the Situation

The L*ord* *said to him, "This is the land I promised on oath to Abraham, Isaac and Jacob when I said, 'I will give it to your descendants.' I have let you see it with your eyes, but you will not cross over into it"* (Deuteronomy 34:4).

Because of his disobedience, Moses wasn't allowed to cross over into the promised land. But God took the great leader to Mount Nebo and allowed him to see that land before he died. Though he had his faults, what an impressive man was Moses! He was the only person who ever spoke with God, face to face. Yet, with Moses—as it is with us—disobedience brings discipline.

Years ago, as I ran from God, I had a terrible automobile accident that caused crippling and pain. I needed a lot of help, both physical and spiritual. And somehow, through the gentle invitation of God himself, I was able to turn to Him with an open heart. In spite of all my anger and pain, I faced Almighty God in openness and received a deep desire to follow Him.

Yes, He disciplines us, but He does it in love. He grieves to see us entangle ourselves in self-destructive actions that limit our potential. Yet He redeems every situation that we offer to Him with an open heart. That is how it was with Moses, and that is how it is with me.

Dear Lord, *like Moses, help me constantly turn to You, to open my heart and life to Your indwelling Spirit. I ask in Jesus' name. Amen.*

Scripture: Deuteronomy 34:1-19
Song: *"Near to the Heart of God"*

From this meditation today, I will pray . . .
Adoration _____

Confession _____

Thanksgiving _____

Supplication _____

From this meditation today, I will . . .
Think _____

Say _____

Do _____

SEARCH THE WORD

Punishment softened by mercy brings a blessing.

January 17

Wherever We Go

*Do not let this Book of the Law depart from your mouth; meditate on it day and night, so that you may be careful to do everything written in it. Then you will be prosperous and successful. Have I not commanded you? Be strong and courageous. Do not be terrified; do not be discouraged, for the L*ORD *your God will be with you wherever you go* (Joshua 1:8, 9).

Scripture: Joshua 1:1-9
Song: *"My Jesus, I Love Thee"*

From this meditation today, I will pray . . .
Adoration _____

Confession _____

Thanksgiving _____

Supplication _____

From this meditation today, I will . . .
Think _____

Say _____

Do _____

Joshua didn't promise the future would be easy. But he knew that obeying God's law would ultimately bring success to God's people.

Years ago, after attending a Christian marriage retreat, my husband, Marshall, and I longed to grow deeper in our relationship to God. Together, we prayed regularly and spent much time reading His Word—and we were soon put to the test! When Marshall's company was bought out, our future was on the line. Things got downright scary. But our prayers for the new company's leaders were answered; they sent a good man to protect Marshall's job.

Yes, after many months of praying and waiting, we were able to rejoice in a negotiator who saved the day for us. Yet it was our God in control. And like Joshua, we grew in our faith that He is with us wherever we go.

Lord, *I praise You for granting me strength and courage as You did Joshua. You are with me and continue to lead the way. You are my All in All. For it is in Your holy name I pray. Amen.*

SPOTLIGHT
Next Week's Lesson

Doing things God's way always pays off in the long run.

January 18

Draw Close

*Joshua told the people, "Consecrate yourselves,
for tomorrow the* Lord *will do amazing things among you"*
(Joshua 3:5).

Most of us know about the ark of the covenant, carried only by the Levites. Worshipers had to stay back from the Ark a thousand yards because of its holiness. It contained the tablets of the Ten Commandments, a jar of manna, and Aaron's staff. What holy and sacred treasures!

The consecration ceremony in this Scripture passage shows us the importance of approaching God with a pure heart. How can we do it?

For one thing, we can simply stop for awhile during our days to enjoy God's intimate presence. In the days of Joshua, the presence of the Lord was, in a sense, "contained" in an external object. But the promise was always underneath: Someday God would actually dwell within His people and lead them from the heart.

We know how that promise unfolded: on the day of Pentecost, the Holy Spirit came to live within every believer. Just as Jesus promised, we worship Him in spirit and truth as He works to purify our lives. Yes, in every age, the call to consecration rings out. For Joshua and his people, it meant staying back. For us—thanks to the cross of Christ—it means drawing ever closer.

Heavenly Father, thank You for the cross of Your Son that brings me access into Your presence. Through Him I pray. Amen.

SEARCH THE WORD

"Create in me a pure heart, O God" (Psalm 51:10).

Scripture: Joshua 3:1-13
Song: *"Have Thine Own Way Lord"*

From this meditation today, I will pray . . .

Adoration _____

Confession _____

Thanksgiving _____

Supplication _____

From this meditation today, I will . . .

Think _____

Say _____

Do _____

January 19

The Original Hippies

*Throughout the period of his separation
he is consecrated to the* LORD *(Numbers 6:8).*

Scripture: Numbers 6:1-8
Song: *"Servant of God, Well Done!"*

From this meditation today, I will pray . . .
Adoration _____
_____
_____

Confession _____
_____
_____

Thanksgiving _____
_____
_____

Supplication _____
_____
_____

From this meditation today, I will . . .
Think _____
_____
_____

Say _____
_____
_____

Do _____
_____
_____

During the 1960s, teenagers began wearing their hair longer as a symbol of rebellion. In ancient Israel, long hair conveyed the opposite attitude. The Nazirite was to use no razor on his head for the entire length of his vow. A man with long hair attracted attention, but in a positive way. He was a Nazirite, a man dedicated to God's service.

The well-known story of Samson begins with the angelic announcement that he is to be a Nazirite. The secret of Samson's strength was not his hair but his vow. Cutting his hair severed the vow, and the Spirit of God (along with Samson's strength) departed.

Cut off from God we are weak. Dedicated to his service, we remain strong.

I have worked with a number of dedicated Christians. I have studied under teachers who were models of Christian humility and wisdom. There was little in their outward appearance that highlighted their dedication to the Lord. But the inner spirit would shine through in such a way that it was as noticeable as shoulder-length hair.

Lord, *use me in Your service. Help me fulfill my vows of dedication and service in each situation I meet this day. In Jesus' name, amen.*

SPOTLIGHT
Next Week's Lesson

Making a promise,
taking a vow, means that
you're committed now.

January 19–25. **Dan Nicksich** *is now entering his 10th year of ministry with First Christian Church in Somerset, Pennsylvania.*

January 20

Choose Him Who Chose

When the angel of the Lord *had spoken these things to all the Israelites, the people wept aloud* (Judges 2:4).

John the Baptist stood up to a king and denounced his sinful behavior. He was imprisoned and later beheaded for his words. The prophet Jeremiah proclaimed the truth, even when he knew a king would be enraged. And Daniel risked the lion's den in defiance of a king's edict.

It makes me wonder: Is pleasing God more important to me than pleasing people? Would I proclaim God's truth, even to a king?

The Bible abounds with examples of those who stood against the ungodly in the face of imprisonment or death. Sadly, we also see those times when the nation of Israel failed to put God ahead of its own self-interest. Yet God's commands were clear: Do not make a covenant with these people, do not follow their gods, do not bow down at their altars.

We all face times when pleasing those around us may seem more important than pleasing God. Sometimes, of course, we can do both! But more often, it's a question of commitment and loyalty to one or the other. May God help us to choose the one who has already chosen us.

O heavenly Father, *may it be that nothing would ever become so important in my eyes that my dedication to You would suffer. In the name of my Lord and Savior, Jesus Christ. Amen.*

SEARCH THE WORD

Let's not make a deal with the devil's children.

Scripture: Judges 2:1-5
Song: *"I'd Rather Have Jesus"*

From this meditation today, I will pray . . .

Adoration _____
_____
_____

Confession _____
_____
_____

Thanksgiving _____
_____
_____

Supplication _____
_____
_____

From this meditation today, I will . . .

Think _____
_____
_____

Say _____
_____
_____

Do _____
_____
_____

January 21

Awesome Responsibility

After that whole generation had been gathered to their fathers, another generation grew up, who knew neither the LORD nor what he had done for Israel (Judges 2:10).

Scripture: Judges 2:6-10
Song: *"Tell It Again"*

From this meditation today, I will pray . . .
Adoration _____
_____
_____

Confession _____
_____
_____

Thanksgiving _____
_____
_____

Supplication _____
_____
_____

From this meditation today, I will . . .
Think _____
_____
_____

Say _____
_____
_____

Do _____
_____
_____
_____

"The church is one generation away from extinction." It's a rather bleak forecast, isn't it? But let's face it: The church is *always* one generation away from extinction. That is, if one generation of parents fails to teach its children about the Lord, we would soon see a repeat of the sad state of affairs depicted in Judges 2:10.

Joshua inspired the people throughout his lifetime. No doubt many had heard of his faithfulness on that day when he and Caleb stood alone among the 12 spies sent to assess the possibilities for conquest in the promised land. They spoke boldly then, saying that with God's help, Israel could surely achieve victory.

But somehow the generation that followed failed to teach its children that kind of vibrant faith in God. The Israelites reached the point where they "knew neither the Lord nor what he had done for Israel."

Let us always remember that each of us has a part in training the next generation. What an awesome responsibility, and what a humbling task!

Lord, *bring me to those young people who could benefit from my Christian example. And give me wise words to say, too, at just the right times. In Jesus precious name I pray. Amen.*

SPOTLIGHT
Next Week's Lesson

The next generation needs to know. Who will tell them?

January 22

Returning His Slingshot

Unlike their fathers, they quickly turned from the way in which their fathers had walked, the way of obedience to the Lord's commands (Judges 2:17).

A 12-year-old boy and a slingshot. Sounds like a recipe for trouble, right? And trouble it was. So Mom took away my slingshot.

I can still recall the day she finally gave it back to me, saying, "Here, I think you're old enough to handle this now." I was 40!

At times, Israel's history reads like the continuing failures of a 12-year-old boy heading in and out of trouble. Judges depicts a particularly distressful time, with Israel failing time and again. God had promised protection, fruitful abundance, and blessings in return for faithfulness. If unfaithful, the people would land in their enemies' hands. Either way, it was their choice, and thus we read that their defeat was "just as he had sworn to them."

A good parent lays out the choices: Obey, and you will be blessed; disobey and face the consequences. God, the most faithful of parents, does the same. Thankfully, He gives us all the grace and strength we need to keep following Him. And when we stumble, He lifts us up that we may start again—even if it's 28 years down the road!

Lord, *open my eyes to the dangers of disobedience today. May I learn from those who are faithful and from those who are not. In Jesus' name, amen.*

Scripture: Judges 2:11-17
Song: *"Falter Not"*

From this meditation today, I will pray . . .

Adoration _____

Confession _____

Thanksgiving _____

Supplication _____

From this meditation today, I will . . .

Think _____

Say _____

Do _____

SEARCH THE WORD

*Doing it "my way"
is learning the hard way.*

January 23

Follow the Leader

When the judge died, the people returned to ways even more corrupt than those of their fathers, following other gods and serving and worshiping them (Judges 2:19).

Scripture: Judges 2:18-23
Song: *"Where He Leads Me"*

From this meditation today, I will pray . . .
Adoration _____
_____
_____

Confession _____
_____
_____

Thanksgiving _____
_____
_____

Supplication _____
_____
_____

From this meditation today, I will . . .
Think _____
_____
_____

Say _____
_____
_____

Do _____
_____
_____
_____

President Roosevelt encouraged his people not to fear "fear itself." John F. Kennedy challenged us to put a man on the moon before the end of a decade. And Martin Luther King, Jr., inspired us with a single, dramatic statement, "I have a dream." Good leaders challenge and inspire like that. They point the way, sometimes into uncharted territory, hopefully onto paths of righteousness.

Israel was good at following the leader. As long as a godly leader pointed the way, the people remained faithful to God. Whenever the good leader died, though, his or her example was quickly forgotten. Israel's history is a series of such failures.

We tend to crave tangible, visible leaders. If they de-emphasize character and morality, many seem to follow suit. We've even heard of those who insist, "Character doesn't count." How sad when those in authority will take such a stance!

God calls His leaders to be examples worthy of following. Are you a leader? Set the right example. A follower? Set your sights on a godly leader.

Lord, *please raise up leaders who are worthy of respect, in Your church and in our nation. May they look to You for guidance. In Jesus' name, amen.*

SPOTLIGHT
Next Week's Lesson

Follow the wrong leader and your life ends up in the ditch.

January 24

By Luck or By Plan?

"We are doomed to die!" he said to his wife. "We have seen God!" But his wife answered, "If the Lord *had meant to kill us, he would not have . . . shown us all these things"* (Judges 13:22, 23).

An old song complains: "If it weren't for bad luck, I'd have no luck at all." But the serious question is: Do you tend to assume something painful is always lurking just around the corner? And is God the one you blame whenever bad things occur?

It's strange how quickly we forget God's abundant blessings when tough times tumble down into our lives. Manoah's wife correctly reasoned that God's blessings are more than adequate proof of His love and acceptance.

One of the best-known verses of Scripture (John 3:16) assures us: God loved us so much that He came to us in person, willingly leaving all the glories of Heaven. If God's intention were to harm us, would He have suffered on our behalf as He did?

In the person of Jesus, we have seen God himself. But in that beautiful vision, we will not die. In fact, because of what we see and believe in His words and deeds, we shall surely live forever. Not by luck, but by plan (from before the foundation of the world), His motive was never anything other than our eternal good.

Father, *help me see the unmistakable signs of Your love in my life. Reassure me whenever I tend to fear the worst. Thank You, in Jesus' name. Amen.*

Scripture: Judges 13:15-23
Song: "Count Your Blessings"

From this meditation today, I will pray . . .

Adoration _____

Confession _____

Thanksgiving _____

Supplication _____

From this meditation today, I will . . .

Think _____

Say _____

Do _____

SEARCH THE WORD

If God shows you His plan, don't panic!

January 25

Come—He Blesses!

*The woman gave birth to a boy and named him Samson. He grew and the L*ord *blessed him*
(Judges 13:24).

Scripture: Judges 13:1-13, 24
Song: *"Growing Dearer Each Day"*

From this meditation today, I will pray . . .

Adoration _____
_____
_____

Confession _____
_____
_____

Thanksgiving _____
_____
_____

Supplication _____
_____
_____

From this meditation today, I will . . .

Think _____
_____
_____

Say _____
_____
_____

Do _____
_____
_____
_____

Israel may have fallen, but God was already planning its deliverance. To a country in oppression and to a woman who was barren came the good news: a son would be born who would one day deliver the nation.

It reminds me of a friend who once sat in a prison cell after being arrested for drunk driving. It was a long night of self-evaluation and introspection. Her life had hit rock bottom, but the good news was that she knew exactly where to look for help. She confessed her failings and renewed her faith in Christ. She would later say that during one very dark night she came to appreciate God's grace.

Even in the midst of our most extreme failures, God extends His good news. No matter the sin, no matter the depths of our self-destruction, God offers His blessings to us as we open our hearts to Him.

How we know our failures! But we often fail to appreciate God's long-standing offer of grace at just the point of our most desperate needfulness. In other words, we don't have to "clean up" to come to Him. We just come; He just blesses.

There are times, **Dear God,** *when I need to spend some serious time in reflection and introspection. Help me examine my life in the light of Your Word, and lead me to repentance. Through Christ I pray. Amen.*

SPOTLIGHT
Next Week's Lesson

When it feels like you're dangling from a cliff, hold on. Help is on the way.

January 26

The Silent Call

[Elisha] took his yoke of oxen and slaughtered them. He burned the plowing equipment to cook the meat and gave it to the people. . . . Then he set out to follow Elijah (1 Kings 19:21).

One chilly evening, hundreds of tiny sparrows landed in the trees and berry bushes outside my window. The flock had found a safe place to rest amidst plentiful food.

But suddenly they departed as a whole. Led by an unnamed leader within, they gave up all they had. And off they flew in a beautiful formation. Each bird knew its place and was totally submitted to it.

I marveled at the complexity of the organization among such simple creatures. It called to mind Psalm 19:1—"The heavens declare the glory of God; the skies proclaim the work of his hands."

Elisha proclaimed God's glory too. He was a family man of means. Yet when God called, Elisha gave up all he had—fortune, family, and freedom. He left it all behind to serve God's servant, Elijah. You see, Elisha knew his place and was totally submitted to it, because he knew the one who called him and promised to lead him.

Lord, *as I submit to Your will, teach me to recognize Your call and follow in Your footsteps. Help me to rest in the knowledge that just as You care for the tiny sparrow, You will care for me. In Christ's name, amen.*

Scripture: 1 Kings 19:15-21
Song: "Great God, A Blessing from Your Throne"

From this meditation today, I will pray . . .

Adoration _____
_____
_____

Confession _____
_____
_____

Thanksgiving _____
_____
_____

Supplication _____
_____
_____

From this meditation today, I will . . .

Think _____
_____
_____

Say _____
_____
_____

Do _____
_____
_____

SEARCH THE WORD
Burning bridges (or plows) may be the fresh start we need.

January 26–February 1. **Author Barbara E. Haley** *has worked as an elementary school teacher and piano instructor. She lives in San Antonio, Texas.*

January 27

The Best I Can Do

Elijah said to Elisha, "Tell me, what can I do for you before I am taken from you?" (2 Kings 2:9).

Scripture: 2 Kings 2:9-15

Song: *"What a Friend We Have in Jesus"*

From this meditation today, I will pray . . .

Adoration _____

Confession _____

Thanksgiving _____

Supplication _____

From this meditation today, I will . . .

Think _____

Say _____

Do _____

Herman Wilkerson believed in prayer. One day, he attended a church service led by a missionary. Afterward, the missionary confessed he was hungry and had no money to buy food. Herman invited the man to his home for dinner, knowing full well there was no food in his house for a proper meal. But Herman prayed, and when he got home, a stranger knocked at his door.

"I accidentally hit this turkey with my car," the stranger said. "I'm just passing through, so I can't use it. But I thought maybe you could." As the two men "gamely" figured out how to prepare and cook that bird, they enjoyed lively fellowship and developed a lasting friendship.

The Bible tells of Elijah being taken into Heaven. Just before he goes, he asks Elisha, "What can I do for you?"

May I suggest that prayer is the most powerful thing we can do for others? What a blessing it would be if every time we prepared to leave someone, we asked, "How can I pray for you before I go?" We would be communicating three important things: we care; we are listening; we know who holds the answer.

Thank You, Father, for caring and for listening to my prayers. Please remind me daily to bless others as I lift up their concerns to You in an attitude of faith and love. In Christ's name, amen.

SPOTLIGHT
Next Week's Lesson

Ask family and friends, "How can I pray for you?"

January 28

Persistence Pays Off

Elisha turned away and walked back and forth in the room and then got on the bed and stretched out upon him once more. The boy sneezed seven times and opened his eyes (2 Kings 4:35).

Scripture: 2 Kings 4:27-37
Song: "God Will Make a Way"

A stone cutter pounded a rock a hundred times—to no avail. But he didn't give up, and with one more strike, the rock split in two.

Did that single blow do the job? No, the break simply required 101 blows. Perhaps the cutter's personal experience, or trust in someone's word, motivated him to keep going.

The prophet Elisha demonstrated this same persistence. He made three attempts to revive a dead child before the boy recovered completely. At one point, the boy's body grew warm. But Elisha didn't accept a partial miracle—he believed God for more. Elisha prayed again, and the boy fully awoke.

How many times do we settle for second best instead of waiting on God's perfect way? We might even give up on praying. But as we read of God's great power, our faith—the power behind our prayers—blossoms and grows. Let us persist, then, in clinging to His almighty presence.

O God, *as I come to You in prayer, remind me to persist and not give up or settle for second best. Thank You for Your promise to supply all of my needs according to Your glorious riches in Christ Jesus. In His name, amen.*

From this meditation today, I will pray . . .
Adoration _____
Confession _____
Thanksgiving _____
Supplication _____

From this meditation today, I will . . .
Think _____
Say _____
Do _____

SEARCH THE WORD
What blessings have we lost by stopping one prayer short?

January 29

Even When We Hurt

Elisha was suffering from the illness from which he died. Jehoash king of Israel went down to see him and wept over him. "My father! My father!" he cried. "The chariots and horsemen of Israel!" (2 Kings 13:14).

Scripture: 2 Kings 13:14-20
Song: *"Sanctuary"*

From this meditation today, I will pray . . .
Adoration _____
_____
_____

Confession _____
_____
_____

Thanksgiving _____
_____
_____

Supplication _____
_____
_____

From this meditation today, I will . . .
Think _____
_____
_____

Say _____
_____
_____

Do _____
_____
_____
_____

Elisha was suffering when Jehoash came to see him. Yet even in his discomfort, Elisha agreed to counsel the king. Even illness couldn't keep Elisha from effective ministry.

A wise person once compared the effect of suffering to that of boiling an egg and a potato. While the egg becomes hard-boiled, the potato emerges soft and pliable. Likewise, suffering may cause us to become calloused and unresponsive or resilient and adaptable.

Suffering is a universal experience, yet we all react differently. Often, pain and hardship limit us or even cause our ministry to grind to a halt. But it doesn't have to. As Billy Graham once said, "The Christian life is not a constant high. I have my moments of deep discouragement. I have to go to God in prayer with tears in my eyes, and say, 'God, forgive me,' or 'Help me.'"

Graham knew this great truth: As we ask God to comfort, strengthen, and use us, He will do it, even amidst our most painful days.

Dear Lord, *thank You that I am not alone in my suffering. Soften my spirit as I remember that You will use this experience to help me fulfill the plans You have for my day. In the name of Jesus I pray. Amen.*

SPOTLIGHT
Next Week's Lesson

"You desire to know the art of living, my friend? . . . Make use of suffering."—H. F. Amiel

January 30

Level Ground

*"I tell you the truth," he continued,
"no prophet is accepted in his hometown"* (Luke 4:24).

The Civil War had ended when General Robert E. Lee visited a church in the north and knelt beside a black man during the Lord's Supper. Later, an observer asked him how he could do that. He replied, "My friend, all ground is level beneath the cross."

Jesus experienced a kind of prejudice when He returned to His hometown. At first the people gloried in His eloquent words and were filled with hope. They focused on what Jesus could do for them, God's chosen people, and they enjoyed the blessings this prophet offered. But they became furious when Jesus spoke approvingly of the healing of Namaan, a Syrian, in Israel's ancient days. That foreigner had been a hated enemy!

Today, we still find it hard to reach out to our so-called enemies as God commands us to do. In fact, we often prefer to stick with our close circle of friends, those from whom we receive so much love and support. But as Charles Swindoll once said, "You can tell a lot about a person by the way they treat those who can do nothing for them."

Dear Lord, thank You for providing for my salvation, though I deserve it not. Help me follow Your example as I extend Your hand of love and grace to all who come into my life. Through Christ I pray. Amen.

Scripture: Luke 4:23-30
Song: *"Blessed Be the Tie That Binds"*

From this meditation today, I will pray . . .
Adoration _____
_____
_____

Confession _____
_____
_____

Thanksgiving _____
_____
_____

Supplication _____
_____
_____

From this meditation today, I will . . .
Think _____
_____
_____

Say _____
_____
_____

Do _____
_____
_____
_____
_____

SPOTLIGHT
Next Week's Lesson
Walk across the room and welcome a stranger.

January 31

Mercy Walk

Be merciful, just as your Father is merciful
(Luke 6:36).

Scripture: Matthew 10:40-43
Song: *"I Want to Be More Like You"*

From this meditation today, I will pray . . .
Adoration _____
_____
_____

Confession _____
_____
_____

Thanksgiving _____
_____
_____

Supplication _____
_____
_____

From this meditation today, I will . . .
Think _____
_____
_____

Say _____
_____
_____

Do _____
_____
_____
_____

One day, a responsible student forgot her homework and came to me in tears. "That's OK," I said, wrapping the child in my arms. "I ate my mercy-flakes this morning. Just bring your work in tomorrow. I'll accept it without penalty."

One of my dictionaries defines mercy as the compassionate treatment of one in distress. It certainly helps the one in need, and I've found that providing relief and comfort makes *me* feel good too. But what about showing compassion to an offender or abuser who seems so clearly undeserving? That's a lot tougher! It's true that such people often don't *deserve* our mercy. But, of course, that's the point: the very definition of mercy makes it an *undeserved* extension of care and favor.

So how can we show mercy, when we don't feel it in our hearts? Like love, forgiveness, or any other Christlike virtue, to offer mercy is a choice of our will.

Today's Scripture passage puts feet to the choice. We are to love, do good to, bless, pray for, and give to those who may never do the same for us. For, as Martin Luther once said, "It is the duty of every Christian to be Christ to his neighbor."

Father, *teach me to be more like You in loving even the most unlovable. For that is exactly how You have treated me! In Christ's name, Amen.*

SPOTLIGHT
Next Week's Lesson

The Lord rewards those who help the hurting.

February

OLD TESTAMENT PEOPLE OF COMMITMENT

*Be merciful, just as your
Father is merciful.*
—Luke 6:36

Photo © istockphoto

February 1

Impossible Dream?

The woman became pregnant, and the next year about that same time she gave birth to a son, just as Elisha had told her (2 Kings 4:17).

Scripture: 2 Kings 4:8-17
Song: *"Awesome God"*

From this meditation today, I will pray . . .

Adoration _____
_____
_____

Confession _____
_____
_____

Thanksgiving _____
_____
_____

Supplication _____
_____
_____

From this meditation today, I will . . .

Think _____
_____
_____

Say _____
_____
_____

Do _____
_____
_____

February 1. Author **Barbara E. Haley** *has worked as an elementary school teacher and piano instructor. She lives in San Antonio, Texas*

Years ago, when the research head of General Motors called a meeting in order to solve a problem, he placed a table outside the meeting room displaying this sign: "Leave slide rules here." This kept his employees from reaching for their slide rules and jumping up to say, "Boss, you can't do that!"

In our Scripture passage today, the Shunammite woman had no son and was married to an old man. From her perspective, having a child was absolutely impossible. So she had simply given up on her dream. But God saw beyond the impossible and blessed her with a son. Even when she couldn't believe the promise, God kept His word. And, of course, that is how He works with us too.

What a wonderful Bible passage to remember when we are praying for a seemingly impossible situation. For as the apostle Paul put it, God is "able to do immeasurably more than all we ask or imagine, according to his power that is at work within us" (Ephesians 3:20).

Dear Father, *it's such a relief to know that my prayers are not limited by what I can imagine or understand. Thank You, in Jesus' name. Amen.*

SPOTLIGHT
Next Week's Lesson

God outgives even our biggest asking and our best thinking.

February 2

Pray Over Your Schedule

In the spring, at the time when kings go off to war, David sent Joab out with the king's men and the whole Israelite army. They destroyed the Ammonites and besieged Rabbah. But David remained in Jerusalem (2 Samuel 11:1).

Time management is one of the most important skills I use in life. I constantly check my calendar and evaluate my priorities to keep myself on schedule and on task.

On those rare occasions when I fail to show up where I have responsibilities, I pay a huge price. I damage my reputation and lose valuable ministry opportunities.

I doubt King David had a Day-Timer™, but however he kept up with his schedule, one spring he decided *not* to go to war with his men, even though that was his custom. As it turned out, the army didn't need David to win their battles.

But because David wasn't where he should have been, he lost his own battle. While the army was away, David succumbed to sexual temptation, and it nearly destroyed him. It did destroy others.

The bottom line for us: As we schedule our days, may we ask God to help us make the best possible choices.

Lord, *as I form my schedule today, help me make choices that will give me the best chance of success in Your kingdom. In Jesus' name, amen.*

Scripture: 2 Samuel 11:1-5
Song: *"Take Time to Be Holy"*

From this meditation today, I will pray . . .

Adoration _____

Confession _____

Thanksgiving _____

Supplication _____

From this meditation today, I will . . .

Think _____

Say _____

Do _____

SEARCH THE WORD
For a consultant to teach you good time management, look heavenward.

February 2–8. **Michael Helms** *is a minister, author, and amateur photographer. He lives with his wife, Tina, in Moultrie, Georgia.*

February 3

Doing the Right Thing

Uriah said to David, ". . . My lord's men are camped in the open fields. How could I go to my house to eat and drink and lie with my wife? . . . I will not do such a thing!" (2 Samuel 11:11).

Scripture: 2 Samuel 11:6-13
Song: *"Find Us Faithful"*

From this meditation today, I will pray . . .
Adoration _____
_____
_____

Confession _____
_____
_____

Thanksgiving _____
_____
_____

Supplication _____
_____
_____

From this meditation today, I will . . .
Think _____
_____
_____

Say _____
_____
_____

Do _____
_____
_____
_____

An accountant once told me she was asked to enter some false numbers into the company's records. She refused, and the owner of the business fired her.

It's not uncommon. In fact, history abounds with stories of people who have set aside their personal well-being to do the right thing. Sometimes what we lose is greater than a job, though. Sometimes our choices put our very lives on the line.

Such was the fate of Uriah, Bathsheba's husband. David brought him back from the war and encouraged him to go home and enjoy his wife. David hoped this would cover his sinful act—and Uriah would think the baby Bathsheba had conceived was his own. But Uriah wouldn't relax while his comrades suffered on the battlefield.

Uriah, countless people in history, and my accountant friend remind us: It takes courage to do the right thing. Sometimes we do it at great cost, but always to the pleasure of God.

Lord, *give me the courage I need to stand firm when tempted to make choices contrary to Your will. Help me be a person of integrity, unwilling to sacrifice morality for pleasure or ethics for gain. May I remember that in all situations I am Your earthly ambassador. Through Christ I pray. Amen.*

SPOTLIGHT
Next Week's Lesson

Do what's right
and leave the consequences
to God.

February 4

Can Others Count on Me?

Put Uriah in the front line where the fighting is fiercest. Then withdraw from him so he will be struck down and die (2 Samuel 11:15).

I met Mrs. Washington on a dirt road in Virginia, Liberia, on the campus of Ricks Institute. She's a refugee of the civil war that ravaged the country for 13 years. Abandoned by all of her children after her husband died, she lives alone in a stick hut on the 1000-acre campus. In a country where there is no Social Security, no welfare, no food stamps, and no government assistance of any kind, children are the life-source for aging parents. When they leave, parents suffer.

How hard it is to be abandoned by those who should support us! I wonder what went through Uriah's mind in those last moments as he noticed his comrades pulling back. Alone, he could hardly defend himself against an overpowering enemy. The pain of abandonment surely pierced his soul before an arrow pierced his heart.

If the Golden Rule serves as our guide, we will not abandon friends in their time of need. If fact, why should we abandon them ever, no matter the situation?

Lord, *thank You for never leaving or forsaking me. As You are faithful to me, help me remain faithful to others. I want my friends and family to be able to count on me through good days and bad, just as I count on You. In the name of the Father, the Son, and the Holy Spirit, I pray. Amen.*

SEARCH THE WORD
An attack by an enemy makes us tough, but betrayal by a friend breaks our hearts.

Scripture: 2 Samuel 11:14-21
Song: *"There's No Disappointment in Heaven"*

From this meditation today, I will pray . . .

Adoration _____

Confession _____

Thanksgiving _____

Supplication _____

From this meditation today, I will . . .

Think _____

Say _____

Do _____

February 5

Grief: Evidence of Love

When Uriah's wife heard that her husband was dead, she mourned for him (2 Samuel 11:26).

Scripture: 2 Samuel 11:22-27
Song: *"Be Still, My Soul"*

From this meditation today, I will pray . . .
Adoration _____
_____
_____

Confession _____
_____
_____

Thanksgiving _____
_____
_____

Supplication _____
_____
_____

From this meditation today, I will . . .
Think _____
_____
_____

Say _____
_____
_____

Do _____
_____
_____
_____

I was 16 years old when I first experienced the death of someone I loved. I was hauling hay with my father. As we passed my grandmother's house, we noticed she had fallen over in the swing on the front porch. I watched as Dad gave her CPR. The color left her skin as she drew her last breath.

Over the next several months I observed the different stages of grief in Mom as she adjusted to life without her mother. I grieved, too, along with our entire family.

At that time I didn't know I'd be a minister, frequently walking with people through their own griefs. Most of the time, someone in my church faces loss and mourning. It's so painful, so difficult.

After Uriah died on the battlefield, Bathsheba, his wife, mourned his death. It was only natural, for grief is the price we pay for loving others. Have you ever thought of it that way? The only way to escape grief is never to have loved. But if we never love, then we never truly live.

Dear Father in Heaven, *if I had my way I'd never deal with grief. It hurts too much. When I have significant loss in my life, remind me that grief is normal and that it's healthy. After a significant period of mourning, bring healing to me and the desire to love again. I pray this prayer in the name of Jesus, my merciful Savior and Lord. Amen.*

SPOTLIGHT
Next Week's Lesson

Better to grieve
because of love
than because of sin.

February 6

Only God Can Do It

Have mercy on me, O God, according to your unfailing love; according to your great compassion blot out my transgressions. Wash away all my iniquity and cleanse me from my sin (Psalm 51:1, 2).

The *Boston Globe* reported in 2006 that scientists are investigating a possible way to cool down the overheated earth and reverse global warming. Could they shoot tons of particles into the atmosphere that would block the sun's rays? One model experiment indicated that if 20 percent of the sunlight over the Arctic Ocean were blocked, it would be enough to restore sea ice there.

We can come up with creative solutions to many of our problems. But the Bible offers no man-made solution to our sin problem. The transgressions we commit against God can be blotted out only by God himself.

David, overcome by his sin with Bathsheba, knew he couldn't fix his problem. Only God, in His great mercy, could rescue David from sin.

What great advances in technology since the days of David! However, nothing has changed when it comes to a soul's salvation. Only God can accomplish it, through the precious blood of His Son.

Father, I am not looking for justice, for I would not survive it. Like David, I need Your mercy. I am not hoping to get what I deserve; I am depending on Your great compassion to forgive me of my sins. In Jesus' name, amen.

SEARCH THE WORD

If Jesus makes you clean, you are clean indeed.

Scripture: Psalm 51:1-9
Song: *"Create in Me a Clean Heart"*

From this meditation today, I will pray . . .

Adoration _____

Confession _____

Thanksgiving _____

Supplication _____

From this meditation today, I will . . .

Think _____

Say _____

Do _____

February 7

In the Restoration Business

Restore to me the joy of your salvation and grant me a willing spirit, to sustain me (Psalm 51:12).

Scripture: Psalm 51:10-19
Song: *"He Keeps Me Singing"*

From this meditation today, I will pray . . .
Adoration _____
_____
_____

Confession _____
_____
_____

Thanksgiving _____
_____
_____

Supplication _____
_____
_____

From this meditation today, I will . . .
Think _____
_____
_____

Say _____
_____
_____

Do _____
_____
_____
_____

For almost a decade, the 1965 Ford Comet deteriorated. Only partially garaged, the back half of the white car was mostly black with stains from the pecan trees above it. That Comet, which belonged to my aging grandmother, was the only car I ever saw her drive.

Before Grandma died, I bought it and had it completely restored, inside and out. What joy on the day when I brought her outside to see that "brand new" work of art!

Life can pile its share of stain on us, can't it? David, marred by his own sin, longed for his joy to be restored to its original condition. So he called out to God for help.

Praise God, He's still in the restoration business. As someone once put it, "There is only one requirement for salvation: we must first be lost." Coming to God, admitting our deep need—the stains of our sinful choices—we ask for what God does best. He extends His loving arms of compassion and opens up the floodgates of grace. He restores us to a new reality: "Therefore, if anyone is in Christ, he is a new creation; the old has gone, the new has come!" (2 Corinthians 5:17).

Lord, *in the rhythm of life, sometimes the cadence becomes erratic. Instead of dancing, I feel agitated by the beat. In such times, bring my heart back into rhythm with Your will. Then will I know joy. Through Christ, amen.*

SPOTLIGHT
Next Week's Lesson

"Hide your face from my sins and blot out all my iniquity" (Psalm 51:9).

February 8

Being God's Messenger

*Then David said to Nathan, "I have sinned against the L*ORD*"*
(2 Samuel 12:13).

"Don't shoot the messenger." It's a common phrase meaning, Why be angry with the one who simply tells us the truth?

It's rare for someone to tell us what we *need* to hear rather than just what we *want* to hear. But mere "yes men" won't help us grow. And such relationships remain superficial at best.

It's risky to speak the unvarnished truth, though. Friendships can become strained. Yet the risks come laced with the rewards of personal growth. We begin seeing personal liabilities that once evaded our vision.

Nathan took a huge risk in going to King David as God's truthful messenger. He didn't accuse directly; he simply told a story that hooked David's heart and held a mirror to his soul. The story of a rich man's thievery became the story of David's own dark deeds with Bathsheba and Uriah.

Thankfully, David was able to respond to the painful revelation: "I have sinned against the Lord." I wonder, though, how I might have responded in a similar situation. Can I look in the mirror and see what's *really* there?

Lord, *I'm not very comfortable pointing out the sin of others. But on occasion, I may need to be a Nathan to someone. Help! In Jesus' name, amen.*

SEARCH THE WORD

Is there someone to whom you need to be a Nathan?

Scripture: 2 Samuel 12:1-7, 13-15
Song: *"Redeemed, Restored, Forgiven"*

From this meditation today, I will pray . . .

Adoration _____
_____
_____

Confession _____
_____
_____

Thanksgiving _____
_____
_____

Supplication _____
_____
_____

From this meditation today, I will . . .

Think _____
_____
_____

Say _____
_____
_____

Do _____
_____
_____

February 9

Transforming Training

The girl pleased him. . . . Immediately he provided her with her beauty treatments and special food (Esther 2:9).

Scripture: Esther 2:1-11
Song: *"More Like the Master"*

From this meditation today, I will pray . . .
Adoration _____
_____
_____

Confession _____
_____
_____

Thanksgiving _____
_____
_____

Supplication _____
_____
_____

From this meditation today, I will . . .
Think _____
_____
_____

Say _____
_____
_____

Do _____
_____
_____

A full year of special treatments and training prepared Esther and the other girls for presentation to the king. They'd be the potential candidates for his next queen. No contender could just rush into the king's presence. First, 12 months of beauty prep!

In *Pygmalion,* by George Bernard Shaw, Professor Henry Higgins had his hands full when he took on the challenge of transforming lowly Eliza Doolittle into a high society lady. Her lower-class upbringing—including her speech, manners, and clothes—had to change so he could pass her off as a well-bred duchess.

I, too, am being transformed so I'll be ready to stand in the presence of God for eternity. My sin stood in the way of my being presentable, but His Son paid the price for my sins. Now His Holy Spirit is busy in my life (and in yours, if Christ is your Savior). He is transforming me, working into me the wonderful fruit of the Spirit: "love, joy, peace, patience, kindness, goodness, faithfulness, gentleness and self-control" (Galatians 5:22, 23).

Thank You, my Father, *for providing salvation for me through Your Son. May I allow Your Holy Spirit to transform me! In Jesus' name, amen.*

February 9–15. **Sue Miholer** *is a newly-retired busy grandmother in Salem, Oregon, where she runs Picky, Picky Ink, her own freelance writing business.*

SPOTLIGHT
Next Week's Lesson

The Holy Spirit's "before" and "after" pictures of us will be truly amazing.

February 10

Special Gifts

So he set a royal crown on her head and made her queen (Esther 2:17).

When we want to show our appreciation to someone, we go out of our way to find the perfect gift. Chocolates? Flowers? A special meal? A fancy card? It has to be something we know the person will value.

I doubt any of us will be able to top what King Xerxes gave Esther—a crown, a banquet in her honor, and a holiday to mark the occasion. He also distributed gifts with "royal liberality."

My king made me His own when I accepted His offer of salvation. Although the day wasn't marked by a crown or calendar change in my honor, He has showered me liberally with His gifts. Even Queen Esther's brilliance fades in light of what God will do for me when I am eternally in His presence.

No matter how you interpret the book of Revelation, for those who are baptized into Christ, the future is full of beautiful things. Heaven will be perfection—beyond anything we can imagine. Just being in His presence will be enough to keep us worshiping Him forever.

I thank You, Father, that You have chosen me to be Your own. What You have given me is beyond imagining, and I can hardly fathom what it will be like to enjoy Your presence throughout eternity. May I live in gratitude for Your immense favor this day! Through my Lord Jesus I pray. Amen.

SEARCH THE WORD

No earthly gifts can compare with our heavenly ones.

Scripture: Esther 2:15-18
Song: *"Love Divine"*

From this meditation today, I will pray...

Adoration _____

Confession _____

Thanksgiving _____

Supplication _____

From this meditation today, I will...

Think _____

Say _____

Do _____

February 11

Right Place, Right Time

Mordecai was sitting at the king's gate
(Esther 2:21).

Scripture: Esther 2:19-23
Song: *"I'll Go Where You Want Me to Go"*

From this meditation today, I will pray . . .

Adoration _____
_____
_____

Confession _____
_____
_____

Thanksgiving _____
_____
_____

Supplication _____
_____
_____

From this meditation today, I will . . .

Think _____
_____
_____

Say _____
_____
_____

Do _____
_____
_____
_____

Heads of state and other powerful individuals have people whose job it is to protect them. In the USA, one of the duties of the Secret Service is to guard the president and vice president.

The Secret Service employs approximately 3,200 special agents, 1,300 uniformed division officers, and more than 2,000 other technical, professional, and administrative support personnel. A Secret Service applicant undergoes a thorough background investigation, including employment history, police records, credit history, school transcripts, neighborhood references, and military records. Then another six or more months of training follows.

But all King Xerxes needed was Mordecai. He uncovered a plot to kill the king and quickly reported it. The perpetrators were executed, a note was entered in the king's records, and that was that. Mordecai had no special training, but God had put him in the place where he'd hear what he needed to hear.

Where has God placed you today? What particular situation has He called you to enter, to make a difference there in God's strength?

Dear Lord, *I know You have placed me where I am today. Keep me alert to what You want me to know and do, that I might bring glory to Your name. All praise to You, in Christ's name. Amen.*

SPOTLIGHT
Next Week's Lesson

Stay alert
for opportunities
to stop evil.

February 12

Let Go of the Banana

If it pleases the king, let a decree be issued to destroy them
(Esther 3:9).

I've heard about a creative way that hunters use to capture a particular kind of monkey in South America. They put a banana in a narrow-mouthed jar and bury the jar in the ground, leaving the top open and exposed. The monkey smells the banana and grabs it. But because the jar is too narrow for him to remove his paw—which now clings tenaciously to the prize—he's caught. He will shriek about his dilemma, but he will not let go.

In our Scripture today, I suppose only one person out of hundreds refused to bow to the king. But it was that one person, Mordecai, who so infuriated Haman. He was in such a rage over the slight that he determined to kill Mordecai—and hatched an even grander scheme when he learned about Mordecai's ethnic heritage.

Like the monkey who won't let go of a banana, Haman was captured by his insistence on getting what he demanded.

Most of us have some monkey-like attitudes, right? We want to hang on to the "banana" of a less-than-God-pleasing attitude or habit. It too can enslave us with anger, bitterness, or just a sad longing for what truly satisfies.

Lord, I want to hold on to wrongs that have been done to me. It's so hard to let go, and I need Your power to do it. Thank You, in Jesus' name. Amen.

SEARCH THE WORD

How hard it is to let go of bad habits!

Scripture: Esther 3:7-13
Song: *"Is Your All on the Altar?"*

From this meditation today, I will pray . . .

Adoration _____

Confession _____

Thanksgiving _____

Supplication _____

From this meditation today, I will . . .

Think _____

Say _____

Do _____

February 13

What's Eating You?

A gallows seventy-five feet high . . .
He had it made for Mordecai
(Esther 7:9).

Scripture: Esther 7:1-10
Song: *"I Surrender All"*

From this meditation today, I will pray . . .
Adoration _____
_____
_____

Confession _____
_____
_____

Thanksgiving _____
_____
_____

Supplication _____
_____
_____

From this meditation today, I will . . .
Think _____
_____
_____

Say _____
_____
_____

Do _____
_____
_____
_____

What we eat can cause chronic indigestion, migraines, and countless other maladies. But often it's not so much what we eat as "what's eating us" that makes us ill.

Unresolved stressful situations can trigger physical symptoms. For example, raging at other drivers raises our blood pressure. If we don't deal with and let go of such stressors, we can actually put our lives in danger.

Haman, consumed by his rage at Mordecai, got the king's permission to do away with all the Jewish people in the kingdom. His fury spelled trouble for him.

The dramatic intensity of today's passage would make a great movie scene. Haman relishes the honor of dining with the king and queen—until Esther reveals her heritage. Haman immediately realizes his life is in danger. He grovels before a Jew for his life, which has been consumed by rage because a Jew would not bow to him. What irony.

What's "eating you" today? Whatever it is, would you like to commit the situation to God? In a simple prayer, just open Your heart to Him. Let Him take away the sting of the hurt.

Lord, *I release to You whatever stands in the way of my growth in Christ. Heal the hurts that come from living here on earth. In Jesus' name, amen.*

SPOTLIGHT
Next Week's Lesson

Bitter anger is an acid
that eats holes
in our souls.

February 14

A New Decree

Now write another decree in the king's name in behalf of the Jews as seems best to you, and seal it with the king's signet ring—for no document written in the king's name and sealed with his ring can be revoked (Esther 8:8).

To counter the decree fashioned by Haman, Esther and Mordecai were to craft a new decree on behalf of the Jews. Jesus, by His death and resurrection, also crafted a decree—a new testament "by His blood"—on our behalf. The law of grace now dictates His dealings with us and our dealings with Him.

When I drove a school bus, I had to follow precise steps upon approaching a railroad crossing. I had to stop a specified distance from the tracks in the farthest right lane, turn on my warning lights, open the door, open the window, and listen for a train. Then I could cross the tracks. (That always reminded me of the rituals the ancient Hebrews had to follow in order to approach God.)

However, when I'm in my car, unless there is a stop sign, I am free to drive across those tracks without stopping. That's a good picture of the easy access we have, because of grace, to the throne of God the Father. Because of the death and resurrection of His Son, the Father bids us draw near.

Thank You, Jesus, that the blood You shed on my behalf gives me instant access to the Lord of All. I pray to the Father in Your name. Amen.

Scripture: Esther 8:3-8
Song: *"I Call the World's Redeemer Mine"*

From this meditation today, I will pray...
Adoration _____

Confession _____

Thanksgiving _____

Supplication _____

From this meditation today, I will...
Think _____

Say _____

Do _____

SEARCH THE WORD
Cleansing rituals are no longer needed; we've been washed in the blood.

February 15

"For Such a Time as This"

Who knows but that you have come to royal position for such a time as this? (Esther 4:14).

Scripture: Esther 4:1-3, 9-17
Song: *"For the Deep Love That Kept Us"*

From this meditation today, I will pray . . .
Adoration _____

Confession _____

Thanksgiving _____

Supplication _____

From this meditation today, I will . . .
Think _____

Say _____

Do _____

My brother-in-law was raised in the Philippines as the son of missionaries. He also spent the majority of his 25-year career with the State Department attached to the embassy in Manila. Even after he retired to teach at a university in the United States, he kept his security clearance so he could fill in overseas when needed.

In the summer of 2001, he was assigned to Manila for six weeks. During that time, rebel forces captured American missionaries Martin and Gracia Burnham. The mission agencies were glad they had someone at the embassy who understood the rebels' mind-set.

Fast forward to summer, 2002. Frank was assigned to Manila for just three weeks that year, but in that exact window of time, Martin and Gracia were shot and released—Martin to God's presence and Gracia to U.S. authorities. Frank was there to assist Gracia with her press conferences (very familiar territory for him). He also worked out many of the details for her return home.

God had uniquely prepared and placed Frank, in His place and at His time, "for such a time as this."

Oh, Lord, I thank You that You uniquely prepare each of us so You can use us to accomplish Your will. Keep me walking close to You so I'm ready for Your plans to unfold. In the name of my Savior, Jesus Christ, amen.

SPOTLIGHT
Next Week's Lesson

Right person, right place, right time:
when it's your turn, take it.

February 16

Treasure This!

After this I looked, and there before me was a door standing open in heaven. And the voice I had first heard speaking to me like a trumpet said, "Come up here, and I will show you what must take place after this" (Revelation 4:1).

A rock? I'd invested hours typing this graduate student's geology thesis . . . and this ugly chalky gray mineral was my compensation? "I'm sorry I can't pay you monetarily, but I hope you'll treasure this. I found two others in the field also." I rolled the knobby hunk between my palms and muttered, "Umm . . . thank you."

He then retrieved it and whacked it in half. Wow! Inside was a cavity populated with purple crystals of indescribable beauty. We were the first to witness their magnificence inside this geode.

When John was given a glimpse into Heaven, he observed splendors so dazzling that he could hardly speak. Lamps blazed. Lightning flashed. Thunder crashed.

While we may not be the first to view a particular wondrously beauty here on earth, it is possible to daily experience, firsthand, the dazzling freshness of God's grace. Whenever we do, let us deeply treasure it.

My Father, *let me always be open to Your matchless beauty amidst the ordinary routines of my days. I love You! In Jesus' name, amen.*

Scripture: Revelation 4:1-6a
Song: *"I Stand in Awe"*

From this meditation today, I will pray . . .

Adoration _____

Confession _____

Thanksgiving _____

Supplication _____

From this meditation today, I will . . .

Think _____

Say _____

Do _____

SEARCH THE WORD

Brief glimpses of Heaven's beauty help us want to make it our home.

February 16–22. **Vicki Hodges** lives in the lap of the Colorado Rockies and works as a Spanish teacher at her local public high school.

February 17

Perpetual Praise

You are worthy, our Lord and God, to receive glory and honor and power, for you created all things, and by your will they were created and have their being (Revelation 4:11).

Scripture: Revelation 4:6b-11
Song: *"Holy, Holy, Holy"*

From this meditation today, I will pray...
Adoration _____

Confession _____

Thanksgiving _____

Supplication _____

From this meditation today, I will...
Think _____

Say _____

Do _____

The school's doors and windows vibrated as each note blasted from the speakers, every beat assaulting the glass and metal frames. This was my first experience chaperoning a hip-hop and rap concert at our local high school. I literally checked my watch every three minutes, wondering how much longer I'd have to endure the psychic battering. When the evening ended, my head's throbbing rivaled that of the school building.

By contrast, John ushers us into the throne room of Heaven to witness a most pleasant, eternal concert. The four creatures, and all those in attendance, worship the Lord continuously in a chain reaction of praise. Time constraints will never limit this concert.

When I consider that God created everything from the substance of His Word and that He sustains everything by His wisdom and power, I am in awe. Worship is the natural overflow of this knowledge, and my entire being throbs with praise.

Heavenly Father, *when I exhaust the words to praise You, it's exciting to think all eternity will be sufficient time to learn to glorify You continuously. Glory to the Father, and to the Son, and to the Holy Spirit; as it was in the beginning, is now, and will be forever! Amen.*

SPOTLIGHT
Next Week's Lesson

And the praise goes on forever and ever and ever . . .

February 18

We're Moving!

*The L*ORD* had said to Abram, "Leave your country, your people and your father's household and go to the land I will show you"* (Genesis 12:1).

Every spring the nerves in my stomach knotted and eventually strangled my emotions. Springtime was our family's D-Day: Dad decided whether or not to sign his newly offered teaching contract for the upcoming school year. Once he accomplished his professional goals in one location, he would accept new challenges . . . and we would have to move. It was wonderful for him, but torment for us kids. I admit that I envied children who could claim a hometown.

God directed Abraham to move, a comand that held both promise and hope. God's agenda targeted big objectives. "*Leave*" packed and delivered a powerful punch: God prepared to revolutionize Abraham's life, and to manipulate the course of history. His goals were deliberate and purposeful.

Ours may not be a drastic calling to move, geographically. Perhaps God is orchestrating a shift in our thought processes or redirecting our areas of service. Possibly, God desires us to pursue a new dream! Whatever the journey, He longs to guide and join us.

Father, *the joy of journeying with You outweighs the tyranny of venturing into the unknown. Thank You for Your good plans. In Jesus' name, amen.*

Scripture: Genesis 12:1-5
Song: *"Move Forward"*

From this meditation today, I will pray . . .

Adoration _____
_____
_____

Confession _____
_____
_____

Thanksgiving _____
_____
_____

Supplication _____
_____
_____

From this meditation today, I will . . .

Think _____
_____
_____

Say _____
_____
_____

Do _____
_____
_____

SEARCH THE WORD

Are you "stuck" or "moving on up"?

February 19

Among the Stars

I will make your descendants as numerous as the stars in the sky and will give them all these lands, and through your offspring all nations on earth will be blessed (Genesis 26:4).

Scripture: Genesis 26:1-5
Song: *"All Heaven Declares"*

From this meditation today, I will pray . . .

Adoration _____
_____
_____

Confession _____
_____
_____

Thanksgiving _____
_____
_____

Supplication _____
_____
_____

From this meditation today, I will . . .

Think _____
_____
_____

Say _____
_____
_____

Do _____
_____
_____

The best estimates indicate that the Milky Way Galaxy contains at least 100 billion stars. And the universe holds approximately 100 billion galaxies, all populated with stars. There are more stars in space than there are grains of sand on the Earth.

Try this: Hold a dime at arm's length and aim at a night sky. That dime would hide about 15 million stars from your view, if it were even possible to see with such power.

Obviously, it was huge when God promised Abraham that his descendants would be as the stars of the universe. Abraham believed God's promise, even though he and Sarah had been unable to have children. The promise referred not only to Abraham's physical offspring, but also to his spiritual children, including all who belong to Jesus, Abraham's divine descendent. As the apostle Paul would write, centuries later: "If you belong to Christ, then you are Abraham's seed, and heirs according to the promise" (Galatians 3:29).

Lord, *give me Your heart and eyes for the lost of all nations. Help me love and serve people, never losing sight of the worth of the individual. For Your love knows no cultural or geographical boundaries. In Jesus' name, amen.*

SPOTLIGHT
Next Week's Lesson

The God who created the galaxies is worthy of our worship.

February 20

The Hard Way

The angel of the Lord *came and sat down under the oak in Ophrah that belonged to Joash the Abiezrite, where his son Gideon was threshing wheat in a winepress to keep it from the Midianites* (Judges 6:11).

Scripture: Judges 6:11-23
Song: *"Faith Is the Victory"*

What is she doing? When I peeked in the kitchen, Aimee's little hands were plunged into the mixing bowl and plastered with eggs, flour, and chocolate chip goo. "I'm just following directions, Mom. It says to mix by hand." Apparently, I hadn't taught her that "mixing by hand" simply meant using a spoon, instead of an electric mixer. Our literalist was doing it the hard way, accidentally.

As the enemy Midianites were so near, Gideon threshed wheat the hard way. He beat the grain in a winepress, since that was quieter and less likely to attract enemy attention. Gideon, a man of valor, rejected the easy way—and even took on additional work from God. Not only would Gideon thresh grain, but he'd also thresh the Midianites!

In our technological age, we expend great energy trying to discover simple, painless means of accomplishing our work. The way is generally hard for a follower of Jesus, but He sufficiently enables and strengthens us to accomplish His will.

Lord, *thanks for equipping me. Help me to serve with a willing mind and daring heart—the right way, easy or hard. Through Christ, amen.*

From this meditation today, I will pray . . .

Adoration _____

Confession _____

Thanksgiving _____

Supplication _____

From this meditation today, I will . . .

Think _____

Say _____

Do _____

SEARCH THE WORD

Be lazy intelligently: do each job right the first time.

February 21

S-O-C-K-S!

That night God did so. Only the fleece was dry; all the ground was covered with dew (Judges 6:40).

Scripture: Judges 6:36-40
Song: *"There Is Joy in the Lord"*

From this meditation today, I will pray . . .
Adoration _____
_____
_____

Confession _____
_____
_____

Thanksgiving _____
_____
_____

Supplication _____
_____
_____

From this meditation today, I will . . .
Think _____
_____
_____

Say _____
_____
_____

Do _____
_____
_____
_____

That's the way it is: *Eso sí que es.* My high school students delighted in the simple technique for remembering this idiomatic expression, "that's the way it is," in Spanish. By rapidly spelling socks, one produces an acceptable pronunciation for these four Spanish words.

My students frequently shout it to their friends outside of school. And in the classroom, if they groan about an assignment, I simply say, S-O-C-K-S to remind them the task is purposeful, nonnegotiable, and I will help them accomplish it.

God revealed His mission to Gideon, a mighty warrior. The assignment seemed impossible; after all, Gideon's clan was the weakest in Manasseh, and he was the least in his family. Gideon wanted verification of the assignment, so he tested God a couple of times. Each time, God patiently reinforced His S-O-C-K-S message to Gideon.

God faithfully demonstrates His power and wisdom, always equipping us to do His will, no matter how mind-boggling the goal might seem. Every time the impossible is accomplished, He is glorified, and that's the way it is.

Lord, *I realize You don't need my help for anything. You set the universe in motion and are capable of doing everything by yourself. But thank You for the privilege of being part of the action. In Jesus' name, amen.*

SPOTLIGHT
Next Week's Lesson

Serving God is a privilege we should eagerly accept.

February 22

Pick Me!

Then I heard the voice of the Lord saying, "Whom shall I send? And who will go for us?" And I said, "Here am I. Send me!" (Isaiah 6:8).

"Staff, this year Anaheim, California, will host the curriculum convention. Three teachers will represent our school. During your convention free time, you might even want to visit Disneyland and the Pacific Ocean. Who wants to go to the convention?" The room exploded with willing volunteers. It's rarely my experience to win something, even if the odds tip in my favor. However, I volunteered and wrote a proposal, listing the reasons I'd make a good attendee. And . . . my principal selected me!

Isaiah, perhaps caught up in the awesomeness of God's presence, volunteered to be God's man. He knew neither the assignment nor what would be required of him. (It's possible the fervor of the nearby seraphim kindled a flame within him.)

Isaiah's passion for serving God, in the capacity of a forgiven sinner, allowed him to welcome any commission from on high. He witnessed God's holiness. What would it take for followers of Jesus to sense His holiness and mission? What would cause us to jump up and down, wave our arms, and yell, "Send me!"?

Lord, *I want a fiery zeal for serving You. Help me love and enlighten others with the truths of Your salvation. Through Christ, I pray. Amen.*

Scripture: Isaiah 6:1-8
Song: *"Here I Am, Lord"*

From this meditation today, I will pray . . .
Adoration _____

Confession _____

Thanksgiving _____

Supplication _____

From this meditation today, I will . . .
Think _____

Say _____

Do _____

SEARCH THE WORD

Are you a willing volunteer or a reluctant draftee in God's army?

February 23

Shining with God's Favor

The Lord saw how great man's wickedness on the earth had become . . . But Noah found favor in the eyes of the Lord
(Genesis 6:5, 8).

Scripture: Genesis 6:1-8
Song: "Father, Whose Everlasting Love"

From this meditation today, I will pray . . .
Adoration _____
_____
_____

Confession _____
_____
_____

Thanksgiving _____
_____
_____

Supplication _____
_____
_____

From this meditation today, I will . . .
Think _____
_____
_____

Say _____
_____
_____

Do _____
_____
_____

Maribeth Parsons' family was gathered in celebration of her 80th birthday. While toddlers bounced in mothers' laps, adults caught up on the latest family happenings. Excited grandchildren crowded about the woman, each wanting to be first with the cards in their outstretched hands. A stack of wrapped presents awaited the arrival of the birthday cake. Around the room, other occupants of Sunny Acres smiled at the charming scene.

Maribeth was a favorite of both staff and residents. She always had a smile or cheerful word for whomever she met. When asked the source of her happy state, she just said, "God's been good to me."

Just as Noah's obedience found favor in God's eyes, Maribeth's life also reflected God's pleasure. In a world gone berserk with mayhem and bedlam, someone whose life reflects the favor of God shines like a diamond. That is the kind of person I want to be, today, tomorrow, and at the end of my days.

Lord, *help me remember that I am Your representative here on earth. Show me ways to share Your love with others. I pray in Jesus' name. Amen.*

SPOTLIGHT
Next Week's Lesson

May your life bring
a smile to God's face.

February 23–28. **Gay Ingram** *enjoys writing from her home in East Texas. Besides devotionals, she has published two novels and a book on her hometown's history.*

February 24

A Willing Offering

The Lord said to Moses, "Speak to the people of Israel, that they take for me an offering; from every man whose heart makes him willing you shall receive the offering for me" (Exodus 25:1, Revised Standard Version).

"Not that shirt, Mom. It's my favorite."

"But Douglas, you haven't worn this in ages." She held up a blue T-shirt.

"It's the only Superman shirt I have, Mom. And I love it even if I can't wear it anymore."

Douglas thought of that shirt in Sunday school class, as he listened to Mr. Brown speak about the people he served as a missionary. "They are very poor. Most live in houses, made of scrap pieces of wood, that have dirt floors." Mr. Brown paused and looked around the room at the attentive, uplifted faces. "But even if all they have to eat is a crusty piece of bread, they will share it with someone who has none."

Douglas thought about Mr. Brown's words all the way home. After lunch he disappeared to his room and stayed for a long time. When he came out, he carried a cardboard box, clothes, and toys spilling over the top. "Here, Mom. Add this shirt to the things you're taking to the homeless shelter."

Father, *help me remember that all I have is on loan from You. Open my eyes to how I can share my blessings with others. I pray in Jesus' name. Amen.*

Scripture: Exodus 25:1-9
Song: *"Lord of My Life!"*

From this meditation today, I will pray . . .

Adoration _____

Confession _____

Thanksgiving _____

Supplication _____

From this meditation today, I will . . .

Think _____

Say _____

Do _____

SEARCH THE WORD

A gift joyfully given is a double blessing.

February 25

Don't Be Distracted

Let me pass through your land; I will go only by the road, I will turn aside neither to the right nor to the left (Deuteronomy 2:27, Revised Standard Version).

Scripture: Deuteronomy 2:26-30
Song: *"The King's Highway"*

From this meditation today, I will pray . . .
Adoration _____
_____
_____

Confession _____
_____
_____

Thanksgiving _____
_____
_____

Supplication _____
_____
_____

From this meditation today, I will . . .
Think _____
_____
_____

Say _____
_____
_____

Do _____
_____
_____
_____

Mrs. Bolton decided to bake a dessert for supper. When she found herself without enough eggs, she called to her son, Jimmy. "You'll need to go to the store, Jimmy. I can't make my chocolate cake without more eggs."

"Yum, chocolate cake. OK, Mom." As he stepped out the door, his friend Steve called. "Want to shoot some hoops?" Jimmy decided it was early and he had time. An hour later, Jimmy set off for the store. Leaving the store, he met up with Roger and Blake. He stopped to talk and, before he knew it, their conversation turned to the next big game. By the time their conversation ended, it had grown dark.

As Jimmy stepped into the kitchen, his mother asked, "Where have you been?" Without waiting for an answer, she said it was so late she hadn't time to bake a cake now. "Your Dad will be home soon, and I need to fix supper."

Sadly, it's so easy to turn aside, even from a once cherished destination. What will it take for you and me to keep our feet on the straight and narrow path Christ has set before us today?

Lord, *I'm tempted to forsake the path you have set before me. Keep me faithful, in spite of the multitude of distractions. In Jesus' name, amen.*

SPOTLIGHT
Next Week's Lesson

Keep my eyes focused on the prize.

February 26

Quick Obedience?

Oh that they had such a mind as this always, to fear me and to keep all my commandments, that it might go well with them and with their children for ever (Deuteronomy 5:29, Revised Standard Version).

"Danny, you still need to sweep the driveway before you go to practice."

"I won't forget, Mom," he replied, his attention focused on the baseball magazine he was reading. His mother left, and the house grew quiet.

Fully engrossed, Danny didn't notice the time going by until he happened to look at the bedside clock. "Ooops!"

With only five minutes to get to the practice field, Danny changed into his uniform. Grabbing his mitt, he flew out the door, hopped on his bike, and pedaled down the street.

That evening, Danny's mother informed him: "Before you're allowed to go to practice again, the driveway must get swept."

Even we adults have our problems responding to God's call in a timely fashion. Why? Perhaps we hope things will "just work out on their own," with little effort on our part. However, the call of God usually involves hard work on behalf of His people. When others need us, we need to respond. Driveways don't clean themselves!

Father, *I want to be quick to obey your commandments. Give me a willing heart and a loving motive, for Your glory. In Jesus' name, amen.*

Scripture: Deuteronomy 5:28-33

Song: *"O Blessed Souls Are They"*

From this meditation today, I will pray...

Adoration _____

Confession _____

Thanksgiving _____

Supplication _____

From this meditation today, I will...

Think _____

Say _____

Do _____

SEARCH THE WORD

When it comes to obeying God, don't procrastinate.

February 27

Attitude of Gratitude

*Take heed lest you forget the L*ORD *your God, by not keeping his commandments and his ordinances and his statutes, which I command you this day: . . . then your heart be lifted up, and you forget the L*ORD *your God, who brought you out of the land of Egypt (Deuteronomy 8:11, 14, Revised Standard Version).*

Scripture: Deuteronomy 8:11-20
Song: *"Hail, Thou Source of Every Blessing"*

From this meditation today, I will pray . . .

Adoration _____

Confession _____

Thanksgiving _____

Supplication _____

From this meditation today, I will . . .

Think _____

Say _____

Do _____

He was born December 4, 1905, in Houston, Texas. At the young age of 19, he inherited the Hughes Tool Company, a million-dollar business. A lifetime aircraft enthusiast, he set many world records, and through his company, pioneered many innovations in aerospace technology.

Cowboy aviator, Hollywood playboy, military contractor, maverick financier— young Howard Hughes captivated the American imagination with his flamboyant lifestyle. But in later life, his eccentricities and excesses degenerated into madness. At his death, Hughes was a stringy-haired old man whose obsessive fear of germs made him a virtual hermit.

Some people live their lives as if every blessing comes from their own efforts. But God calls us to a continuous attitude of gratitude.

Every blessing comes from His gracious hand. Take heed!

Father, *I acknowledge that everything I have comes from your loving heart. Let me live my days in thankfulness, pointing to Your unconditional favor. In the name of Your Son, my Savior, I pray. Amen.*

SPOTLIGHT
Next Week's Lesson

"Let him who boasts boast in the Lord" (2 Corinthians 10:17).

February 28

Protective Love

*What does the L*ORD *your God require of you, but to fear the Lord your God, to walk in all his ways, to love him, to serve the L*ORD *your God . . . to keep the commandments and statutes of the L*ORD*, which I command you this day for your good?* (Deuteronomy 10:12, *Revised Standard Version*).

"Judy, will you go collect the books for Library Hour from Mrs. Johnston?" The Johnstons lived only two streets away in their neighborhood, and Lacy Johnston was Judy's best friend.

Sack in hand, Judy turned the corner beside a yard enclosed in a white picket fence. A yellow sign reading "Beware of Dog" hung on its gate. As she passed, a rottweiler rushed toward her, barking furiously. Judy picked up a stick and began poking through a gap, laughing at the dog's aggressive reaction. Suddenly, the dog took a flying leap over the fence and pushed Judy to the ground.

Arms covering her face, Judy crouched in fear of the dog's attack. But the dog's owner quickly came to the little girl's rescue, and Judy ran home. The phone rang as Judy's mother comforted her. "Yes, I understand," Judy's mother said as she hung up. "Didn't you see the sign, Judy? It was there for your good, to protect you from harm."

Father, *help me see that Your commandments are not harsh. Through them You protect me from my own self-destructive attitudes and behaviors. I love You because You first loved me! Thank You, in Jesus' name. Amen.*

Scripture: Deuteronomy 10:12-21

Song: *"Ye Righteous in the Lord Rejoice"*

From this meditation today, I will pray . . .

Adoration _____

Confession _____

Thanksgiving _____

Supplication _____

From this meditation today, I will . . .

Think _____

Say _____

Do _____

SEARCH THE WORD

God's laws are not a fence to lock us in but to keep us safe.

"**Y**ou are worthy, our Lord and God, to receive glory and honor and power, for you created all things, and by your will they were created and have their being"
—Revelation 4:11

March

THE PROMISE OF NEW LIFE

"You show that you are a letter from Christ. . . ."
—2 Corinthians 3:3

Photo © Getty Images

March 1

Come Home to Peace

I will gather you from the nations and bring you back from the countries where you have been scattered, and I will give you back the land of Israel again (Ezekiel 11:17).

Scripture: Ezekiel 11:14-21

Song: *"Return, O Wanderer, to Thy Home"*

From this meditation today, I will pray . . .

Adoration _____
_____
_____

Confession _____
_____
_____

Thanksgiving _____
_____
_____

Supplication _____
_____
_____

From this meditation today, I will . . .

Think _____
_____
_____

Say _____
_____
_____

Do _____
_____
_____

Ezekiel announced that the scattered Israelites would return to their homeland some day. It happened most recently in 1948, when the "new" Jewish state was re-constituted once again. Was this the final return of God's people before the day of the Lord? We don't know for sure, but we can watch with faith as history unfolds before us.

There's an application here for us too. We often feel scattered, don't we? But what does it take to bring us "back home" to God's peace (see Philippians 4:7)? For me, it requires carving out times for quietness and prayer.

Of course, my initial impulse is to seek some form of escape or entertainment. Yet when I've stayed quiet for a while, I've found the need for escape lessening. Soon the desire to get away from my hurts gives way to a deeper desire for the one who can heal them. As the great 17th-century preacher John Bunyan once put it: "If we have not quiet in our minds, outward comfort will do no more for us than a golden slipper on a gouty foot."

Dear God, *keep bringing Your people home—including me, this very day. I pray in the name of Jesus, my Savior and Lord. Amen.*

SPOTLIGHT
Next Week's Lesson

God created, man destroyed, God restores—
that's the Bible story.

March 1. **Gary Allen** *is editor of* Devotions. *He lives in southwest Georgia with his wife and Yorkshire Terrier, Robbie Burns. Tim and Dan are his two adult sons.*

March 2

Who's in Charge Here?

I have installed my King on Zion, my holy hill
(Psalm 2:6).

"Who are the authorities at school?"
"My teachers, the principal, the bus driver."
"What about at home? Who's in charge there?"
"Mom!"

I had to laugh at this definitive answer, straight from the lips of a 9-year-old. She knew exactly who was in charge of her life.

Who is the authority in your life? It's a valid question, no matter who you are or what position you hold. Even those enjoying positions of power in this world will one day stand before the King of kings. The wise ruler recognizes this and governs accordingly.

Who is the authority in your life? You may never rise to such a grandiose position as those who rule over nations. Yet it's vitally important that you live as one who recognizes His authority.

We live in an age where it seems more common to question, resist, or defy authority. Some would even stand in defiance of God's divinely installed king. What about you—who is the authority in your life?

Lord, help me submit to Your authority in the most practical ways today. May I follow the King of kings in all things. In Jesus' name, amen.

SEARCH THE WORD

The authority is "the one who writes it." God is the Word; He is the author.

Scripture: Psalm 2:4-11

Song: *"King of Kings"*

From this meditation today, I will pray . . .

Adoration _____

Confession _____

Thanksgiving _____

Supplication _____

From this meditation today, I will . . .

Think _____

Say _____

Do _____

March 2–8. **Dan Nicksich** serves as senior minister of First Christian Church in Somerset, Pennsylvania. He and wife Donna have two sons, Andrew and Derek.

March 3

Share the Gift

*I have other sheep that are not of this sheep pen.
I must bring them also. They too will listen to my voice,
and there shall be one flock and one shepherd* (John 10:16).

Scripture: John 10:11-18
Song: *"Bring Them In"*

From this meditation today, I will pray . . .
Adoration _____
_____
_____

Confession _____
_____
_____

Thanksgiving _____
_____
_____

Supplication _____
_____
_____

From this meditation today, I will . . .
Think _____
_____
_____

Say _____
_____
_____

Do _____
_____
_____
_____

One of the best-known pictures of Jesus is that of the shepherd who leaves the 99 sheep behind to go and search for the one missing lamb. But I like John's picture of Jesus as well—that of a shepherd who brings *other* sheep in and makes them part of the flock as well.

I doubt the apostles understood the worldwide implications of these words of Jesus. How could they possibly know He was referring to a harvest among Gentiles when He referred to "other sheep that are not of this sheep pen"? How could they ever envision the world we live in today—and the penetration of the gospel to virtually every corner of the earth?

I was once challenged by a preacher who said, "We have received the greatest gift in the world. Why are we so selfish with it?" In other words, there are other sheep not yet part of the flock. What can we do to bring them in? Why hold so tight to the greatest gift mankind could ever receive?

Dear Father in Heaven, *I confess my complacency in taking Your Word to others. I acknowledge my fear and ask that You renew my heart and open my eyes to openhearted people. I pray this prayer in the name of Jesus, my merciful Savior and Lord. Amen.*

SPOTLIGHT
Next Week's Lesson

Every sheep needs
a shepherd,
a Good Shepherd.

March 4

His Dream Job

You have granted him the desire of his heart and have not withheld the request of his lips
(Psalm 21:2).

It was the job he'd been dreaming about for a long time. He was called in for a second interview, this one with a vice president of the firm.

"How do you feel about traveling for the company?"

"Well, I don't mind traveling, but I have to tell you that I'm a Christian. If it ever got to the point where traveling interfered with my family and my time of worshiping with them, I'd have to do something about it."

Zack could hardly believe what he had just said. He realized this bold statement could cost him his dream job. The silence was deafening. After a moment that stretched to an eternity, the other man smiled and said, "I like that."

No matter what we stand to lose (even a dream job), why not proclaim our dedication and thanks to the Lord? Even with his dream job on the line, Zack proclaimed his devotion to God and his family. Since we trust in Him, let us not be shaken. Zack was hired—and God was glorified.

Lord, *remind me that in putting You first I stand to reap the greatest of blessings. Indeed, it is You who grant the desires of my heart. Help me to glorify You with my life. In Jesus' name I pray. Amen.*

Scripture: Psalm 21:1-7
Song: *"Be Glorified"*

From this meditation today, I will pray . . .

Adoration _____

Confession _____

Thanksgiving _____

Supplication _____

From this meditation today, I will . . .

Think _____

Say _____

Do _____

SEARCH THE WORD

Dream jobs become nightmares, when God is left outside.

March 5

When You Need to Talk

You love righteousness and hate wickedness; therefore God, your God, has set you above your companions by anointing you with the oil of joy (Psalm 45:7).

Scripture: Psalm 45:1-7

Song: *"What a Friend We Have in Jesus"*

From this meditation today, I will pray . . .

Adoration _____
_____
_____

Confession _____
_____
_____

Thanksgiving _____
_____
_____

Supplication _____
_____
_____

From this meditation today, I will . . .

Think _____
_____
_____

Say _____
_____
_____

Do _____
_____
_____
_____

Paul McCartney, best known as one of the Beatles, revealed in December 2006 that he had been seeing a psychiatrist for help following the breakup of his marriage. His explanation was unapologetic and to the point: "It's not a bad idea to have someone to talk to."

We all need someone to talk to. Even the best-known fictional heroes are firmly linked to their sidekicks. Who thinks of Batman without quickly connecting him with Robin? Robin Hood had Little John, and the "Lone" Ranger was something of a misnomer—since he was rarely without his friend Tonto.

The psalm-writer sings the praises of his king. His praise speaks of a relationship of shared joy and mutual respect. Yet he firmly understands that God is the source of the king's strength and blessings. Men may triumph over their enemies, but it is God who grants the victory. It is God who raises humans to positions of power and might. For no king, no matter how mighty he may be, will endure forever. Wise are those who serve the king whose throne endures forever.

Thank You, God, for my close friends. They bring comfort in times of sorrow, encouragement amidst despair. Through Christ my Lord, amen.

SPOTLIGHT
Next Week's Lesson

Shepherds anoint sheep for healing; God anoints His shepherd for our healing.

March 6

Whatever You Want

*Endow the king with your justice, O God,
the royal son with your righteousness*
(Psalm 72:1).

After Solomon offered a thousand burnt offerings, God responded: "Ask for whatever you want me to give you" (2 Chronicles 1:7).

Rather than riches or long life, Solomon asked for wisdom. Faced with the daunting task of ruling Israel after David's death, Solomon sought God's assistance. God not only granted his request, he also blessed him with what he did not ask: riches *and* long life.

Many know Solomon as the wisest man ever to walk the earth. Few know that David, his father, had also prayed that Solomon would receive God's guidance in order to govern wisely.

What do you wish for your children? While Psalm 72:20 reveals this to be a prayer of David, it reads much like a prophecy of Solomon's reign. David understood the relationship between God's wisdom and success in Solomon's divinely appointed task.

Do you see your children (or children you know) filling a role in God's kingdom? Do you pray accordingly?

Lord, guide children and teens that they might seek You always. Help me to be a good example, and, if possible, a good mentor too. Instill within all of our youth the desire to seek Your will, especially when they face tough ethical choices and temptations. Through Christ I pray. Amen.

Scripture: Psalm 72:1-7

Song: *"Happy the Home When God Is There"*

From this meditation today, I will pray . . .

Adoration _____

Confession _____

Thanksgiving _____

Supplication _____

From this meditation today, I will . . .

Think _____

Say _____

Do _____

SEARCH THE WORD

Praying for righteous children is a big step toward having righteous children.

March 7

When God Takes an Oath

*The L*ORD *has sworn and will not change his mind:
"You are a priest forever, in the order of Melchizedek"*
(Psalm 110:4).

Scripture: Psalm 110
Song: "'Tis So Sweet to Trust in Jesus"

From this meditation today, I will pray . . .
Adoration _____
_____
_____

Confession _____
_____
_____

Thanksgiving _____
_____
_____

Supplication _____
_____
_____

From this meditation today, I will . . .
Think _____
_____
_____

Say _____
_____
_____

Do _____
_____
_____
_____
_____

Did you ever cross your heart and hope to die? Did you ever swear on a stack of Bibles? Do you remember any childhood pacts to be best friends forever?

Jesus says any such oaths are unnecessary. Our yes should be yes and our no should be no. In other words, we should be people known so much for honesty and integrity that anything beyond our word wouldn't be required.

The writer of the book of Hebrews quotes Psalm 110:4 to show that Jesus is the indestructible, eternal high priest. He also makes the point that God cannot lie; therefore, any oath He has taken can be trusted throughout eternity. In the same way, any promise He has given stands forever.

The Lord will not change His mind. He has redeemed you and empowered you to serve Him as a minister of the new covenant. The Lord has given His word that He will be with you no matter what difficulty comes your way. It is His oath, His promise to you. Are God's promises sufficient for you?

What great assurance we have, **O Lord,** *since all the wonderful promises You have given are sure to be fulfilled! I give You praise, in the name of the Father, the Son, and the Holy Spirit, amen.*

SPOTLIGHT
Next Week's Lesson

The new shepherd is a priest as well, capable of intervening for our welfare at every turn.

March 8

Appreciate Him!

*I will bless them and the places surrounding my hill.
I will send down showers in season; there will be showers of blessing*
(Ezekiel 34:26).

Christine couldn't stop praising God. "Eva will be 2-years-old in another month, and I don't think there's been a day we haven't thanked God for her. And now we have a healthy baby boy too. We are so blessed. What have we done to deserve all this?"

The day of delivery often brings a mixture of thanksgiving, exhaustion, and relief. But Christine was obviously expressing what, for her and her husband, Dan, has become a daily habit of praise and thanksgiving. Most of us have received showers of blessings from God. Sadly, we often fail to appreciate those blessings on a day-in, day-out basis. Christine reminded me to give thanks again for an often unappreciated blessing—my family.

God is the shepherd who guides, supplies, and protects His people from all that could possibly harm them. Yet the ancient Israelites needed frequent reminders to *appreciate* their shepherd. Let it never be said of us that we failed to see how blessed we are!

Dear Father in Heaven, *how inspiring to hear Your name lifted in praise! Thank You for allowing me to share in the joy of birth and new life. Help me to live each day in remembrance of Your great goodness. I pray this prayer in the name of Christ my Lord. Amen.*

Scripture: Ezekiel 34:23-31
Song: *"There Shall Be Showers of Blessing"*

From this meditation today, I will pray . . .

Adoration _____
_____
_____

Confession _____
_____
_____

Thanksgiving _____
_____
_____

Supplication _____
_____
_____

From this meditation today, I will . . .

Think _____
_____
_____

Say _____
_____
_____

Do _____
_____
_____

SEARCH THE WORD

Showers of blessing should never be met with a drought of thanksgiving.

March 9

Serenity Prayer

Give us aid against the enemy, for the help of man is worthless
(Psalm 60:11).

Scripture: Psalm 60:1-5, 11, 12
Song: *"Peace, Troubled Soul"*

From this meditation today, I will pray . . .
Adoration _____
_____
_____

Confession _____
_____
_____

Thanksgiving _____
_____
_____

Supplication _____
_____
_____

From this meditation today, I will . . .
Think _____
_____
_____

Say _____
_____
_____

Do _____
_____
_____

My favorite written prayer is "the Serenity Prayer," in which we ask God for ability to face the things we can't change, the courage to change the things we can, and the wisdom to know the difference. Many people, like me, have prayed those words when they've felt challenged, overwhelmed, or powerless. The prayer often appears on walls at the meeting places for addiction-recovery groups, as well as in hospitals and churches.

I don't pray the Serenity Prayer because of an addiction to alcohol or drugs. No, my particular compulsion is far more subtle but just as powerful. I don't know of any meetings for people like me, but if there were one, I'd have to stand up and announce: "Hello, my name is Lisa, and I'm a control freak."

But the events of the past year have shown me that trying to control my life is like trying to hold back the tide with my hands. All my efforts to be strong fell apart, and I was left with this truth: God's abiding love restores me. With God, I am serene, despite the storms.

Lord, *thank You for Your strong, gentle arms that wrap around me, encouraging me to put all my trust in You. In the name of Jesus, amen.*

March 9–15. **Lisa Konzen** *is an administrative assistant and freelance writer. She enjoys reading, cooking, and taking lazy afternoon naps with her cat, Simone.*

SPOTLIGHT
Next Week's Lesson

Looking for renewed respect—
from friends and enemies—
is a worthy goal.

March 10

Under the Light?

Restore us, O God Almighty; make your face shine upon us, that we may be saved (Psalm 80:7).

When my mother was in the hospital last year, I visited her almost every night after work. She enjoyed the visits, but she always worried about my safety at night. So, after kissing me good night, she'd ask me the same question, night after night, until it got to be our little joke: "Are you parked under the light?"

However, no night I visited her was ever darker than the one in which she passed away. Suddenly, it seemed that even if I'd parked under a search light, I would still be engulfed in darkness.

But when I was too sad to find my own way to the light, Christ reached down to me through the members of my church family. They rallied around me. They helped me in so many ways, never drawing attention to themselves, but always reflecting God's glory. Some made meals, others helped me clean up and organize Mom's house to sell it. Still others just sat with me as I cried. Through them, God's light warmed me, saved me from despair, and renewed my spirit.

Sometimes the dark is so deep that I can almost feel it. But then I lift my head, **Savior,** *and I see You. Your love shines through Your servants, piercing the blackness and filling me with light. Help me to be a reflection of Your light to others this day. In Your name I pray. Amen.*

SEARCH THE WORD

Darkness so heavy it weighs one down can be lifted by one small ray of the Light.

Scripture: Psalm 80:1-7
Song: *"The Light of the World Is Jesus"*

From this meditation today, I will pray . . .

Adoration _____

Confession _____

Thanksgiving _____

Supplication _____

From this meditation today, I will . . .

Think _____

Say _____

Do _____

March 11

Mondaymorningitis

I will listen to what God the Lord will say; he promises peace to his people, . . . but let them not return to folly (Psalm 85:8).

Scripture: Psalm 85:1-9
Song: *"Father, Speak Your Word Again"*

From this meditation today, I will pray . . .
Adoration _____
_____
_____
Confession _____
_____
_____
Thanksgiving _____
_____
_____
Supplication _____
_____
_____

From this meditation today, I will . . .
Think _____
_____
_____
Say _____
_____
_____
Do _____
_____
_____
_____

A disease runs rampant throughout churches in America, afflicting people of all ages, races, and genders. Its name: Mondaymorningitis. This tragic condition is marked by enthusiastic worship and attention to the sermon on Sunday, followed by spiritual amnesia the next day. Sufferers are usually well-meaning, regular churchgoers. But they find the cares and demands of the workaday world crowding out the message of the gospel they've heard only 24 hours earlier.

Some complications of this disease include irritable mood, loss of satisfaction in one's prayer life, and weakness of spirit. Researchers believe some of the causes may be mental distractions (such as children running late for school) bosses breathing down one's neck, and a spouse who once again forgot to take out the trash. (Yes, I did the research myself.)

There is only one cure. It is drastic, but 100% guaranteed: Daily doses of time spent quietly with the Savior have proven quite effective. (A common side effect is peace; take as directed by your divine physician.)

Healer of my soul, *I too soon forget the message of Your love. The closeness I feel to You on Sunday evaporates with the jarring alarm clock on Monday morning. Forgive me, Lord! In Jesus' name, amen.*

SPOTLIGHT
Next Week's Lesson

When God's people gain respect, so does God. Are you an attractor or a detractor?

March 12

Restored to God—and Renewed

*Restore us to yourself, O Lord, that we may return;
renew our days as of old* (Lamentations 5:21).

It was an old, broken-down wooden chair that my father, recently deceased, had made for me many years before. Dad had taken great pride in crafting the child-sized chair. But what once had been my favorite perch was now busted in the middle, with the paint chipped and peeling. I was ready to toss it in the trash pile, until a friend from church stopped me.

"Would you mind if I take a stab at it?" Denny asked. He explained that his hobby was restoring furniture. I knew he'd worked on a piece for a mutual friend, so I decided to let him try.

About ten days later, he returned with a chair I didn't recognize at first. He hadn't just *restored* the chair to its former charm. He *renewed* it, making it better than it had ever been before.

God does that with us. When we repent, He doesn't just return us to the way we were before. He restores us to himself, to a new and better way that only He can give. That's spiritual renewal, from the inside out.

Master Craftsman, *who created the universe, I'm astounded that You love me so much. Your love transforms me, a lump of clay that You breathe the breath of life into, day by day. Because of Your mercy, I am a new creation. Help me to live for You every day of my life. In Jesus' name, amen.*

SEARCH THE WORD
Broken hearts and spirits need only one thing: the touch of the Master's hand.

Scripture: Lamentations 5:15-21
Song: *"Let the Beauty of Jesus"*

From this meditation today, I will pray . . .

Adoration _____

Confession _____

Thanksgiving _____

Supplication _____

From this meditation today, I will . . .

Think _____

Say _____

Do _____

March 13

The Unruly Calf

*I have surely heard Ephraim's moaning: "You disciplined me like an unruly calf, and I have been disciplined. Restore me, and I will return, because you are the L*ORD *my God"* (Jeremiah 31:18).

Scripture: Jeremiah 31:7-9, 16-20
Song: *"O Gift of Gifts!"*

From this meditation today, I will pray . . .
Adoration _____
_____
_____

Confession _____
_____
_____

Thanksgiving _____
_____
_____

Supplication _____
_____
_____

From this meditation today, I will . . .
Think _____
_____
_____

Say _____
_____
_____

Do _____
_____
_____
_____

The artist Winslow Homer painted a picture called "The Unruly Calf." In it, a young boy tugs on a rope attached to a calf. The boy is obviously struggling, but the stubborn calf refuses to be led.

Today's verse brought that painting to mind. While God is certainly stronger than any young boy, man, or mountain, He still calls us an unruly calf. But this makes no sense. Surely, if our God is that strong, we couldn't refuse to be led by Him, right?

But that is the mystery and wonder of His loving gift of free will to us. God graciously allows us to make our own choices. He will not overpower us into submission. Rather, He desires our willing acceptance of His leading so we may respond in heartfelt love.

Along with that loving gift of free will comes a great risk. If we remain in disobedience, and like an unruly calf refuse to be led by Christ, we may find ourselves outside the pasture.

Good Shepherd of sheep *(and unruly calves), Your yoke is easy and Your burden is light. Help me to follow You freely—with joy and peace in my heart—without stumbling. Through Christ I pray. Amen.*

SPOTLIGHT
Next Week's Lesson
When we let God take our reins and let His whisper fill our ears, we become broken creatures in His service.

March 14

Restored for Service

Therefore this is what the Lord says: "If you repent, I will restore you that you may serve me"
(Jeremiah 15:19).

Many of my friends are retired from regular employment, but they don't sit back in rocking chairs with nothing to do. Most of them seem busier now than when they drew a paycheck. They stay active for the glory of God, and they say they enjoy volunteering because they "love feeling useful."

We all need direction and purpose in life, don't we? Maybe that's why books like *The Purpose-Driven Life*, by Rick Warren, are so successful. Warren speaks to the fact that we human beings are on a constant quest, a seemingly endless search for meaning in our lives.

But as noble as that search may be, it can be dangerous if it leads us to focus purely on our own self-fulfillment. In fact, turning inward in pure self-interest is what sin is all about. Christ calls us to repent—literally, to turn around—so that the focus of our search moves us toward Him. Then we can find the true fulfillment Warren describes. It's something my retired friends already know: Serving God restores us as nothing else can.

Dear Lord, You have redeemed me for a purpose. I am called to be Your servant, Your hands and feet in this world, and a voice of eternal praise in the next. Thank You for saving me and giving me the most wonderful reason to live. In the name of Jesus, Lord and Savior of all, I pray. Amen.

Scripture: Jeremiah 15:15-21
Song: *"All for Jesus"*

From this meditation today, I will pray . . .
Adoration _____

Confession _____

Thanksgiving _____

Supplication _____

From this meditation today, I will . . .
Think _____

Say _____

Do _____

SEARCH THE WORD
Don't let God restore you unless you want to serve Him endlessly.

March 15

Hearts of Flesh

*I will give you a new heart and put a new spirit in you;
I will remove from you your heart of stone and give you a heart of flesh*
(Ezekiel 36:26).

Scripture: Ezekiel 36:22-32
Song: *"Give Me Thy Heart"*

From this meditation today, I will pray . . .
Adoration _____
_____
_____

Confession _____
_____
_____

Thanksgiving _____
_____
_____

Supplication _____
_____
_____

From this meditation today, I will . . .
Think _____
_____
_____

Say _____
_____
_____

Do _____
_____
_____
_____

Stones can be quite handy. They can prop a door open or line a pathway. The big ones can even be climbed on for exciting recreation. But there's one thing about stones that makes them difficult: They're awfully hard to move.

Imagine having a heart of stone, literally. On average, you'd be carrying around a 10.5-ounce lump in your chest (9 ounces if you're a woman). Of course, you wouldn't be carrying it anywhere, because, as noted, stone is awfully hard to move. And a heart of stone couldn't contract to pump blood through your body. You'd be a corpse—"stone-cold" dead.

I know this is just a silly analogy. But think of it in spiritual terms. Sin creates a heart of stone in us, making us incapable of really living. Christ died and rolled away the stone, though, not just the one at His grave, but also the stony places in our hearts. We did nothing to earn this gift. Yet, because of His mercy, He gives us hearts of flesh, hearts that live in and for Him. What a blessing!

My Lord God, *You've chiseled away the stone of my heart, giving me new life. I know I don't deserve such love, and I also know I could never have removed that stone myself. But now that You've redeemed me, help me to serve You with every beat of my heart. In Christ's name, amen.*

SPOTLIGHT
Next Week's Lesson

God's child is softhearted,
as He is.

March 16

God Will Do Something New

*Forget the former things; do not dwell on the past.
See, I am doing a new thing!*
(Isaiah 43:18, 19).

Twelve years ago the company I worked for relocated. I had invested 20 years and loved my job; it was a difficult time of transition. But God led me to a special promise that helped me look to the future.

I'm going through another change in my career right now. After managing a team for five years, I've chosen, for reasons too numerous to mention, to step down into more of a service role. I wonder: Will it work out? Will I love it as much as I've loved my old job?

And once again I'm reminded of today's Scripture—the same passage that encouraged me 12 years ago; the same passage that I shared with a friend at work this week; the same passage that began my week of assigned devotional writing.

Obviously, God wanted to get my attention! He has reminded me of His power and faithfulness with Israel and of His power and faithfulness today for my own future. He wants me to remind you of the same things.

Lord, forgive me for not trusting You after You've proven Yourself over and over again. Help me look to the future, to the new thing You will do, and not dwell in the supposed security of the past. Through Christ, amen.

Scripture: Isaiah 43:14-21
Song: *"The Guiding Hand"*

From this meditation today, I will pray . . .
Adoration _____
_____
_____

Confession _____
_____
_____

Thanksgiving _____
_____
_____

Supplication _____
_____
_____

From this meditation today, I will . . .
Think _____
_____
_____

Say _____
_____
_____

Do _____
_____
_____

SEARCH THE WORD

Memory can be a curse if it blinds one to God's new plan.

March 16–19, 22. **Maralee Parker,** *a new grandma in Elgin, Illinois, invests her days working on publications at Judson University in the adult education division.*

March 17

Soar Like an Eagle

*Those who hope in the L*ORD *will renew their strength.
They will soar on wings like eagles; they will run and not grow weary,
they will walk and not be faint* (Isaiah 40:31).

Scripture: Isaiah 40:25-31
Song: "It Is Well with My Soul"

From this meditation today, I will pray . . .

Adoration _____
_____
_____

Confession _____
_____
_____

Thanksgiving _____
_____
_____

Supplication _____
_____
_____

From this meditation today, I will . . .

Think _____
_____
_____

Say _____
_____
_____

Do _____
_____
_____
_____

Do you know that an eagle can soar above storms? The eagle can tell when a storm is coming and will fly to a high spot, ready to catch the winds that will lift it above the storm.

I love that image! I have a lot of storms in my life, many related to our 18-year-old autistic/bipolar daughter. Life is stressful most of the time, so I often remind myself of the promises found in these verses. It's wonderfully encouraging, and incomprehensible, to know that the almighty creator of the universe—the one who hung the stars in place and calls each one by name—gives me strength and power each day.

Yes, the soaring eagle gives me a visual to cling to as I'm going through yet another stormy day. I remind myself that because of the grace and strength God gives, I can choose to rise above my circumstances and soar, just as eagles do. It all depends upon waiting on the Lord. We can rise above it all, as we wait patiently on Him for our needed strength, guidance, and peace.

Almighty God and Heavenly Father, *help me trust You through the storms of life. Remind me that You hold all power and that You're able to help me with anything that comes my way. In Jesus' name. Amen.*

SPOTLIGHT
Next Week's Lesson

Out of breath. A feeling we all know. A second wind, the wind of the Spirit, is what we need.

March 18

A New Covenant

In the same way, after the supper he took the cup, saying, "This cup is the new covenant in my blood, which is poured out for you" (Luke 22:20).

Scripture: Luke 22:14-23
Song: *"The Old Rugged Cross"*

How's your memory?

I'm not too proud to confess that I struggle these days with remembering. So I make use of practical reminders on a regular basis. I need them in order to accomplish everything I must get done in a day. When I'm out in the car, I'll call myself on my work phone and leave a message to remind me about something. Or I'll send an e-mail from work to my home computer. I also use computer pop-up windows to help me remember.

I tell my family that I have too many details to be responsible for, and that's why I have these problems. Nevertheless, reminders are essential to my success in life these days.

So I'm thankful that Jesus, in all of His omniscience, knew that I would need a reminder. May I never forget the great sacrifice He made for me on the cross of Calvary. He told His disciples to take the bread, and the cup, that they might remember Him often. We need to do the same. Don't forget.

O Lord, *how can I give enough thanks to You, the one who willingly poured out Your life for me? May I never forget your amazing, merciful sacrifice on my behalf. Because of Jesus, I pray. Amen.*

SEARCH THE WORD

Important things are sometimes forgotten. Some important things must not be forgotten.

From this meditation today, I will pray . . .

Adoration _____

Confession _____

Thanksgiving _____

Supplication _____

From this meditation today, I will . . .

Think _____

Say _____

Do _____

March 19

Be Reconciled

We are therefore Christ's ambassadors, as though God were making his appeal through us. We implore you on Christ's behalf: Be reconciled to God (2 Corinthians 5:20).

Scripture: 2 Corinthians 5:16-21
Song: *"I Come to the Cross"*

From this meditation today, I will pray . . .
Adoration _____
_____
_____

Confession _____
_____
_____

Thanksgiving _____
_____
_____

Supplication _____
_____
_____

From this meditation today, I will . . .
Think _____
_____
_____

Say _____
_____
_____

Do _____
_____
_____
_____

It's my observation that some teen girls seem to enjoy living in a constant state of drama. I've seen this over and over in my daughter's life. She and her friend can get "bent out of shape" over the most trivial things—sometimes evoking tears, hurt feelings, and angry words. Often phone calls are ignored—thanks to caller I.D.—or the phones themselves are slammed down without even a decent good-bye.

More than once I've had to serve as mediator between my daughter and her girlfriend. It happens regularly when they're together (and we parents are far away from home), and a rift develops between the girls. Those times are stressful for everyone. We talk it out, and they eventually reconcile. Then everyone heaves a sigh of relief when they come back together, ready to forgive and move on.

Thus it is with God and us. He wants us to be reconciled to Him, and it can only happen through Christ. Isn't it wonderful that God provided the mediator? He sent Christ for us so we can be reconciled to Him forever.

Merciful Father, *thank You for loving me so much that You sent the answer before I knew there was a problem. Thank You for reconciling me to You, through Your Son, Christ Jesus. In His name I pray, Amen.*

SPOTLIGHT
Next Week's Lesson

Saved by CPR—
all God's children have
Christ-Produced Reconciliation!

March 20

The Pathway to Hope

*The LORD is good to those whose
hope is in him, to the one who seeks him
(Lamentations 3:25).*

Directing our thoughts into dark memories of mistakes made, sins committed, and sufferings endured can lead us to despair. What starts as a simple pity-party can quickly degenerate into a major depression. Once in such gloomy depths, it's hard to pull oneself out into the sunshine again.

Jeremiah knew all about sorrow that comes from sad thoughts, as he remembered what the Israelites had lost because of their sins. But he also knew exactly what he needed to do whenever his inner turmoil became overwhelming: He turned his thoughts to the Lord. He remembered God's great love for him; he took comfort in knowing that he could always count on the Lord to be there for him, no matter what he was going through. Each morning brought a brand new start and another opportunity to experience God's great faithfulness. Such thoughts put him back on the right path.

Which path are you on today? If your thoughts are gloomy, spend some time remembering how much God loves you and how He has provided for you in the past. Put yourself on the pathway to hope.

Gracious Father, help me remember the ways you have blessed my life. Fill my heart with joy and hope, as I walk today's path in your presence. Amen.

Scripture: Lamentations 3:19-31
Song: *"Whispering Hope"*

From this meditation today, I will pray . . .
Adoration
Confession
Thanksgiving
Supplication

From this meditation today, I will . . .
Think
Say
Do

SEARCH THE WORD
Every day begins with a "Y" intersection: should I take Hope Avenue or Despair Descent?

March 21, 22. **Cheryl J. Frey** *runs an editorial services out of her home in Rochester, New York. She spends her spare time with family—especially her grandchildren.*

March 21

How to Escape Quicksand

*[The LORD] lifted me out of the slimy pit,
out of the mud and mire; he set my feet on a rock*
(Psalm 40:2).

Scripture: Psalm 40:1-5
Song: *"My Hope Is Built"*

From this meditation today, I will pray . . .
Adoration _____
_____
_____

Confession _____
_____
_____

Thanksgiving _____
_____
_____

Supplication _____
_____
_____

From this meditation today, I will . . .
Think _____
_____
_____

Say _____
_____
_____

Do _____
_____
_____
_____

Would you like to know how to escape from quicksand? Today's psalm has good advice on that subject. Contrary to the scary images from the movies where people are sucked under quicksand never to reappear, scientists now know that a person can float out if they stay calm. Rather than flailing around in a panic trying to pull yourself out, just relax, stretch out on your back to increase the surface area, and wait for your legs to pop free. Moving your legs in a circular motion will stir in water and help you float out eventually.

Although David might not have been in quicksand, he was stuck in a slimy mudpit. And he knew what to do: he cried out to the Lord and waited patiently for God to pull him out and set his feet on the rock.

When the trials of life are grabbing us and pulling us under, our first impulse is to panic and try to fight our way out. But the best escape from a terrible mess that has us trapped is to cry out a hearty "Help!" to the Father, relax, and wait patiently for Him to rescue us.

Heavenly Father, *how I long for the faith to stop trying so hard to save myself. Remind me when I am the most desperate to relax into your arms of love and trust You to rescue me. In the name of Jesus, my Savior, I pray. Amen.*

SPOTLIGHT
Next Week's Lesson

Gasping or grasping?
An easy choice when God's
hand is extended.

March 22

Do You Hear What I Hear?

I will attach tendons to you and make flesh come upon you and cover you with skin; I will put breath in you, and you will come to life. Then you will know that I am the Lord (Ezekiel 37:6).

It's cicada time in the Midwest. Cicadas are shrimp-size creatures with transparent wings and red eyes that come alive every 17 years. If you live in an area with old trees, you may be "blessed" with hoards of them, several million per acre. When they sing their cicada song, it can sound like a 747 airplane overhead.

They crawl out of the ground, fight to get out of their outer shell, and then look for a mate. After they're successful, the male dies and the female lays eggs in trees. Later, the eggs hatch into nymphs, which fall from the trees and burrow into the ground, where they snack on tree-root sap. At the appropriate time—exactly 17 years later—they claw their way up and out into the world, and the whole cycle is repeated. God has truly created an amazing world!

In Ezekiel's passage, we see another illustration of His awesome power with raising the dry bones. He can do anything. Nothing is too hard for the Lord!

Creator of all, *I am in awe of the ways You reveal Yourself in our world. Help me to realize that my amazement should turn toward You, in glorifying You. You are worthy of admiration and praise! I love You, and I pray this prayer in the name of Jesus, my Savior and Lord. Amen.*

SEARCH THE WORD

Tendons, flesh, skin, breath—even spirit—God can give new life.

Scripture: Ezekiel 37:1-14
Song: *"This Is My Father's World"*

From this meditation today, I will pray . . .

Adoration _____

Confession _____

Thanksgiving _____

Supplication _____

From this meditation today, I will . . .

Think _____

Say _____

Do _____

March 23

That First Bath

Wash yourselves and be clean!
(Isaiah 1:16, *New Living Translation*).

Scripture: Isaiah 1:12-17
Song: *"Are You Washed in the Blood?"*

From this meditation today, I will pray . . .
Adoration _____
_____
_____

Confession _____
_____
_____

Thanksgiving _____
_____
_____

Supplication _____
_____
_____

From this meditation today, I will . . .
Think _____
_____
_____

Say _____
_____
_____

Do _____
_____

When my second child was born, I was offered the "privilege" of cutting the umbilical cord and watching baby's first bath. I accepted, of course! When it came time for the bath, my 8-pound, 3-ounce boy began screaming at the top of his little lungs. He didn't like the bath at all. It was all I could do to keep from crying in sympathy.

In retrospect, I can understand my son's problem. He was used to a nice, warm environment inside Mommy. But change begins with new life. Besides, he really needed that bath.

As Christians, when we're baptized we are washed clean of our unrighteousness by the Holy Spirit. We are made new, a new creation. Our sin is separated from us "as far as the east is from the west." While we sometimes "get dirty" with poor decisions, we remain in a position of acceptance before the Father, all because of Christ and His cross. Certainly, there are consequences for our decisions. But we can boldly enter the throne room of God because we have been cleaned.

Dear Father, *thank You for washing away my sin. Help me remember that You now have a plan for my life. In Jesus' name, amen.*

March 23–29. **Pete Anderson** *is a fourth-grade teacher who lives in Ocala, Florida, with his wife of almost 25 years and the younger of his two boys.*

SPOTLIGHT
Next Week's Lesson

Spotless white robes will replace sin-stained laundry when God is the cleaner.

March 24

The Waters of Rebirth

He saved us, not because of righteous things we had done, but because of his mercy. He saved us through the washing of rebirth and renewal by the Holy Spirit (Titus 3:5).

"What can wash away my sin? Nothing but the blood of Jesus!" That is what the old hymn says, and it is so true. Jesus redeemed us through the washing of rebirth, and we are renewed by the Holy Spirit.

Clearly, we cannot earn salvation. No amount of money I give, nor amount of service I do, can earn me rebirth. I can only accept God's gift of salvation by faith. I accept what He did on the cross for me—His death and His resurrection—by faith. And I enter into the waters of baptism, what Paul calls the washing of rebirth. To God be the glory!

Just as we take a shower to wash away any dirt from our physical bodies, so Christ washes us to cleanse us completely. Nothing is overlooked, nothing is left uncleaned.

Don't you enjoy the waters as you bathe? Likewise, the washing of rebirth is just as glorious—even more so. In it Christ gives us himself—the living water.

Dear Heavenly Father, *thank You for saving me through the life and death of Your precious Son, Jesus. Thank You for the waters of rebirth, and thank You for Your Holy Spirit who renews me daily. In the name of the Father, the Son, and the Holy Spirit, I pray. Amen.*

Scripture: Titus 3:1-7
Song: *"Nothing but the Blood"*

From this meditation today, I will pray . . .
Adoration _____
Confession _____
Thanksgiving _____
Supplication _____

From this meditation today, I will . . .
Think _____
Say _____
Do _____

SEARCH THE WORD

Sin always makes one feel dirty. Some like the feeling. The wise ask for God's cleansing.

March 25

Like Spring Rains

As surely as the sun rises, he will appear; he will come to us like the winter rains, like the spring rains that water the earth
(Hosea 6:3).

Scripture: Hosea 6:1-6

Song: *"The Water of Life"*

From this meditation today, I will pray . . .

Adoration _____

_____

_____

Confession _____

_____

_____

Thanksgiving _____

_____

_____

Supplication _____

_____

_____

From this meditation today, I will . . .

Think _____

_____

_____

Say _____

_____

_____

Do _____

_____

_____

_____

"April showers bring May flowers." I said that many times while growing up to demonstrate my superior knowledge of Spring weather patterns. I also said, "Rain, rain, go away; come again another day. Little Phillip (my younger brother) wants to play!" When I was young, I wanted to be outside playing, but the rain would prohibit my fun.

I'm older now, and I know we need the spring rains to water our earth. If anything is going to grow—from grass to crops, from weeds to trees—we need the rain. (Thankfully, we have had the beginning of the end to the drought here in Florida this month.)

And just like the rain that our earth needs, we humans need Jesus. "As surely as the sun rises, he will appear," the prophet Hosea said. We don't know exactly when the rains will come, but we know they *will* come. Likewise, we may not know when Jesus will return, but we know He *will* indeed come to earth again, just as He promised (see John 14:3 and Acts 1:11).

Father, *I am thankful for the rain that waters the earth. I know that just as it will rain, Your Son will return one day. Help me to live each day knowing that He may enter into my world at any moment. In Christ's name, amen.*

SPOTLIGHT
Next Week's Lesson

Life depends on water.
Spiritual life depends
on living water.

March 26

Are You Prospering?

He is like a tree planted by streams of water, which yields its fruit in season and whose leaf does not wither. Whatever he does prospers (Psalm 1:3).

Ever been to a riverbank? It seems that most riverbanks abound with lush vegetation: green grass, leafy trees, thriving plants. Any plant blessed enough to be near a river gets all of the water it needs. The roots of the tree can even grow under or into the river to get needed moisture. Trees simply thrive when planted near a river.

Maybe we ought to live like trees planted near streams of water. I don't mean that we need leaves or a broad trunk! But I do mean that we should be solidly "planted" by our living water, Jesus. Then the "bad weather" that comes into our lives won't seem so devastating. As art critic John Ruskin once said: "Sunshine is delicious, rain is refreshing, wind braces up, snow is exhilarating; there is no such thing as bad weather, only different kinds of good weather."

When our faith, our trust, our lives are *in* Jesus, we thrive, no matter the weather. Then the fruit of our labor is full and sweet to our Savior. While we are "doing His good will, He abides with us still." So may our lives be firmly rooted in Christ.

Dear Lord, help my fruit, my testimony, to be strong and sweet for Your sake. Help me thrive in my relationship with You. Through Christ, amen.

Scripture: Psalm 1
Song: *"Like a River Glorious"*

From this meditation today, I will pray . . .
Adoration _____
_____
_____

Confession _____
_____
_____

Thanksgiving _____
_____
_____

Supplication _____
_____
_____

From this meditation today, I will . . .
Think _____
_____
_____

Say _____
_____
_____

Do _____
_____
_____
_____

SEARCH THE WORD
Rooted in the living water or in the arid desert of sin? That is the choice.

March 27

Give Me Living Water

If you only knew the gift God has for you and who I am, you would ask me, and I would give you living water
(John 4:10, *New Living Translation*).

Scripture: John 4:7-15
Song: *"Nearer, My God, to Thee"*

From this meditation today, I will pray . . .

Adoration _____
_____
_____

Confession _____
_____
_____

Thanksgiving _____
_____
_____

Supplication _____
_____
_____

From this meditation today, I will . . .

Think _____
_____
_____

Say _____
_____
_____

Do _____
_____
_____
_____

Legend says that as the "unsinkable" ship Titanic sank, music swelled above the chaos. The hymn, "Nearer, My God, to Thee" was being played on deck by a small ensemble. As hundreds of passengers without lifeboats jumped into the frigid waters of the North Atlantic, death was inevitable. The hymn was prophetic, for most of those hapless victims were only moments from encountering the living God. How many met Him as Savior . . . and how many met Him as judge?

In contrast to those deathly Atlantic waters, the water Jesus offers is living. Christ isn't offering water whereby we will be thirsty again. He is offering life-giving water for eternity. He is offering salvation. Anyone who partakes of this water will never thirst again.

This simple passage of Scripture reminds me that everyone needs the living water. And, as Christians, we are called to share this water with others . . . or the lost will find themselves in dark, uninviting waters indeed.

O great and merciful Father, *thank You for Jesus, my Savior. Help me to be nearer to You, O Lord, and give me the words to say and the boldness to speak so others can know the life-giving waters of salvation. In the precious name of Jesus, I pray. Amen.*

SPOTLIGHT
Next Week's Lesson

When Ezekiel spoke of a life-giving river, did he have a vision of Christ? We do.

March 28

He's in the Cleaning Business

"Blessed are those who wash their robes, that they may have the right to the tree of life and may go through the gates into the city" (Revelation 22:14).

Death. It's not a popular subject to write about, talk about, or dream about. Yet we will probably all experience it. Unless Jesus returns before our physical death, our lives on this earth will end in a grave. But death is *not* the end of the story for Christians; it's the next step. The Bible reminds us: "away from the body and at home with the Lord" (2 Corinthians 5:8).

Each believer can face death with courage and be sure of a future with Christ. Have you made some bad decisions or done some terribly wrong things in your past? You can come. The simple message of the Bible is that anyone can come and wash their robes and be made clean. In order for us to enter the heavenly city and enjoy eternal life, Jesus first makes us clean. I am so thankful on this Saturday in March 2009 that God is still in the "cleaning business"!

One last thing: We are the bride of Christ. The Spirit *and* the bride say, "Come!" You're invited!

Merciful Father, *thank You for saving my soul and cleansing me. Thank You for offering the water of life freely to all who desire to come. Help me to extend that invitation to others too. In the name of Jesus, amen.*

Scripture: Revelation 22:12-17
Song: *"For Those Tears I Died"*

From this meditation today, I will pray...
Adoration _____
_____
_____

Confession _____
_____
_____

Thanksgiving _____
_____
_____

Supplication _____
_____
_____

From this meditation today, I will...
Think _____
_____
_____

Say _____
_____
_____

Do _____
_____
_____
_____

SEARCH THE WORD
Only those dressed appropriately enter Heaven's gates. A clean, white robe will suffice.

March 29

Water from the Sanctuary

Fruit trees of all kinds will grow on both banks of the river. Their leaves will not wither, nor will their fruit fail. Every month they will bear, because the water from the sanctuary flows to them (Ezekiel 47:12).

Scripture: Ezekiel 47:1-12
Song: *"I've Got a River of Life"*

From this meditation today, I will pray...
Adoration _____
_____
_____

Confession _____
_____
_____

Thanksgiving _____
_____
_____

Supplication _____
_____
_____

From this meditation today, I will...
Think _____
_____
_____

Say _____
_____
_____

Do _____
_____
_____
_____

I live in Florida. If you don't, you may have images of fruit trees in full bloom, lots of sunshine, and a certain "mouse" that is widely popular down here. And while these images are, for the most part, true, they are not absolutes. Our fruit trees aren't always in bloom. And while we certainly have a good deal of sunshine, we do have rain, hurricanes, and our share of bad weather. (Let's not talk about Mickey.)

Our Scripture today has Ezekiel at the entrance of the temple. He observes water coming out from under the threshold, and he receives this promise: The trees will bear fruit every month.

Imagine a place where fresh fruit is always available. A place with abundant fresh water. That is our destination. And while some people may believe that, if you live right, you will go to Florida when you die, we know that if you trust Jesus, you'll spend eternity with Him (probably not in Florida).

Father, *thank You for the encouragement of knowing that You have me in the palm of Your hand. Help me appreciate the beauty in what You have created—especially the glory of Your plan of salvation. In Jesus' name, amen.*

SPOTLIGHT
Next Week's Lesson

"The river of water,
as clear as crystal,
flowing from the throne of God"
(Revelation 22:1).

March 30

Greater Than Foolishness

The word of the cross is foolishness to those who are perishing, but to us who are being saved it is the power of God (1 Corinthians 1:18, *New American Standard Bible*).

I thought divorce was my way out of the constant pain in my heart. God surely couldn't want me to be so unhappy or desire our children to live with such angry, bickering parents. In my misery, I prayed, "God, please come into my life. I've made such a mess of things without You, and I desperately need Your wisdom. I don't know anything about the Bible, but help me follow Your directions."

I soon sensed God saying to me, "Ask your husband's forgiveness." I thought, *Will that really change anything?* The Holy Spirit continued to prompt me, "Pray for your husband, be submissive to him." It was all foolishness to my way of thinking. Yet, as I acted on God's leading, my husband began to respond in loving ways, and the Lord restored our marriage.

Yes, He revived a love that was dead. Thirty-four years later, I am still thankful: God's wisdom was greater than my foolishness.

Lord, *You rescued me from my foolishness by Your great wisdom. Thank You for bringing Your great power into my life. In Jesus' name, amen.*

Scripture: 1 Corinthians 1:18-25
Song: *"The Cross of Jesus"*

From this meditation today, I will pray . . .
Adoration _____

Confession _____

Thanksgiving _____

Supplication _____

From this meditation today, I will . . .
Think _____

Say _____

Do _____

SEARCH THE WORD
Some look at the cross and see foolishness. Others look at the cross and see God's wisdom and grace.

March 30, 31. **Marty Prudhomme** *is a great grandmother who teaches Bible studies and leads a friendship-evangelism ministry called Adopt a Block.*

March 31

Jesus, the Prophesied

He was pierced through for our transgressions, He was crushed for our iniquities; The chastening for our well-being fell upon Him, and by His scourging we are healed (Isaiah 53:5, *New American Standard Bible*).

Scripture: Isaiah 53:1-9

Song: *"Sweet Savior, in Thy Pitying Grace"*

From this meditation today, I will pray . . .

Adoration _____
_____
_____

Confession _____
_____
_____

Thanksgiving _____
_____
_____

Supplication _____
_____
_____

From this meditation today, I will . . .

Think _____
_____
_____

Say _____
_____
_____

Do _____
_____
_____
_____

I stood in the hospital room watching Sam as he slept. (This was his third heart attack.) I prayed, "God, please let Sam wake up so I can tell him about Jesus. Don't let him leave this life unless he goes with You."

I gave him a little nudge. As Sam opened his eyes, I reassured him, "God must be keeping you alive for a purpose." Sam agreed with me. We talked for awhile, and then I asked him, "Have you considered the possibility you may not live through the next attack? Where would you spend eternity?"

Sam's answer amazed me. He said, "I have never thought about it." So that day I told Sam about Jesus, who suffered and died for his sins. Sam accepted God's forgiveness that day in his hospital room.

Isaiah predicted Messiah's sufferings thousands of years ago, but he never saw this prophecy's fulfillment. We now know the great truth: The chastening for our well-being fell on Jesus of Nazareth, the incarnate Lord. Because of His infinite sacrifice, we can live forever.

Thank You, **Father,** *for salvation through the atoning death of Jesus. Help me tell others the good news of Your Son. In His name I pray. Amen.*

SPOTLIGHT
Next Week's Lesson

Predictive prophecy pictures a coming reality. The cross paints Isaiah's picture blood red.

April

THE DAWN OF NEW LIFE

*"Therefore my heart is glad and my tongue rejoices;
my body also will live in hope."*
—Acts 2:26

Photo © iStockphoto

April 1

Humble Enough?

"You don't know what you are asking," Jesus said. "Can you drink the cup I drink or be baptized with the baptism I am baptized with?"
(Mark 10:38).

Scripture: Mark 10:32-45

Song: *"Behold My Servant, See Him Rise"*

From this meditation today, I will pray . . .

Adoration _____
_____
_____

Confession _____
_____
_____

Thanksgiving _____
_____
_____

Supplication _____
_____
_____

From this meditation today, I will . . .

Think _____
_____
_____

Say _____
_____
_____

Do _____
_____
_____

My friend Regina serves her husband and children faithfully, without complaint, while living in a simple house trailer. She has allowed many hurting teens to live with her family from time to time. Regina serves in the church nursery, and occasionally she cooks for sick people in the community.

And more than once Regina has come to my rescue when I've been rushing to finish a church project. Regina doesn't have much by worldly standards, but she is a loyal, humble servant who lays down her life every day for her Lord Jesus. What a godly example to me!

Many people crave honor and desire power, but do not realize the price that comes with elevated positions. James and John wanted to be honored and raised above the rest of Jesus' disciples. Jesus knew they didn't understand the meaning of greatness in His kingdom. Honor there comes only to those humble enough to receive it.

Lord, *I want to serve You without complaint. By Your grace, help me to lay down my life in Your service, starting today with the smallest acts of kindness and love. I pray in the name of Jesus, my Savior and Lord. Amen.*

April 1, 2, 4, and 5. **Marty Prudhomme** is a great grandmother who teaches Bible studies and leads a friendship-evangelism ministry called Adopt a Block.

SPOTLIGHT
Next Week's Lesson

Can you, are you willing to take up Jesus' cross to the death?

April 2

Appropriate Tears

God, with undeserved kindness, declares that we are righteous. He did this through Christ Jesus when He freed us from the penalty for our sins (Romans 3:24, New Living Translation).

Steve lives alone in a little yellow house and rides his bicycle to his job at a donut shop several miles away. I met Steve while working in his neighborhood with our church's "Adopt a Block" ministry. As I stood in his front yard talking to Steve, his eyes began to fill with tears. The smell of alcohol was evident on his breath (at only 10:30 in the morning.)

"I remember everything you said to me last week," Steve said. I had prayed with him then, "Lord, please give Steve favor at work and let him know Your love for Him."

The idea that I would come to tell him about God's gift of love amazed him. Steve knew he was a sinner; no one had to tell him that. But the reality that God sent His Son to redeem him brought Steve to tears.

It truly is a profound reality: When we trust God's loving kindness, we are declared righteous, placed in right standing with God, freed from the penalty of sin. Upon such a pronouncement of pardon, tears are thoroughly appropriate!

Father, *You loved me when I was so unlovable. Now help me to love others with Your kind of love. In Christ's holy name I pray. Amen.*

SEARCH THE WORD

Tears of repentance are lovely prisms of the soul.

Scripture: Romans 3:21-26
Song: *"Love Divine"*

From this meditation today, I will pray . . .
Adoration _____
_____
_____

Confession _____
_____
_____

Thanksgiving _____
_____
_____

Supplication _____
_____
_____

From this meditation today, I will . . .
Think _____
_____
_____

Say _____
_____
_____

Do _____
_____
_____
_____

April 3

Spotless!

Their sins and lawless acts I will remember no more
(Hebrews 10:17).

Scripture: Hebrews 10:10-18
Song: *"Nothing but the Blood of Jesus"*

From this meditation today, I will pray . . .
Adoration _____
_____
_____

Confession _____
_____
_____

Thanksgiving _____
_____
_____

Supplication _____
_____
_____

From this meditation today, I will . . .
Think _____
_____
_____

Say _____
_____
_____

Do _____
_____
_____

I once lost a dryer load of my own clothes because of stains I couldn't get out. This unhappy event started innocently enough with my throwing a pair of my young daughter's jeans into the washer along with several of my best dresses. Unknown to me there were three crayons in one of her pockets. The clothes all made it safely through the wash cycle, since I used cold water. However, once the crayons encountered the heat of the dryer, they quickly melted and spread in interesting patters over my clothes. Stained beyond salvaging, they all had to be thrown away.

Realizing my shortcomings in the stain department, I'm happy to know that the job of removing the stain of sin from my soul is not up to me. Because of Jesus' one time sacrifice on the cross for my sins, I can wear a spotless robe of righteousness. Washed in His blood, I bear no trace of the former stains—they are both gone and forgotten. Hallelujah, what a Savior.

*Thank You, **Lord**, that we "have been made holy through the sacrifice of the body of Jesus Christ." You have provided the cleansing that we could never achieve on our own. Help us to keep our hearts pure and free from sin. In Jesus' name, amen.*

SPOTLIGHT
Next Week's Lesson

"What can wash away my sin? Nothing but the blood of Jesus."

April 3. **Cheryl J. Frey** runs an editorial services out of her home in Rochester, New York. She spends her spare time with family—especially her grandchildren.

April 4

Flee from Sin

Flee immorality. Every other sin that a man commits is outside the body, but the immoral man sins against his own body (1 Corinthians 6:18, *New American Standard Bible*).

Cindy was sexually abused by her mother's boyfriend when she was 8-years-old. She now lives with her grandparents in a tiny house, where she sleeps on the sofa.

Cindy has suffered tremendously during her young life. Her mom never really wanted to hurt her child, but that's exactly what happened as she kept making bad decisions. Mostly, her mom "just wanted to have fun;" she certainly didn't want God telling her what to do.

Like Cindy's mother, many people believe God is trying to spoil their fun. All those rules and commandments! But God warns us not to sin, simply because it will destroy us and our families. As Benjamin Franklin once said: "Sin is not harmful because it is forbidden, but it is forbidden because it is hurtful."

If only we would believe it: God wants us to be filled up, overflowing with abundant life, joyful and productive. But the self-destructiveness of sin leaves us hopeless and hurting. So . . . flee!

Dear Lord, *I know my body is the temple, the dwelling place, of the Holy Spirit. You gave Your life so I could be washed clean. Please help me flee immorality and live a holy life. Help me remember that Your rules and commands indicate Your deep care for me. In Jesus' name, amen.*

SEARCH THE WORD

Are you afraid enough of sin to run away? Are you wise enough to be afraid?

Scripture: 1 Corinthians 6:12-20
Song: *"Yield Not to Temptation"*

From this meditation today, I will pray . . .
Adoration _____
_____
_____

Confession _____
_____
_____

Thanksgiving _____
_____
_____

Supplication _____
_____
_____

From this meditation today, I will . . .
Think _____
_____
_____

Say _____
_____
_____

Do _____
_____
_____

April 5

Life Out of Death

*"Father, forgive them; they do not know what they are doing."
And they cast lots, dividing up His garments among themselves
(Luke 23:34, New American Standard Bible).*

Scripture: Luke 23:32-47

Song: *"It Is Not Death to Die"*

From this meditation today, I will pray . . .

Adoration _____
_____
_____

Confession _____
_____
_____

Thanksgiving _____
_____
_____

Supplication _____
_____
_____

From this meditation today, I will . . .

Think _____
_____
_____

Say _____
_____
_____

Do _____
_____
_____
_____

Each year I visit my friends Gail and Greg in Oregon—where the ocean is wild and dazzlingly beautiful and where the forests are vast, gigantic, and gorgeous. But last year I saw a forest that had burned during an extremely dry summer season. Black, charred trees stretched for miles.

Such devastation made me want to cry. But Gail said: "Fire cleanses the land, ridding it of dead and diseased trees. New growth comes out of these fires." In fact, certain seeds lay dormant until there's a forest fire. Only under great heat will these seeds open and take root, creating a healthy new tree. From destruction comes beauty.

Christ, too, gave us beauty for our ashes. Those who crucified Him didn't know that His violent death would give us the greatest victory of all time.

Christ still uses the "fire storms" in our lives to give us the greatest triumphs. Are we willing to endure, though, when the heat soars?

Dear Father in Heaven, *I thank You for the salvation and peace that came from Your suffering on the cross. Help me to be convinced, daily, that all of my trials can be redeemed for the good by Your power. Help me even to be willing to suffer for Your sake that Your glory may become evident to all. In the name of Jesus, my merciful Savior and Lord. Amen.*

SPOTLIGHT
Next Week's Lesson

The shadow of the cross
exists everywhere
without the Sonrise!

April 6

God's Promises

We tell you the good news: What God promised our fathers he has fulfilled for us, their children, by raising up Jesus (Acts 13:32, 33).

Life can be so sad. This afternoon, I've learned that two people who are dear to me have both been placed under hospice care. They were surrogate father and mother to me when I needed guidance early in my ministry. They live in a distant city. Not long ago, when I phoned them at the nursing home where they live, I identified myself, as I always do, "Hi, Drexel here."

There was a long pause at the other end of the line, and then he said: "I don't know who you are." This was the man who had helped to mold my life over many years. His response stunned me.

I don't like sad endings. But this week's reading reminds me that beyond all our earthly grief, discontent, and distress, there is a happier ending ahead. The power by which God the Father raised Jesus is the same power that will resurrect us to new life some day. Then we will know for sure that the words of the old gospel song are true: "It will be worth it all, when we see Jesus."

Help me to remember, **God,** *that Your promises are filled with hope and joy—and the sure prospect of Heaven. Through Christ, amen.*

Scripture: Acts 13:26-33
Song: *"Standing on the Promises"*

From this meditation today, I will pray . . .

Adoration _____
_____
_____

Confession _____
_____
_____

Thanksgiving _____
_____
_____

Supplication _____
_____
_____

From this meditation today, I will . . .

Think _____
_____
_____

Say _____
_____
_____

Do _____
_____
_____

SEARCH THE WORD
Earthly bad news is easily overwhelmed by heavenly good news.

April 6–12. **Drexel Rankin**, *now retired, served the Christian Church (Disciples of Christ) as an ordained minister for more than 35 years.*

April 7

Remembering in Prayer

Ever since I heard about your faith in the Lord Jesus and your love for all the saints, I have not stopped giving thanks for you, remembering you in my prayers (Ephesians 1:15, 16).

Scripture: Ephesians 1:15-23
Song: *"Help Us Accept Each Other"*

From this meditation today, I will pray . . .

Adoration _____
_____
_____

Confession _____
_____
_____

Thanksgiving _____
_____
_____

Supplication _____
_____
_____

From this meditation today, I will . . .

Think _____
_____
_____

Say _____
_____
_____

Do _____
_____
_____
_____

For a whole week I fished with my son and three of my friends. We experienced good fishing and bad during those days—times when smallmouth bass and walleyes were plentiful, and days when it was tough to find a fish anywhere in the lake.

What a special time for us! We were so active. We traveled, boated, fished, and ate together. I learned what had unfolded in the lives of my friends since we'd last been together. And I discovered in more depth what was happening in the life of my son and his family.

There were times, however, when I simply wanted stillness and quiet. I took several long walks up a dirt road, away from camp. During those unscheduled times of quiet, I reflected on the struggles of my son and friends—and the hopes they harbored for better days.

I prayed during those undisturbed walks, giving thanks—and also interceding for these beloved ones, that they continue growing in Christ. Isn't this how Paul recalled the believers in Ephesus? His heart was constantly pulled back to prayer and thanks for those he loved.

Lord, *for family and friends who love me, advise me, help me, and lead me—may I always give thanks. In the name of Christ, amen.*

SPOTLIGHT
Next Week's Lesson

If Christ be not risen, death wins. Surrender to Him or surrender to death.

April 8

Never Futile!

If the dead are not raised, then Christ has not been raised either. And if Christ has not been raised, your faith is futile (1 Corinthians 15:16, 17).

I look into the sky and think I can see forever, billions of miles into the universe. Of course, it is nighttime. During the day, when all is sunlit and bright, I can see no farther than our sun. But when the darkness enfolds me, then and only then am I able to see thousands of suns, billions of miles away.

Only in the darkness can I see forever.

Have you noticed that, in the midst of crisis, we often sense more fully the presence of our resurrected Christ? When I feel lost, sick, tired, dejected, and dying the risen Christ propels himself into my life. He is always there, always in the midst of my life, even when impenetrable darkness seems to surround me. In fact, the darkness itself can help me perceive Him.

The resurrection reminds me that Christ is not bound by space or time. He is not bound by a tomb with a rock in front of it. He is present in my life, here and now. And my faith never was futile—nor shall it ever be!

O Lord, *for Your ever-present love that overcomes the darkness of life, I thank You. May I experience the resurrected Christ in every moment of life that You grant me. And may I rejoice amidst every trial, for You are there with me in all circumstances. In Jesus' name, amen.*

SEARCH THE WORD
Faith and futility—not doubt—are the opposite ends of the spiritual spectrum. Where do you stand?

Scripture: 1 Corinthians 15:12-26
Song: *"Because He Lives"*

From this meditation today, I will pray . . .
Adoration _____
_____
_____

Confession _____
_____
_____

Thanksgiving _____
_____
_____

Supplication _____
_____
_____

From this meditation today, I will . . .
Think _____
_____
_____

Say _____
_____
_____

Do _____
_____
_____

April 9

The Thursday Before

Having been buried with him in baptism and raised with him through your faith in the power of God, who raised him from the dead (Colossians 2:12).

Scripture: Colossians 2:6-15
Song: *"Lead Me to Calvary"*

From this meditation today, I will pray...
Adoration _____
_____
_____

Confession _____
_____
_____

Thanksgiving _____
_____
_____

Supplication _____
_____
_____

From this meditation today, I will...
Think _____
_____
_____

Say _____
_____
_____

Do _____
_____
_____
_____

On the Thursday before the first Easter, Jesus breaks the bread and pours the cup as He gathers His disciples around a table in an upper room. "This is my body, which is for you," He tells them. "This cup is the new covenant in my blood" (see 1 Corinthians 11:24, 25). It is a glorious meal, but betrayal looms in the darkness. And, even in His faithfulness, Jesus struggles in Gethsemane, sweating great drops of blood while contemplating the horror of Friday's cross.

Too often, we Christians arrive at the joy of Easter Sunday without experiencing the pain and agony of Thursday and Friday. Without these two days, the story is incomplete.

Today, as we prepare for the "Hallelujah" of Sunday, let us grapple with, and agonize through, the events of Thursday and Friday. After all, there is no resurrection if there has been no death. And, as Paul tells us, in baptism it is just as if we ourselves were put to death there with Christ. Only then are we free to love and serve Him by faith. What a Savior we have!

Father, *help me to rejoice in Christ's life while recalling His sobering command: "Take up your cross and follow me." In His name, amen.*

SPOTLIGHT
Next Week's Lesson

Medical science is impotent in stopping death, but God is omnipotent. He can.

April 10

Good Friday—Today

*Now if we died with Christ,
we believe that we will also live with him*
(Romans 6:8).

Good Friday recalls the day of Christ's death, and Easter Sunday is the day we celebrate His resurrection. Without these two days, we are left with an interesting teacher whose influence somehow outlived Him. That's the spiritual equivalent of very watered-down soup!

Otherwise, we end up seeing a God who is life-sized, manageable, marginally helpful, but not likely to ask much of us. These two days compel us to see that our reconciliation with God will not be accomplished on our own terms. We cannot write the script.

The bread, the wine, the thorns, the wood, the nails, the death, burial, and resurrection. Apart from those, we will not know God.

By Friday evening, evil appears to have the final word. Jesus has breathed His last. The tomb embraces Him. The entrance, sealed securely, seems to speak of what might have been.

It's important that we recall the whole story that climaxes in the glory of the resurrection.

Transform my life, **Dear God,** *into a close walk with You that takes me down pathways of both dying and rising. Give me the courage to "let die" everything in me that refuses to follow Your will each day. And raise up in me all the lovely fruits of Your Spirit. I pray in Jesus' name, amen.*

SEARCH THE WORD
The Christian can call the day his Lord died "Good Friday" because he knows there is a "Great Sunday"!

Scripture: Romans 6:3-11
Song: *"Lift High the Cross"*

From this meditation today, I will pray . . .

Adoration _____

Confession _____

Thanksgiving _____

Supplication _____

From this meditation today, I will . . .

Think _____

Say _____

Do _____

April 11

Waiting for the Dawn

Since, then, you have been raised with Christ, set your hearts on things above, where Christ is seated at the right hand of God (Colossians 3:1).

Scripture: Colossians 3:1-11
Song: *"Are Ye Able, Said the Master"*

From this meditation today, I will pray . . .
Adoration _____
_____
_____

Confession _____
_____
_____

Thanksgiving _____
_____
_____

Supplication _____
_____
_____

From this meditation today, I will . . .
Think _____
_____
_____

Say _____
_____
_____

Do _____
_____
_____
_____
_____

The Saturday before the first Easter was a time of fearful anxiety. The disciples were ready to pack it in, call it quits. All they had hoped for was gone. Their dreams were shattered. For them, Jesus had summed it up perfectly: "It is finished."

Paul, however, knew that the outcome was hardly gloomy; instead, it was glorious. And, since Christ arose from the dead, we who are "in Him" through baptism are raised to new life as well. The apostle's writings constantly reflect this great truth of our identification with Christ and His work of salvation. For example:

"If we died with Christ . . ." (Romans 6:8).

"I have been crucified with Christ . . ." (Galatians 2:20).

"Since you died with Christ . . ." (Colossians 2:20).

On the surface, not much about the Christian life is unique. Christians look the same, suffer the same pains, and die the same deaths as others. Yet, Christians live on the basis of "the hope that is stored up" for them in Heaven (see Colossians 1:5). And that hope rests solely on the one who went there before them, direct from a cold grave.

God, *help me recall my identification with Christ's death, burial, and resurrection. May I walk in newness of life this day! In Jesus' name, amen.*

SPOTLIGHT
Next Week's Lesson

The Christian's body faces death as inevitable, but the Christian spirit senses resurrection and eternality.

April 12

Resurrection Day!

He is not here; he has risen!
(Luke 24:6).

Scripture: Luke 24:1-12
Song: *"Thine Is the Glory"*

I remember how much I enjoyed going to the Saturday morning movie matinees as a boy. It wasn't just the idea of going to the movie; it was also the feeling of *urgency* that gnawed inside of me.

You see, the reason I just couldn't miss a Saturday morning kids' show was because they came as unending serials that linked together from week to week. And each week always ended in some dreadful event that put the hero's life in danger—concluding with the words: "To Be Continued". The same design shows through in our cliff-hanger TV shows today.

The women who went to visit the tomb on that first Easter morning were startled by the question of the two men inside. And the disciples treated the tale of the returning women as an idle story.

What resulted, however, quickly showed that this saga of Jesus Christ would be labeled: "To Be Continued." There was more to come.

Because Christ lives, we too are resurrected from the darkness of sin. In Christ, we are made alive, born anew. And because of Easter, our story, also, is "To Be Continued" eternally.

Almighty Father, help me always to rejoice in Your mighty work of salvation on my behalf. I pray through my deliverer, Jesus. Amen.

From this meditation today, I will pray . . .

Adoration _____

Confession _____

Thanksgiving _____

Supplication _____

From this meditation today, I will . . .

Think _____

Say _____

Do _____

SEARCH THE WORD

Across the gate of every cemetery, every mausoleum door, the words should be written: "Jesus is not here!"

April 13

Listen!

He is not here; he has risen, just as he said
(Matthew 28:6).

Scripture: Matthew 28:6-10
Song: *"Christ Has Arisen, Alleluia"*

From this meditation today, I will pray . . .
Adoration _____
_____
_____

Confession _____
_____
_____

Thanksgiving _____
_____
_____

Supplication _____
_____
_____

From this meditation today, I will . . .
Think _____
_____
_____

Say _____
_____
_____

Do _____
_____
_____

I didn't listen when experienced gardeners told me, "Take it slowly. Buy only one or two rose bushes until you know how to take care of them." Instead, I bought over a dozen. I lost half of them during the first winter. Now, even the remaining bushes need more maintenance than I had imagined. How I wish I had started out small. How I wish I had listened!

The women who came to Jesus' tomb to anoint a dead body had trouble listening too. Repeatedly, Jesus had told them He would rise on the third day. But they thought they knew better. After all, didn't they see Him crucified only days before? Didn't they watch as His disciples placed His lifeless body in a tomb? What Jesus had said didn't make sense in light of what they had seen and how they felt. So they went to the tomb expecting to find a corpse.

He is risen! What Jesus said would happen, happened. No doubt the women were much better listeners after their experience. And so am I.

Thank You, **Lord Jesus,** *for being my risen and living Savior. Teach me to open my ears to the sound of Your voice. Instruct me in Your ways, O Lord, for Your servant is listening. In Your name I pray. Amen.*

SPOTLIGHT
Next Week's Lesson

Witnesses have used their senses to establish reality—eyes, ears, touch. They use their tongues to testify.

April 13–19. **Patricia Mitchell,** *former Editorial Director at Hallmark Cards, writes from the home she shares with two people and four cats in Kansas City, Missouri.*

April 14

What's in a Name?

Jesus said to her, "Mary"
(John 20:16).

Scripture: John 20:11-18

Song: *"The Name of Jesus"*

I've become better at remembering names. When I'm introduced to someone, a few little "tricks" have been helping—like quickly repeating the person's name aloud, or associating the name with something I notice about the person's appearance. I'm more successful, however, when I simply focus my full attention on the one standing before me. Then, the next time we meet, I can usually extend one of the grandest human compliments: using his or her own name.

I know how good it feels when someone I've met remembers my name. It tells me I'm not just another face in the crowd. I'm not anonymous, not invisible; someone thought enough of me to remember my name. Those people remind me that even the Lord knows me by name—just as he knew Mary. No one is too "small" for His notice. No name is too difficult or too foreign for Him to pronounce.

Census figures tell us that the world's population tops 6.5 billion. Even so, Augustine's words still hold true: "God loves each of us as if there were only one of us." He calls me—and He calls you—by name.

Thank You, **Heavenly Father,** *that You have chosen to honor me by adopting me into Your family. Thank You for desiring such a close, personal relationship with me! All praise to You, through Christ my Lord! Amen.*

SEARCH THE WORD

*Jesus loves me,
this I know, for He calls
His sheep by name.*

From this meditation today, I will pray . . .

Adoration _____

Confession _____

Thanksgiving _____

Supplication _____

From this meditation today, I will . . .

Think _____

Say _____

Do _____

April 15

Along the Road

He asked them, "What are you discussing so intently as you walk along?" They stopped short, sadness written across their faces (Luke 24:17, *New Living Translation*).

Scripture: Luke 24:13-23, 28-31
Song: *"Lord, Take My Hand and Lead Me"*

From this meditation today, I will pray...
Adoration _____
_____
_____

Confession _____
_____
_____

Thanksgiving _____
_____
_____

Supplication _____
_____
_____

From this meditation today, I will...
Think _____
_____
_____

Say _____
_____
_____

Do _____
_____
_____
_____

Someone once said, "I didn't know I'd have to be torn down before I could be built up." Certainly the disciples on the road to Emmaus had been torn down. They had heard Jesus teach and had watched Him perform miracles. They had followed Him and placed their hope in Him, only to see Him crucified and buried. Granted, a rumor floated around about an empty tomb, but who knew? No wonder the disciples walked along with "sadness written across their faces."

When life tears us down, sadness seems the only logical response. Missed opportunities. Financial setbacks. A broken marriage. Sickness and disability. The loss of a loved one. But while things crumble, Jesus builds. On the road to Emmaus, He walked along with the despondent disciples, teaching them, strengthening their faith, and opening their eyes to their risen Lord and Savior. In the same way, He walks along with His "torn down" disciples of today. He comforts, encourages, and strengthens.

Thank You, Lord, for walking with me in those times when I feel most alone. Build in me compassion, understanding, and wisdom so that I too may walk along with others and build them up in love. In the name of the Father, the Son, and the Holy Spirit, I pray. Amen.

SPOTLIGHT
Next Week's Lesson

Many walk away from the cross and tomb confused and subdued. Meeting Jesus changes everything.

April 16

Show Me

Then Jesus told him, "Because you have seen me, you have believed; blessed are those who have not seen and yet have believed"
(John 20:29).

I live in Missouri, the Show-Me state. One story attributes that motto to Willard Duncan Vandiver, Missouri's state representative in Congress early in the 20th century. He once said that "frothy eloquence neither convinces nor satisfies me. I am from Missouri. You have got to show me."

The disciple Thomas made a similar statement. Sure, he had heard talk of Jesus' resurrection. Talk, however, didn't convince him and didn't satisfy him. "You've got to show me," he told the other disciples. So Jesus showed him His hands and His side. And what Thomas saw convinced him. He bowed down and worshiped His Lord and Savior.

After His resurrection, Jesus physically appeared to many. Most people, though, from the beginning of time until today, have never seen His nail-wounded hands and His spear-pierced side. But that doesn't mean He has nothing to show us. He shows us His truth in Scripture, His love among believers, and His blessing on faith that has not seen yet still believes.

Dear God, *keep me faithful to Your Word, and show me the way that leads to You, even when I find it hard to believe. In Christ's name I pray. Amen.*

Scripture: John 20:24-29
Song: *"I Am Content, My Jesus Ever Lives"*

From this meditation today, I will pray . . .
Adoration _____
_____
_____

Confession _____
_____
_____

Thanksgiving _____
_____
_____

Supplication _____
_____
_____

From this meditation today, I will . . .
Think _____
_____
_____

Say _____
_____
_____

Do _____
_____
_____

SEARCH THE WORD

What will it take to convince some that Jesus is alive? His coming again? Too late!

April 17

Comfort Zone

Simon Peter said, "I'm going fishing"
(John 21:3, New Living Translation).

Scripture: John 21:1-14
Song: *"In Thee Is Gladness"*

From this meditation today, I will pray . . .
Adoration _____
_____
_____

Confession _____
_____
_____

Thanksgiving _____
_____
_____

Supplication _____
_____
_____

From this meditation today, I will . . .
Think _____
_____
_____

Say _____
_____
_____

Do _____
_____
_____
_____

"When things get tough, the tough get going." The rest of us run to our comfort zones, right? Some people watch TV or listen to music. Others cook, garden, or go for a walk. Some eat; I sew. After the astonishing events of Jesus' trial, crucifixion, and resurrection, Peter . . . went fishing.

In upsetting or traumatic times, we're eager to get back to normal. We fly to familiar surroundings. We regain control by doing something we know we can do—an activity (or non-activity) that brings us peace. But deep down inside, we know our lives have changed, as the lives of Jesus' disciples certainly had. Because of His glorious resurrection, they were no longer just fishermen. Now they were preachers of the good news to all the world.

When the Holy Spirit works faith in the heart, lives change. We're no longer satisfied by the temporary "comforts" this world offers. No matter what's going on in our lives, our comfort comes from Christ, who calls each one of us to rest at ease in His peace and love.

Lord, *thank You for understanding my worries and fears. Thank You for being there for me through all the times of my life. Though the world may change around me, in You I have comfort, security, and peace. In the precious name of Jesus I pray. Amen.*

SPOTLIGHT
Next Week's Lesson

If one believes Jesus is risen, he will go "fishing," fishing for unbelievers.

April 18

Tell the Story

What I received I passed on to you as of first importance: that Christ died for our sins according to the Scriptures, that he was buried, that he was raised on the third day according to the Scriptures (1 Corinthians 15:3, 4).

"We desperately need a teacher for fourth grade. Will you do it?" Not being a trained teacher, I couldn't picture myself taking on a weekly after-school religion class. Besides, it would mean leaving early from work every Wednesday, which would mean reporting to work earlier on Thursday morning. Ouch! Since the commitment was for only one semester, however, I decided to go ahead. That was ten years ago, and counting.

I've picked up a few teaching techniques along the way. I can name no better role model, however, than the apostle Paul. Paul simply taught the gospel message that was passed on to Him from the apostles and other eyewitnesses of the risen Lord. He stuck to the facts and let the Holy Spirit take care of the rest.

Children receive the gospel only if we pass it on to them. Is there a little one in your life who has not heard about Jesus and His love?

Thank You, **Lord,** *for everyone in my life who has gladly and willingly passed on to me the message of salvation by grace. Bless them, Lord, for all they have done to enlighten, encourage, and inspire me in my faith-walk. In the name of Jesus, Lord and Savior of all, I pray. Amen.*

Scripture: 1 Corinthians 15:1-8
Song: *"I Love to Tell the Story"*

From this meditation today, I will pray . . .
Adoration _____

Confession _____

Thanksgiving _____

Supplication _____

From this meditation today, I will . . .
Think _____

Say _____

Do _____

SEARCH THE WORD

What is of first importance to you? The facts of the gospel? How do you show it?

April 19

Well Dressed

I am going to send you what my Father has promised; but stay in the city until you have been clothed with power from on high (Luke 24:49).

Scripture: Luke 24:44-53
Song: *"Holy Spirit, Light Divine"*

From this meditation today, I will pray . . .
Adoration _____
_____
_____

Confession _____
_____
_____

Thanksgiving _____
_____
_____

Supplication _____
_____
_____

From this meditation today, I will . . .
Think _____
_____
_____

Say _____
_____
_____

Do _____
_____
_____
_____
_____

I was pleased with myself for having landed an elegant designer dress on sale. The first time I wore it, a colleague, who had formerly worked as a buyer at an upscale department store, spotted it right away. At first glance, she could name the designer, and she knew exactly where I had bought it!

The spiritual clothing we wear every day is just as noticeable. Our loved ones, friends, associates, and even strangers hear our words and observe our actions. They recognize love, joy, gentleness, and kindness when they see it. They can readily spot peace, patience, goodness, faithfulness, and self-control. These things stand out, especially in a world accustomed to much the opposite.

As the Holy Spirit continues to work in you, your "spiritual clothing" becomes even more elegant, more attractive, more remarkable to others. Christians who see it won't need to ask, "Where did you get that?" They know! But someone else might not know. What will you tell them about the power-clothing you're wearing?

Lord, *clothe me with Your power so that my words and actions, my thoughts and attitudes, reflect the riches of Your spiritual graces. In all I do, let others see evidence of Your work in my heart. In Jesus' name, amen.*

SPOTLIGHT
Next Week's Lesson

Do you feel clothed in power or undressed by weakness? Witnesses know power.

April 20

My Mother's Likeness

Don't you know me, Philip, even after I have been among you such a long time? Anyone who has seen me has seen the Father. How can you say, "Show us the Father?" (John 14:9).

One day I said, "Whenever I look in the mirror, I see my mother." This puzzled my small grandson, for he knew my mother had died several years ago. He stared at me and asked, "How can that be?"

My grandson never knew my mother and didn't realize how much I look like her. But it isn't only my physical appearance that so resembles Mom. She influenced the way I think and act, and she instilled many of her character traits in me. Mother is the one who taught me to sew and cook, to be a good wife and mother, and to care for my home. I even teach a Sunday school class of preschoolers in the same room where she taught little ones for many years.

My mother was a godly woman, and I am pleased to follow in her footsteps. It is a good reminder to look in the mirror each day and see Mother looking back at me. I hope I will leave a good image to reflect in the lives of my children and grandchildren.

Dear Father, *thank You for sending Jesus into the world to reveal Your character and Your love. I come to You in His name. Amen.*

Scripture: John 14:8-14
Song: *"O to Be Like Thee!"*

From this meditation today, I will pray . . .

Adoration _____

Confession _____

Thanksgiving _____

Supplication _____

From this meditation today, I will . . .

Think _____

Say _____

Do _____

SEARCH THE WORD

A careful look at Jesus gives a very good look at the Father.

April 20–26. **LeAnn Campbell** is a retired special education teacher. She and her husband have six children, eleven grandchildren, and two great-grandsons.

April 21

A Sorry Sight

I will not accuse forever, nor will I always be angry, for then the spirit of man would grow faint before me—the breath of man that I have created (Isaiah 57:16).

Scripture: Isaiah 57:14-21

Song: *"Afflicted Saint, to Christ Draw Near"*

From this meditation today, I will pray . . .

Adoration _____

_____

_____

Confession _____

_____

_____

Thanksgiving _____

_____

_____

Supplication _____

_____

_____

From this meditation today, I will . . .

Think _____

_____

_____

Say _____

_____

_____

Do _____

_____

_____

_____

One morning after breakfast, I tossed a leftover waffle outside for our little dog, Muffin. My husband and I went for our daily walk, and Muffin trotted alongside with the waffle in her mouth. Later in the day the waffle was gone, but the next morning it reappeared—dirty and tasteless (in our opinion), because Muffin had buried it for a while. But she dug it up to carry around again. This went on for several days, and the waffle looked more unappetizing every time she dug it up.

Muffin's waffle was a lot like we are when someone makes us angry. Perhaps we bury our feelings for a while—but not too deep. We want to keep them close enough to the surface so we can dig them up to drag around again. But as today's Scripture tells us, it is not good always to be angry, for that makes a person's spirit grow faint. Just as that waffle looked worse every day, anger and accusations drag us down to a pretty sorry sight.

Dear Lord, *I don't want to carry anger around, nor do I want to direct it toward others. When I'm angry, help me to forgive the one who has hurt me, even though I may need to hold him accountable. Also, help me direct all that energy toward the problem—and a solution. In Jesus' name, amen.*

SPOTLIGHT
Next Week's Lesson

Dorcas was a witness to Christ's power. Her poverty did not hinder His riches.

April 22

Mercy in Little Things

The Lord *has heard my cry for mercy; the* Lord *accepts my prayer* (Psalm 6:9).

Five months after Mom's death from Alzheimer's disease, the doctor gave us the diagnosis for my mother-in-law: "Alzheimer's," he said. How could we face this memory-robbing disease a second time? We cried to God for mercy. He didn't cure the Alzheimer's—it lasted 25 years from my mother's first symptoms in the 1960s until my mother-in-law's death in 1999. Even though we lived with the disease all those years, we know God heard and answered our cries. His mercy came to us in small, everyday ways.

Friends let us know they cared. One asked, "Is your mother having problems?" Just five words, but they were enough to show her concern. In the later years, a support group formed where we could share with other families our struggles and victories. Monthly suppers with my husband's siblings turned out to be an invaluable support system when we had to make tough decisions about my mother-in-law's care.

We have wonderful memories of both mothers. There are funny and touching stories to share when our families get together. Each rings with the mercy of God.

God, *thank You for the mercy of others that conveys Your own goodness. May the good memories be the ones we remember. In Jesus' name, amen.*

Scripture: Psalm 6
Song: *"He Leadeth Me"*

From this meditation today, I will pray . . .

Adoration _____

Confession _____

Thanksgiving _____

Supplication _____

From this meditation today, I will . . .

Think _____

Say _____

Do _____

SEARCH THE WORD

The one who cries for mercy will see God's mercy at every hand.

April 23

Sustain Me

The L*ord* *will sustain him on his sickbed and restore him from his bed of illness*
(Psalm 41:3).

Scripture: Psalm 41
Song: *"Precious Lord, Take My Hand"*

From this meditation today, I will pray . . .
Adoration _____
_____
_____

Confession _____
_____
_____

Thanksgiving _____
_____
_____

Supplication _____
_____
_____

From this meditation today, I will . . .
Think _____
_____
_____

Say _____
_____
_____

Do _____
_____
_____
_____

The college instructor asked questions on the history test that she had not covered in class, and I knew my grade would be bad, maybe even failing. That was 30 years ago, and now I've forgotten whether my score was good or bad on that test. What I do remember is how I worried over that grade. Although I should have turned my concerns over to God and asked Him to sustain me, I came home and fretted. I stretched out on the couch, covered up with an afghan, and gave in to my misery.

The test was already over, and all my anxiety couldn't change a thing. But like so many problems that plague us, my worries about the test grew worse during the nighttime. And as morning dawned, the stress had made me physically ill.

What anxiety I could have saved myself if I had only done as David did when he was ill! He asked God for mercy and acknowledged that God would sustain him. Then he moved on to heartfelt worship: "Praise be to the Lord, the God of Israel, from everlasting to everlasting. Amen and Amen" (Psalm 41:13).

Heavenly Father, *may I never forget that You are faithful to sustain me. I pray that I will come to You for mercy every day, rather than wasting energy with unnecessary worrying. Through Christ I pray. Amen.*

SPOTLIGHT
Next Week's Lesson

Dorcas did not bodily rise from her sickbed, but praises quickly did from those she blessed.

April 24

"I'm Sorry"

"Return, faithless people; I will cure you of backsliding."
"Yes, we will come to you, for you are the Lord *our God"*
(Jeremiah 3:22).

"**I**'m sorry, Mom."
"I didn't mean to do it, Dad."
What parent hasn't heard these words at least once? The broken dish, wrecked car, stolen goods—children face many temptations and often backslide.

When one of our daughters was small, she eyed the clear plastic cane-shaped tube of candy near the cash register. After we left the store, I realized she had the colorful cane in her hand. We went back inside, and I stood beside her while she gave the candy to the clerk and apologized for taking it. The clerk accepted the candy, but she felt sorry for my little girl because I made her return it.

My daughter probably wasn't sorry that day, for she wanted the candy and didn't get it. But she learned that it's wrong to walk out of a store with something unless you've paid for it.

We don't always learn our lessons that quickly. Many of us, children and adults, are guilty of backsliding before we honestly admit that we're sorry and ready to change our ways.

Father, *thanks for Your forgiveness when I confess that I'm wrong. And thank You for restoring our fellowship so quickly. In Jesus' name, amen.*

Scripture: Jeremiah 3:19-23
Song: *"Lord, I'm Coming Home"*

From this meditation today, I will pray . . .

Adoration _____

Confession _____

Thanksgiving _____

Supplication _____

From this meditation today, I will . . .

Think _____

Say _____

Do _____

SEARCH THE WORD

Here's the problem with backsliding: getting closer to where you don't want to be and farther from where you do.

April 25

When I Need Help

O Lord my God, I called to you for help and you healed me
(Psalm 30:2).

Scripture: Psalm 30:1-5
Song: *"God Will Take Care of You"*

From this meditation today, I will pray . . .
Adoration _____
_____
_____

Confession _____
_____
_____

Thanksgiving _____
_____
_____

Supplication _____
_____
_____

From this meditation today, I will . . .
Think _____
_____
_____

Say _____
_____
_____

Do _____
_____
_____
_____

Throughout the week, as we camped in a wooded park, a flock of geese wandered through the campsites. One afternoon as we finished our lunch of hotdogs and chips, two of the geese came close to investigate. My sister-in-law tossed them a piece of bread, and the largest goose grabbed it. The piece was too large for him, so he pulled off a hunk and left the remainder on the ground.

He swallowed the bread—but it stuck on the way down! His neck began to convulse, and we knew he was in trouble, unable to finish swallowing. He'd take a tentative step toward the piece of bread still on the ground, but then backed away as he continued his struggle to swallow. None of us knew how to help him, for we knew the goose would either run away or attack if we tried to catch him. After several minutes, he managed to swallow the first bite and then grabbed the other piece.

I didn't know how to help the struggling goose, but when I have trouble I can call on God for help. He knows me through and through. And since most every problem I have is some form of "heart trouble," He is the perfect Physician to come to my aid.

Thank You, God, for all the times You've been there, ready to help when I've called. Praise You for Your goodness and grace! In Jesus' name, amen.

SPOTLIGHT
Next Week's Lesson

Good deeds have the sweet smell of gladness, even when the smell of death is nearby.

April 26

Use Those Abilities!

Peter went with them, and when he arrived he was taken upstairs to the room. All the widows stood around him, crying and showing him the robes and other clothing that Dorcas had made while she was still with them (Acts 9:39).

When our four daughters were small, their grandma crocheted each of them a red coat. The girls proudly wore those coats all winter. Grandma made them because she loved her granddaughters and wanted them to have beautiful clothes. The next year she crocheted extra lengths so they could wear their coats for another year.

When the pretty coats were finally outgrown, we had to put them away. But the girls still remember what Grandma did for them. She knew how to use a crochet hook, and it was a wonderful way to express her love.

Our Scripture reading today is about another woman who made clothing for her friends and neighbors. Dorcas must have been a fine seamstress, and she used her skill to make robes and clothes. When she died, the widows she'd befriended cried as they showed their garments to Peter.

Some of us can sew or crochet; others wield a hammer, a paintbrush, or concoct great recipes. What a privilege it is to use our talent and experience to help others.

Dear God, *guide me in using the spiritual gifts and abilities You've given me. Should I read to a shut-in, visit a grieving person, or provide transportation for someone with no car? Thank You, in the name of Jesus. Amen.*

SEARCH THE WORD

What will people miss when they no longer have you?

Scripture: Acts 9:32-43
Song: *"Give of Your Best to the Master"*

From this meditation today, I will pray...
Adoration _____

Confession _____

Thanksgiving _____

Supplication _____

From this meditation today, I will...
Think _____

Say _____

Do _____

April 27

Soaring Above the Canyon

You yourselves have seen what I did to Egypt, and how I carried you on eagles' wings and brought you to myself (Exodus 19:4).

Scripture: Exodus 19:1-8
Song: *"I Must Tell Jesus"*

From this meditation today, I will pray . . .

Adoration _____

_____

_____

Confession _____

_____

_____

Thanksgiving _____

_____

_____

Supplication _____

_____

_____

From this meditation today, I will . . .

Think _____

_____

_____

Say _____

_____

_____

Do _____

_____

_____

The eagle stretched out its powerful wings and soared high above the canyon floor. It seemed to float effortlessly on the wind. I had come to the Grand Canyon to remember my maker. The majestic depths and vibrant colors of the canyon were awe-inspiring. Its vast beauty gave glory to the creator.

A week earlier, I had been diagnosed with cancer. The full extent of its invasive attacks was not yet known. I cried to the Lord and asked Him to keep the cancer from also attacking my soul with fear, doubt, and distrust.

As the eagles soared gracefully over the seemingly endless canyon, God reminded me: He promised to carry me on wings like eagles. If I rested on Him as the eagle rested on the wind currents, He would carry me over the canyons of seemingly insurmountable circumstances. He would save me from the depths of despair. From there, I would begin to see things from His perspective.

Creator of All, *You are my maker, and You know everything about me. You promise to carry me through every circumstance that You allow into my life. Help me to trust You completely. In Jesus' name, amen.*

April 27–30. **Julie Kloster** *is a teacher, speaker, and freelance writer. She also enjoys singing with her church worship team. She lives in Sycamore, Illinois.*

SPOTLIGHT
Next Week's Lesson

Chosen! Chosen! Chosen! That is Paul's word about us in Ephesians 1. "He chose us." Hallelujah!

April 28

Depending on a Promise

If the inheritance depends on the law, then it no longer depends on a promise; but God in his grace gave it to Abraham through a promise (Galatians 3:18).

My 7-year-old daughter, Sarah, put her hand over her eyes to shade the stage lights. She scanned the audience. I smiled and waved. Sarah's little sisters bobbed up and down in excitement on their grandparents' laps. Sarah bit her lip and blinked hard when she saw that the seat next to me was still empty.

Sarah's daddy had promised to try to make it home from a business trip to attend her Christmas pageant, but an unexpected snowstorm was delaying flights. Suddenly, the back door to the auditorium opened. Her snow-covered daddy arrived just in time.

Sometimes it's quite difficult for people to keep their word; sometimes they fail. God, however, always keeps His promises. Abraham believed God and His promise to provide him an eternal inheritance. This promise was fulfilled in Jesus. Abraham did not receive eternal life by keeping the law—it hadn't even been given yet! No, Abraham was saved by faith, through Christ's work on the cross, just as we are. We can trust our ever faithful God to keep every promise He makes.

Faithful God and keeper of promises, *I look with expectant hope to the promise of eternity with You. In the name of Your Son, Jesus, amen.*

SEARCH THE WORD
"Standing on the promises" is the wisest, safest, most joyous place to stand.

Scripture: Galatians 3:15-18
Song: *"All I Need"*

From this meditation today, I will pray . . .
Adoration _____

Confession _____

Thanksgiving _____

Supplication _____

From this meditation today, I will . . .
Think _____

Say _____

Do _____

April 29

Pardon Me!

*So the law was put in charge to lead us to Christ
that we might be justified by faith*
(Galatians 3:24).

Scripture: Galatians 3:23-29
Song: *"This Is How It Feels to Be Free"*

From this meditation today, I will pray . . .
Adoration _____
_____
_____

Confession _____
_____
_____

Thanksgiving _____
_____
_____

Supplication _____
_____
_____

From this meditation today, I will . . .
Think _____
_____
_____

Say _____
_____
_____

Do _____
_____
_____
_____

"The law, whether human or divine, is no respecter of persons," said President Ford. It was September 8, 1974, and Ford was about to pardon former President Nixon for his role in the Watergate scandal. Ford continued, "I, Gerald R. Ford, President of the United States . . . do grant a full, free, and absolute pardon unto Richard Nixon for all offenses against the United States." At that moment, regardless of any guilt that might be proven by the law, Richard Nixon was free from punishment for any wrongdoing.

We humans, too, stand in need of a pardon. We have broken God's law. Yet God's law helps us to recognize that we are sinners in need of the Savior.

By God's wonderful grace, He offers all-sufficient pardon and eternal salvation. Through repentance and faith in Jesus Christ, we can become children of God, being baptized into His body. We thus receive a "full, free, and absolute pardon" in Christ. Released from the curse of sin, we can sing and shout God's praise with exuberant joy.

Father, *thank You for the cross of Your Son, Jesus. He took the punishment that I deserved. How wonderful and glorious Your love for me must be! Now I am forgiven and free. May I give You glory and praise all the days of my life. In the holy name of Jesus, my Lord and Savior, I pray. Amen.*

SPOTLIGHT
Next Week's Lesson
Do you have someone who would say, "Ever since I heard about your faith, I have not stopped giving thanks for you"? (See Ephesians 1:15, 16.)

April 30

Fully Adopted, Fully Loved

When the time had fully come, God sent his Son, born of a woman, born under law, to redeem those under law, that we might receive the full rights of sons (Galatians 4:4, 5).

A splotch of "Molokai Blue" paint adorned Caitlyn's hair. She grinned. "I'm almost done painting her room," she said. "Carpeting comes tomorrow."

Caitlyn's 10-year-old daughter, Bridget, danced around her. "We want her room to be ready when we get the call to come and get her," Bridget explained. "Her name is Holly."

Bridget's family was adopting a baby girl from China. "We already love her, and we don't even know her yet," Bridget explained. "I have always wanted a baby sister. I can hardly wait!"

Under Roman law, an adopted child had all the legal rights of a biological child, even if the adopted child had formerly been a slave. The child wasn't second-class, but equal to other children in the family in every way.

The apostle Paul wanted the Galatians to understand that this is how God adopts us. We become His children, and He becomes our "Abba, Father" or "Daddy, God." As adopted children, we are first-class heirs to His kingdom.

Daddy God, *thank You for adopting me fully and completely as Your own dearly loved child. Thank You for the promise of eternity with You, as an heir to Your kingdom. In Christ's precious name, amen.*

Scripture: Galatians 4:1-7

Song: *"Redeemed, How I Love to Proclaim It!"*

From this meditation today, I will pray . . .

Adoration _____

Confession _____

Thanksgiving _____

Supplication _____

From this meditation today, I will . . .

Think _____

Say _____

Do _____

SEARCH THE WORD

When God adopts, it is for love, and it is forever.

"They worshiped him . . . with great joy." —Luke 24:52

May

THE FRUITS OF NEW LIFE

*The people all responded together,
"We will do everything the L*ORD *has said."*
—Exodus 19:8

Photo © Getty Images

May 1

What List Am I On?

Everyone who has left houses or brothers or sisters or father or mother or children or fields for my sake will receive a hundred times as much and will inherit eternal life (Matthew 19:29).

Scripture: Matthew 19:23-30
Song: *"All As God Wills"*

From this meditation today, I will pray . . .

Adoration _____
_____
_____

Confession _____
_____
_____

Thanksgiving _____
_____
_____

Supplication _____
_____
_____

From this meditation today, I will . . .

Think _____
_____
_____

Say _____
_____
_____

Do _____
_____
_____

May 1–3. **Julie Kloster** *is a teacher, speaker, and freelance writer. She also enjoys singing with her church worship team. She lives in Sycamore, Illinois.*

"A nine-figure fortune won't get you much mention these days, at least not on these pages," said Forbes.com on September 21, 2006. For the first time in history, the nation's wealthiest Forbes 400 each had at least $1 billion dollars! Forbes also noted that eight members on the list the year before had died. One couple had dropped off the list because they had given $1 billion dollars to charity.

Wealth in this world is highly acclaimed, but what is the *eternal value* of financial gain? We may not be on the Forbes 400 list, but if our name is written in the Lamb's Book of Life, we have eternal treasure. The tempting but temporal trappings of this world will never compare to the unending blessings of those Christ has redeemed.

Jesus made it clear that financial wealth can stand in the way of our understanding of the need for a Savior. God is the God of the impossible, however, and He can change the heart of any person. Are we willing to use all that we have for God's kingdom?

O Lord, all good things come from You. Use all the gifts that You have given to me for Your honor and glory. In Jesus' name, amen.

SPOTLIGHT
Next Week's Lesson
It's better to be in God's elect ("included in Christ") than in Forbes 400.
(Ephesians 1:13)

May 2

More Christlike

The fruit of the Spirit is love, joy, peace, patience, kindness, goodness, faithfulness, gentleness and self-control. Against such things there is no law (Galatians 5:22, 23).

"If you plant an apple seed, will you grow an orange tree?" I asked a group of preschoolers.

They laughed. "No! An apple tree!"

"You are silly," a curly-headed 4-year-old told me.

"You are right!" I answered. "The type of plant that grows depends on the seed that we plant."

This basic principle is true for our spiritual lives, as well. If the Holy Spirit is planted in our hearts and we listen to His voice, we will bear the fruits of the Spirit. If we do not keep in step with the Spirit, though, we will produce the acts of our own sinful nature. Without the Holy Spirit being planted in our hearts, we will be unable to consistently grow His fruit, the evidence that He is there.

God alone can plant the Holy Spirit in our hearts. He does this when we repent of our sins and are baptized into Christ. Once the seed is planted, we can listen to the Spirit's voice and grow to the heights of spiritual maturity. As we grow in the Spirit of Christ—amazingly—we become more and more like Christ himself.

Spirit of God, *fill me with Your presence that I may bear Your fruit. I want to hear Your voice and follow You. Teach me through Your Word how to be more like Jesus. For in His name, I pray. Amen.*

SEARCH THE WORD

No good government makes laws against good behavior. Every bad government does.

Scripture: Galatians 5:16-25
Song: *"Spirit of the Living God"*

From this meditation today, I will pray . . .
Adoration _____

Confession _____

Thanksgiving _____

Supplication _____

From this meditation today, I will . . .
Think _____

Say _____

Do _____

May 3

Guaranteed!

Having believed, you were marked in him with a seal, the promised Holy Spirit, who is a deposit guaranteeing our inheritance until the redemption of those who are God's possession—to the praise of his glory (Ephesians 1:13, 14).

Scripture: Ephesians 1:3-14
Song: *"He the Pearly Gates Will Open"*

From this meditation today, I will pray . . .
Adoration _____

Confession _____

Thanksgiving _____

Supplication _____

From this meditation today, I will . . .
Think _____

Say _____

Do _____

I painted the white wicker chair, replaced the worn cushion with a new one in modern colors, and tucked it into a corner of the sun room. It was a treasure to our family—a piece of inheritance to add to our collection of items left behind by those we loved.

In the corner of one bedroom is a small, marble-topped dresser. Its edges are rough with use. The latch hangs crooked. Still, it is a treasure to us, having once belonged to my grandmother.

We have a few beautiful pieces of old china, several tarnished pieces of silver, an embroidered tablecloth on a small round table in our dining room, and an old German knife. They are all relics of the past that are now marked with age and use. Yet they are precious to us because we've inherited them from precious people.

Christians have an inheritance in Heaven that will never perish, spoil, or fade. At baptism, the Holy Spirit takes up residence in our hearts. His presence is a seal, a divine promise, guaranteeing our eternal inheritance.

Holy Spirit, *thanks for living in me as a promise that I belong to God. I am so grateful for Your ever-present sustaining grace. Through Christ, amen.*

SPOTLIGHT
Next Week's Lesson

No fading stamp on the hand,
no perishable membership card—
we have better: the seal of the Spirit.

May 4

Grace Has Come

Grace and truth came through Jesus Christ
(John 1:17).

Most of the time, Christians press on in their daily lives with God by faith, not experiencing visions or special revelations. But I believe God does sometimes break through in a special way. It happened to me once.

A group of us was praying in a friend's house, and the Lord Jesus stood in our midst. I seemed to see His feet as He stood there. He was very real to me, and He said, "You are acceptable to Me." His presence was like a beautiful perfume, which lingered with me for some days, then faded. Faith had to take over once again.

I was so overcome by the sweetness of His presence that I forgot to pass on the message! I knew it was for someone else at that meeting who truly needed encouragement in Christian growth—a person struggling with doubt and truth, with law and grace.

The apostle John wrote about the Jesus He knew well; he had experienced the Lord's grace and truth firsthand. We can experience it too. We may not see Him with physical sight until we stand before Him. But we can receive His goodness any time we open our hearts.

Lord, by Your grace, You forgive me and accept me. Now my heart is free to proclaim Your goodness to all in my world. In Jesus' name, amen.

SEARCH THE WORD

Grace and truth—what more could one want?

Scripture: John 1:14-18
Song: *"Here Is Love"*

From this meditation today, I will pray . . .

Adoration _____

Confession _____

Thanksgiving _____

Supplication _____

From this meditation today, I will . . .

Think _____

Say _____

Do _____

May 4–10. **Marion Turnbull** and her husband, now retired in Manchester, UK, raised a family in England, then served together as missionaries in Africa.

May 5

Powerful Enough to Wait

The LORD *will wait, that He may be gracious to you*
(Isaiah 30:18, *New King James Version*).

Scripture: Isaiah 30:15-21
Song: *"We Rest on Thee"*

From this meditation today, I will pray . . .
Adoration _____
_____
_____

Confession _____
_____
_____

Thanksgiving _____
_____
_____

Supplication _____
_____
_____

From this meditation today, I will . . .
Think _____
_____
_____

Say _____
_____
_____

Do _____
_____
_____
_____

We hear a lot today about terrorists, young men ready to sacrifice everything, even their own lives, for their cause. They kill and maim in their zeal for their religion.

To many people, Paul was a terrorist. Extremely zealous for his religion, he dragged Christians into prison and death, thinking he was doing the will of God. When Jesus met him—and he saw that the whole time he had been fighting *against* God—he reeled into a state of collapse for days. He said that everything he had considered his best assets—pride in his national and religious heritage and all his own efforts to be righteous before God—he now counted these things as rubbish compared with knowing the Lord Jesus.

In that context, I find today's verse amazing. The Lord is waiting to be gracious to me? He waits until I come to the end of my own zealous efforts to earn His favor, until I give up the fight, until I simply allow Him to show me compassion. Some gods need to be supported and defended so they may go forth in power—not ours. He is powerful enough to wait; He leads His people with grace.

Thank You, LORD, *for being so patient with me. I will wait for You and receive all that You want to pour out upon me. Through Christ, amen.*

SPOTLIGHT
Next Week's Lesson
The best that may be said of our lives in transgressions and sins is that's where we "used to live"
(Ephesians 2:2).

May 6

Hospitality or Fame?

I would rather be a doorkeeper in the house of my God than dwell in the tents of the wicked (Psalm 84:10).

I knew a gentle Welshman (now with his Lord) who was once a champion boxer. His name was Gerault James, and he came from a humble home. But a famous fight promoter spotted his talent. There is big money in boxing, and Gerault was on the way up from the beginning.

Gerault was a Christian. One day during a training session in the boxing ring, Gerault's small New Testament fell out of his dressing robe onto the floor. The fight promoter was watching and saw what it was. He climbed up and kicked the New Testament right out of the ring. "You can forget all *that*!" he said. "No place in your life for that now, my boy!"

Gerault knew he had to make a choice. Go on in his boxing career and make the kind of money he had dreamed about . . . or follow Jesus.

He chose Jesus. He and his wife ran a small hotel in Aberystwyth, Wales, and served God's people for many years. Such a choice is not too difficult for most Christians, those who have tasted that the Lord is good. In Gerault's case it meant preferring a life of kind hospitality to one of fame and affluence.

Not just to the door, **Father,** You call me to enter right in to Your blessed presence. What can tempt me away from You? In Jesus' name, amen.

SEARCH THE WORD

Lifestyle and career choices reflect priorities and faith. Do mine?

Scripture: Psalm 84:8-12
Song: *"Close to Thee"*

From this meditation today, I will pray . . .
Adoration _____
_____
_____

Confession _____
_____
_____

Thanksgiving _____
_____
_____

Supplication _____
_____
_____

From this meditation today, I will . . .
Think _____
_____
_____

Say _____
_____
_____

Do _____
_____
_____
_____

May 7

He Knows My Pain

Although He was a son, He learned obedience by what He suffered (Hebrews 5:8).

Scripture: Hebrews 4:14–5:10
Song: *"God with Us"*

From this meditation today, I will pray . . .
Adoration _____
_____
_____

Confession _____
_____
_____

Thanksgiving _____
_____
_____

Supplication _____
_____
_____

From this meditation today, I will . . .
Think _____
_____
_____

Say _____
_____
_____

Do _____
_____
_____

My sister lost her 19-year-old son in an accident. She had been looking for God for many years, and neither of us could understand this terrible tragedy. How can we? However, she went on to find Jesus, and I was able to direct her to a church near to where she lived.

One day she phoned me and said, with tears, "Isn't God good? He's given me a Christian friend who also lost a child—and she knows how it feels."

The friend, Norah, had a beautiful married daughter who died while giving birth. She took my sister into her arms and comforted her as I, who never lost a child, could not. Significant loss and pain had developed that extra dimension in Norah's life.

Not that God *wants* us to suffer; Jesus has suffered enough for all of us. But without experiencing a little pain, how can we know what it feels like?

My Jesus, Eternal Son of God, King of kings, needed this dimension too. He is so much more glorious because of it.

I cannot help but worship You, Lord, so perfect in every way. You are not a high priest untouched by my sufferings. Thus You are able to comfort me in my worst times, knowing my pain. Please help me to rely on You amidst all circumstance, rejoicing in Your goodness. Through Christ, amen.

SPOTLIGHT
Next Week's Lesson

He is the God who is "rich in mercy." We must never forget that.
See Ephesians 2:4.

May 8

Behave Like the Father

Just as he who called you is holy, so be holy in all you do
(1 Peter 1:15).

Many people come to the UK from other countries with different cultures, customs, and laws. They want to stay here and be considered British. However, if they do, some things will have to change. They are not now under the laws of their own country, tribe, or family. If they are accepted into our society, they must behave themselves as British citizens. If not, they will be sent back home (in theory, anyway). The same is true of any country.

I am so glad I have been accepted into the family of God by a new birth. Now I have a wonderful Father who is holy. He calls me to be like Him, letting go of all that clings to me from my old life.

Yes, He calls His children to behave as He behaves, to forget the old ways. It's an impossibly high standard, of course. That's why He promises His indwelling Spirit to transform us by His grace in ways that we could never accomplish on our own. Ultimately, then, our goal is not so much to be *like* Him as to *grow close* to Him. Then, paradoxically, we do become more and more like Him as our lives in Him unfold. Thanks be to God!

Dear Heavenly Father, *may I never look to the ways of this world to govern my behavior. I want to walk close to You daily, that You may work Your own character deep into my life. Thank You, in Jesus' name. Amen.*

SEARCH THE WORD

Holiness is seldom a daily conversation, but it must be a daily commitment.

Scripture: 1 Peter 1:10-16
Song: *"Trust and Obey"*

From this meditation today, I will pray . . .

Adoration _____
_____
_____

Confession _____
_____
_____

Thanksgiving _____
_____
_____

Supplication _____
_____
_____

From this meditation today, I will . . .

Think _____
_____
_____

Say _____
_____
_____

Do _____
_____
_____
_____

May 9

His Shining Face

The LORD *make his face shine upon you and be gracious to you*
(Numbers 6:25).

Scripture: Numbers 6:22-27

Song: *"That I Should Gain"*

From this meditation today, I will pray . . .
Adoration _____
_____
_____

Confession _____
_____
_____

Thanksgiving _____
_____
_____

Supplication _____
_____
_____

From this meditation today, I will . . .
Think _____
_____
_____

Say _____
_____
_____

Do _____
_____
_____
_____

Someone very close to me came to our house one day. "I want God," she said. "Tell me how I can get Him." What a joy to lead her to Jesus! "Now," she said, "I must do something for God."

Because I knew Jean so well, I knew she had a great guilt, and she was feeling she must sacrifice something for God, to somehow atone for her past. So, looking her straight in the eye, I said, "When Jesus died on the cross, He wiped your slate clean. There is nothing left to pay, you know." The relief and joy showed in her eyes.

It's true. Consider the ancient Israelites, for example, who had so often been grumblers and idolaters in their relationship with God. Yet God pronounced His blessing on these constantly rebelling people and put His name on them. The Lord intended only good for them. Therefore, ever so patiently, by His infinite mercy, He redeemed and blessed them.

The enemies of God run before His angry face. But when He looks upon His people, we see only His shining countenance, the face of love and grace.

Gracious Father in Heaven, *I come to You, not fearing any condemnation for my past failings. I come in the name of Your beloved Son, who always sees Your face; in Him I am blessed. Thank You, in His name. Amen.*

SPOTLIGHT
Next Week's Lesson

The glow of goodness and grace—is it radiating from your face?

May 10

The Results: Up to Him

We are God's workmanship, created in Christ Jesus to do good works, which God prepared in advance for us to do
(Ephesians 2:10).

Patricia St. John looked back on her life. "With so little to show for it, what had the years really achieved?" she wondered. Let's look . . .

She trained as a nurse and cared for the many wounded and shattered people of London during wartime bombings. Later, she went to Africa with her brother, helping him at a Christian hospital in a Muslim land. Seeing the need, she went to live alone in a hill town to care for the sick and preach Jesus in word and deed to the poor. After some years she was forced to move, but not before some found the Savior and willingly suffered for their faith.

She wrote favorite children's books, which still bless many children (including mine). She researched and wrote a book about revival in Rwanda; helped care for her brother's children and the little persecuted Christian community; nursed her mother in old age; helped her sister in war-torn Lebanon; blessed children everywhere.

Achieved? She had only taken up what came to hand. That is all we can do—take the steps prepared in advance for us. God will assess the results.

I thank You, **Father,** *that You have work prepared for me to do. I take up what comes to my hand—and I do it with joy. In Christ I pray. Amen.*

SEARCH THE WORD
God provides possibility; His children must provide product.

Scripture: Ephesians 2:1-10
Song: *"I Want to Serve the Purpose of God"*

From this meditation today, I will pray . . .

Adoration _____

Confession _____

Thanksgiving _____

Supplication _____

From this meditation today, I will . . .

Think _____

Say _____

Do _____

May 11

Shadow Creatures

He reveals the deep things of darkness and brings deep shadows into the light (Job 12:22).

Scripture: Job 12:13-25
Song: "The Light of the World Is Jesus"

From this meditation today, I will pray...
Adoration _____
_____
_____

Confession _____
_____
_____

Thanksgiving _____
_____
_____

Supplication _____
_____
_____

From this meditation today, I will...
Think _____
_____
_____

Say _____
_____
_____

Do _____
_____
_____

An almost cartoonish image presents itself in this verse. We can imagine a hideous, snaggletoothed shadow creature—long operating under the happy delusion that it wields an unbeatable power—suddenly yanked from the shadows and forced into the blinding light of God. The creature, assumed to be an unstoppable power, has no choice but to kneel beneath the far mightier authority.

The believer looks around at this world and observes with sadness many wicked people flaunting their immoralities. Like the soldiers who crucified Jesus, they spit in the face of God. And it wounds those of us who love Him. However, it might help us to have compassion if we remember that these shadow creatures lurk behind every sinning person. They perform their awful ministry from the secrecy of deep shadow.

We can chase away some of the shadows of our world with our small lights. But we know that one day the great light will come; it will permanently disable every creature of shadow.

Light of the world, *living in this shadowy place is difficult! I long for the day when Your beauty illuminates the universe. In Jesus' name, amen.*

May 11-17. **Rhonda Brunea** *lives in a tiny town in New York state with her kids and her Lord. She is encouraged by recalling that she has family everywhere*

SPOTLIGHT
Next Week's Lesson

Ephesians 3 might be titled "Paul and the Mystery of God," but God's plan is no longer hidden.

May 12

Secret Society

Blessed are your eyes because they see, and your ears because they hear (Matthew 13:16).

Christians are members of the ultimate secret society. Nothing sinister, just secret. Some of us are blessed to live in countries where we may openly profess our belief in Christ. Even with this freedom, our unbelieving neighbors often won't have a clue what we're talking about. We simply see things with different eyes than those who see only with their natural eyes. We are perceived as simple-minded and odd, at best. Being misunderstood can grow burdensome.

From time to time, we recognize one of our own as we pass through the ordinary hours of our days. We clasp hands and smile. We confess, "I'm a believer too." And for a moment we recall with relief that there are others like us, those who see what we see and hear what we hear.

Actually, there are brothers and sisters everywhere, in every imaginable guise. They too are listening for God's voice, peering intently into the things of the Spirit and then carrying them out into a largely blind and deaf society to give away. How blessed to be a member of this secret society!

Dear Lord, help me to remember that I'm part of a beautiful family of believers who love You as I do. Many more would love You if they only knew You. Give me courage to speak up! In the name of Christ, amen.

SEARCH THE WORD

Blessed eyes help the blind see; blessed ears help the deaf hear.

Scripture: Matthew 13:10-17
Song: *"Open My Eyes, Lord"*

From this meditation today, I will pray...

Adoration _____

Confession _____

Thanksgiving _____

Supplication _____

From this meditation today, I will...

Think _____

Say _____

Do _____

May 13

Behind the Veil

No wise man, enchanter, magician or diviner can explain to the king the mystery he has asked about, but there is a God in heaven who reveals mysteries (Daniel 2:27, 28).

Scripture: Daniel 2:25-30
Song: *"Be Thou My Vision"*

From this meditation today, I will pray . . .
Adoration _____
_____
_____

Confession _____
_____
_____

Thanksgiving _____
_____
_____

Supplication _____
_____
_____

From this meditation today, I will . . .
Think _____
_____
_____

Say _____
_____
_____

Do _____
_____
_____
_____

Maria wants nothing more in the world than to train her children in godliness. She wants to protect them from the deceit of the world. But cruel circumstances constantly intervene to make her good intentions impossible. So she watches helplessly as her beloved children slip farther and farther from God. Her agonized prayer comes through in one word: *"Why?"*

Why? So much we don't know! God has veiled His universe in mystery. When it serves His purposes, He lifts the edge of the veil ever so slightly, revealing a bit of the secret. As when a magician reveals a trick, the child of God experiences a moment of delighted "Aha." Then comes the relief of understanding—and finally the question, "Why didn't I see that before?"

We aren't allowed to observe much that transpires behind the veil separating us from Heaven. Thus our ignorance gives rise to painful questions. But perhaps there is a more helpful response than questioning God: trust. For her part, Maria has determined to wait with a patient heart . . . until she is given a peek behind the veil.

O God, *so often I'm confused, and sometimes I just have to weep. Yet I will trust in the one who holds the key to all mysteries. In Jesus' name, amen.*

SPOTLIGHT
Next Week's Lesson
Isaiah knew it would come: "The glory of the Lord will be revealed, and all mankind together will see it" (Isaiah 40:5).

May 14

Teamwork

Surely the Sovereign Lord *does nothing without revealing his plan to his servants the prophets* (Amos 3:7).

The owner of the store gathers her employees for a meeting. "This," she says, "is what I plan to do." She gives her workers an overview of what she intends to accomplish. Then she assigns specific tasks to each person. Her team waits, listening, ready to do all that their employer requires.

They want to please their superior, and so they listen carefully, fully intending to follow her plan. She, in turn, realizes that her workers need certain information in order to function best in their positions. While she may not reveal every detail of her grand plan, she will let them in on all they need to know.

Similarly, God honors His "team" by trusting us to help Him carry out His work in the world. As someone has said, "We are the only hands and feet that Jesus has on earth until He comes again." Our part is to listen carefully for His plan to be revealed, since to obey we must first hear the orders.

Let us give plenty of time to listening, then. What is the Spirit of God revealing to His workers today? What does the master require of His team?

Master, *You have a plan, and nothing will thwart it. What would You say to me? Your servant is listening. Through Christ I pray. Amen.*

SEARCH THE WORD
Want to know God's plan? Give careful attention to His revelation. It's there.

Scripture: Amos 3:1-8
Song: *"It Is No Secret"*

From this meditation today, I will pray . . .
Adoration _____

Confession _____

Thanksgiving _____

Supplication _____

From this meditation today, I will . . .
Think _____

Say _____

Do _____

May 15

Childlike Wisdom

I praise you, Father, Lord of heaven and earth, because you have hidden these things from the wise and learned, and revealed them to little children (Matthew 11:25).

Scripture: Matthew 11:25-30
Song: *"I Know Whom I Have Believed"*

From this meditation today, I will pray...
Adoration _____

Confession _____

Thanksgiving _____

Supplication _____

From this meditation today, I will...
Think _____

Say _____

Do _____

A small boy clambers onto the lap of his grandfather with no hesitation or embarrassment. He turns wide eyes to the beloved face, waiting for one of the old man's amazing stories. The boy's heart is ready to accept whatever Grandpa says. He reposes in the complete comfort born of long trust. In this attitude of heart and mind, he sees miracles and wonders everywhere.

A young man returns from the university. He has learned to filter everything through his critical thinking skills. He stands stiffly before his grandfather and shakes his hand. Grandfather's stories meet a knowing smile and a skeptical lift of one brow. He loves his grandpa, but the older man has diminished in his eyes. The young man has learned to doubt and question everything.

The grandfather has much wisdom to offer his grandson. But he is wise enough to know that he must wait for the boy to grow up a little more before he will hear. One day he will regain his childlike wisdom, and then he will again see invisible wonders.

Father, *sometimes I think too much! I know You don't expect me to take everything in blind faith, but there are some things that must be believed to be seen. Help me to cultivate a childlike heart. In Jesus' name, amen.*

SPOTLIGHT
Next Week's Lesson

Children play Hide 'n Seek, but the wise and learned must seek God's hidden thing, the gospel.

May 16

The King's Guard

Men ought to regard us as servants of Christ and as those entrusted with the secret things of God (1 Corinthians 4:1).

A wise king needed servants to guard his most precious and secret treasures. "They must be strong," the king said to his counselors. "Unintimidated by the enemy, stalwart in the face of discouragement and fear, and willing to do all that I command."

"Then the applicants must be dreadfully serious?" asked one.

"Oh, not at all," replied the king. "I could not trust one who had no joy. No, I want those who know when to laugh—and laugh well, at that."

"So you desire those who are popular in the taverns?"

"Certainly not! They must be sober of mind—friendly, and yet able to hold close the secrets with which I will entrust them. They must be honest, self-controlled, skilled in arms, and protective of the lowly."

"Oh, king," said an elder counselor, trembling. "I fear that we may not find such servants."

"I say that you will. I have summoned them, you see, men and women of noble character to guard the secret things of the kingdom. I am drawing them to myself, and they will come."

My King, I am humbled and honored that You have entrusted me with the precious secrets of the soul. Thanks to You, through Christ! Amen.

SEARCH THE WORD

Trusted with the secrets of God—what a privilege we share!

Scripture: 1 Corinthians 4:1-5
Song: *"Why Me, Lord?"*

From this meditation today, I will pray . . .

Adoration _____

Confession _____

Thanksgiving _____

Supplication _____

From this meditation today, I will . . .

Think _____

Say _____

Do _____

May 17

The Best Revenge

His intent was that now, through the church, the manifold wisdom of God should be made known to the rulers and authorities in the heavenly realms (Ephesians 3:10).

Scripture: Ephesians 3:1-13
Song: *"All My Hope on God Is Founded"*

From this meditation today, I will pray . . .

Adoration _____
_____
_____

Confession _____
_____
_____

Thanksgiving _____
_____
_____

Supplication _____
_____
_____

From this meditation today, I will . . .

Think _____
_____
_____

Say _____
_____
_____

Do _____
_____
_____
_____

"I know. Hank will be sorry when he sees me living it up."

"That's not what I meant, Carol. I mean living really well, God's way—forgiving the one who hurt you, praying for him and moving on with your life, with all that you're meant to be here on planet Earth."

"Oh, I know I'm supposed to do all that, but how can I? After the way he betrayed me? Forget it."

"OK," Linda replied quietly. "Then Satan wins."

"What?"

"Either you can let the enemy stomp all over you and make you bitter—useless as a warrior of God—or you can stand up and kick him in the face. You can choose God's way and prove to the enemy what a loser he is."

Carol sipped her coffee. "Well," she finally laughed, "I guess maybe it is time I helped God to prove His point. I'll live so well, I'll make that nasty Satan sorry he ever got in my face."

"That's my little warrior.

"O God, *sometimes Your way doesn't seem very satisfying. I'd like to exact a little sweet revenge. Help me choose Your way, instead, against those other dubious "rulers and authorities." In the name of Christ my Lord, amen.*

SPOTLIGHT
Next Week's Lesson

The church's task?
Making known the manifold
wisdom of God—it's that simple!

May 18

Drifting from Doctrine?

As for you, speak the things which are proper for sound doctrine
(Titus 2:1, *New King James Version*).

As I lay in the rowboat, the sun was warm, the breeze cool, and the clouds drifted along like passing friends. Nothing much was happening, except a gentle rocking. I didn't notice a slow, steady drift to deeper water, along with an ever-growing wind . . .

Some years ago the press attacked former Vice President Dan Quayle, for stating that, all else being equal, it was better for children to be raised by two parents rather than just one. Yes, there are great single parents. But wasn't Quayle right? After all, the role of father and mother was God's idea from the beginning.

My point: Previous generations would have labeled Quayle wholesome and wise, but the popular view has drifted far from such traditional perspectives. Have we in the church drifted too? Maybe we haven't noticed! Maybe we haven't looked out from our small boat as we warm ourselves in the sun. God hasn't changed. But how much have we sought to change Him?

Father, *don't let us get too comfortable in our boat. And please keep us from merely drifting with the current of the world. Help us be strong, even in the face of constant peer pressure. In the name of Christ I pray. Amen.*

Scripture: Titus 2:1-13
Song: *"Blow the Trumpet in Zion"*

From this meditation today, I will pray . . .

Adoration _____

Confession _____

Thanksgiving _____

Supplication _____

From this meditation today, I will . . .

Think _____

Say _____

Do _____

SEARCH THE WORD

Doctrinal shift is worse than tectonic shift. Earthquakes and disaster loom.

May 18–24. **Daniel Varnell** *is a scientist living in Delaware with his wife and three daughters. He serves God and the local church as a teacher and author.*

May 19

The Goodness of Togetherness

*It is not good that man should be alone;
I will make him a helper comparable to him*
(Genesis 2:18, *New King James Version*).

Scripture: Genesis 2:18-25
Song: *"In the Garden"*

From this meditation today, I will pray...
Adoration _____
_____
_____

Confession _____
_____
_____

Thanksgiving _____
_____
_____

Supplication _____
_____
_____

From this meditation today, I will...
Think _____
_____
_____

Say _____
_____
_____

Do _____
_____
_____
_____

My dad's side of my family amazes me. Not one divorce can be found in my generation nor the next generation—and none in any previous generation.

Something else unusual about Dad's family: the amount of time spent *as* family. My parents wouldn't even go to a wedding unless children were included. I remember Dad and Mom—together—bringing my brother and me to music lessons. While my brother was being instructed, Dad would walk with me, maybe get a candy bar, or sit in the car with me.

God formed Eve so she and Adam could be together. And *together* they were to "be fruitful and increase in number; fill the earth," (Genesis 1:28). A woman came from a man and they, together, were complete.

Why no divorces in my dad's family? Spouses taking time together, with the children watching. What better way is there?

Dear Father in Heaven, *my heart melts as I contemplate the glories of Your grace. I am amazed at Your desire for fellowship with human beings and Your call to us to form community among ourselves. Thank You for the goodness of togetherness! If some are away from family today, I pray for holy bridges over the distance. In the name of Jesus, amen.*

SPOTLIGHT
Next Week's Lesson

From the beginning God's plan for the family remains: mutual love, mutual submission.

May 20

In the House

That you shall say, "It is the Passover sacrifice of the Lord, who passed over the houses of the children of Israel in Egypt when He struck the Egyptians and delivered our households"
(Exodus 12:27, *New King James Version*).

Twelve-year-old Ruth Becker recalled the terrible night. She watched as an officer grabbed her sister, another grabbed her brother. They placed them in a lifeboat. Her mother screamed, and they let her on, then they were gone. Moments later, Ruth was thrust into Lifeboat #13—and soon the mighty ship *Titanic* sunk beneath the sea.

Ruth's household was divided during that tragedy. But have you noticed in Scripture how God so often saves *by household*? In Egypt, God saved the people of Israel by household. In a boat, God saved Noah's household. Angels went to Lot's household and saved them.

The jailor of Paul and Silas—and the jailor's whole household—came to Christ. At Peter's preaching, God saved the household of Cornelius.

Ruth Becker and her family survived and were eventually reunited. They were a household again and could testify to salvation from ice-cold waves. We too can be households like that. Saved from sin, our whole families can point to the goodness and grace of God.

Father, *show each of us where we can be in a godly family that we might together experience Your mercy and serve You.*

Scripture: Exodus 12:21-28
Song: *"You Are My Hiding Place"*

From this meditation today, I will pray . . .
Adoration _____

Confession _____

Thanksgiving _____

Supplication _____

From this meditation today, I will . . .
Think _____

Say _____

Do _____

SEARCH THE WORD

The house where God lives, lives also a blessed family.

May 21

Let Us Learn!

*Prize [wisdom] highly, and she will exalt you;
she will honor you if you embrace her*
(Proverbs 4:8, *Revised Standard Version*).

Scripture: Proverbs 4:1-9

Song: *"My Soul Follows Hard After Thee"*

From this meditation today, I will pray . . .

Adoration _____

_____

_____

Confession _____

_____

_____

Thanksgiving _____

_____

_____

Supplication _____

_____

_____

From this meditation today, I will . . .

Think _____

_____

_____

Say _____

_____

_____

Do _____

_____

_____

_____

My neighbor, one of the greatest men I've known, passed away a few weeks ago. He fought battles in North Africa, survived a concentration camp in Siberia, and even worked on the Apollo space program. My girls adopted him as a grandfather.

He was passionate about freedom. Having been denied it, he knew its value. He also spoke often about being raised in Poland. In the school system there, if he and his friends didn't apply themselves and learn their lessons, then their parents would have to pay for their schooling. So they had extra incentive to study, to give serious attention to gaining understanding and wisdom.

In today's Scripture, God gives us plenty of incentive to embrace the instruction of a father, to retain the lessons taught us, and to find wisdom in it all. If we do these things, then we will be promoted and honored.

My neighbor found knowledge and wisdom through the lessons taught in his youth and through Jesus Christ. Our heavenly Father brings us lessons in many ways, even amidst the ordinary situations we'll face today. Therefore, let us learn.

God, *in prayer, in the Word, and in all things You bring me lessons I need. Give me a heart always ready to learn from You. Through Christ, amen.*

SPOTLIGHT
Next Week's Lesson

The successful family is filled with the wisdom of God.

May 22

In . . . In . . . In . . .

Let the word of Christ dwell in you richly in all wisdom, teaching and admonishing one another in psalms and hymns and spiritual songs, singing with grace in your hearts to the Lord (Colossians 3:16, *New King James Version*).

As the couple embraced, tears streamed down the faces of the Mayan pastor and his wife. They were on a marriage retreat and, for the first time, the pastor saw his wife as a partner in ministry. For the first time she felt included.

A key word in the book of Colossians is "in." Paul wrote to the saints in Colossae, who had hope *in* Heaven, which they learned about *in* the Word, which was told them *in* truth, *in* wisdom, and *in* good works. With Christ dwelling *in* them, they were called *in*to one body to admonish each other *in* psalms, *in* hymns, *in* spiritual songs, with grace *in* their hearts. They were *in* ministry with each other, with Paul and with God.

Look around: with whom are you *in* this Christian journey? You may be overlooking a great partner or your own family. What affects one, affects another—and the whole body of Christ. We are all *in* Christ, members of His body together.

Father, *how wonderful to walk with You and my brothers and sisters in Christ. Open my eyes to my partners in Your work. Help me always to walk in loving, respectful relationships with them. In Jesus' name, amen.*

SEARCH THE WORD

Which is better: to be in or out, as far as Christ is concerned?

Scripture: Colossians 3:12-24
Song: *"In Him We Live and Move and Have Our Being"*

From this meditation today, I will pray . . .

Adoration _____
_____
_____

Confession _____
_____
_____

Thanksgiving _____
_____
_____

Supplication _____
_____
_____

From this meditation today, I will . . .

Think _____
_____
_____

Say _____
_____
_____

Do _____
_____
_____

May 23

Don't Be a Cowbird

If anyone does not provide for his own, and especially for those of his household, he has denied the faith and is worse than an unbeliever (1 Timothy 5:8, *New King James Version*).

Scripture: 1 Timothy 5:1-8
Song: *"Servant of God, Remember"*

From this meditation today, I will pray . . .
Adoration _____
_____
_____

Confession _____
_____
_____

Thanksgiving _____
_____
_____

Supplication _____
_____
_____

From this meditation today, I will . . .
Think _____
_____
_____

Say _____
_____
_____

Do _____
_____
_____
_____

Do you know about cowbirds? They will remove an egg from another bird's nest and destroy it. They lay their own egg in its place and abandon it to the owner of the nest. Sometimes their egg is rejected.

The proper name of the cowbird is *Molothrus ater*. Molothrus refers to a vagabond or parasite—one who surely fails to provide for others.

Paul's instructions to Timothy were sometimes meant to exhort or encourage. But in today's Scripture, Paul simply commands. Sometimes God's Word is candid and direct, because sometimes we need strong medicine. I don't want to be compared to a bird that acts like a parasite. And I certainly don't want to be considered worse than one who denies my Lord Jesus. Therefore, I must provide for others, especially those in the church.

These harsh words point us in the right direction, because they come from one who loves us deeply. He calls us to love others in return. So . . . who should I help today and tomorrow, and how?

Father, *let my thoughts and ways be open to Your correction. Pick me up, gently, and point me in the right direction. Help me to be a blessing to someone this day. In the name of Your Son, my Savior, I pray. Amen.*

SPOTLIGHT
Next Week's Lesson

At the heart of love
is providing for, providing
all good things to the one loved.

May 24

Together Forever

This is a great mystery, but I speak concerning Christ and the church (Ephesians 5:32, *New King James Version*).

At church a woman confided to me that she didn't feel close to God and didn't think God loved her. I was saddened by her sadness. She seemed to walk with one foot in the world and one in church. And she found no joy.

Our Scripture readings this week have highlighted family. Look now at the great picture God lays out for us. Marriage shows how the living church should relate to Christ. Love, covenant, communication, purpose, preparation—all these go into a marriage and a home. Do you feel close to Christ? (You should feel like His bride.)

God had one grand purpose in creating humankind. It wasn't to subdue the earth (that came later); it wasn't to fight back against Satan. No, it was to create a people who would spend time—and eternity—*with* Him. All things, from evangelism to worship, are part of this plan.

With His disciples listening, Jesus closed His earthly ministry before the cross with these words: "Father, I desire that they also whom You gave Me may be with Me where I am" (John 17:24, *NKJV*). He wants to be close to us, forever. Know it. Feel it, right now.

Father, *may I see my life from Your perspective. You made me so You could be with me in Heaven, forever. I take a moment now to bask in that amazing truth. How You love me! How I love You! Through Christ, amen.*

SEARCH THE WORD
In purpose, in commitment, in joy—who is closer than bride and groom? And who is closer that Christ and His bride?

Scripture: Ephesians 5:21–6:4
Song: *"Draw Me Close"*

From this meditation today, I will pray . . .
Adoration _____

Confession _____

Thanksgiving _____

Supplication _____

From this meditation today, I will . . .
Think _____

Say _____

Do _____

May 25

Running to the Source

*Guide me in your truth and teach me,
for you are God my Savior, and my hope is in you all day long*
(Psalm 25:5).

Scripture: Psalm 25:1-5

Song: *"Guide Me, O Thou Great Jehovah"*

From this meditation today, I will pray . . .

Adoration _____

Confession _____

Thanksgiving _____

Supplication _____

From this meditation today, I will . . .

Think _____

Say _____

Do _____

When my children were young, I often overheard something like this:

"Is *not!*"
"Is *too!*"
"Is *not!*"
"Is *too!*"

These debates usually ended with the children running to me to settle the dispute. They wanted an ultimate answer. My response? "Yes, it's brother's turn to go first."

But sometimes their discussions would concern serious matters, like "Why are there street people?" I didn't always have answers for such harder questions, but I pointed them to the one who did. We would read His Word, pray, and talk about what actions we could take to best please our Lord.

We children of God sometimes foolishly debate questions without running to our heavenly Father for the ultimate truth. Why is this? Don't we value His truth?

Father, *give me the confidence of a child in looking to You to provide insight and direction amidst each situation today. In Jesus' name, amen.*

SPOTLIGHT
Next Week's Lesson

There is a war in progress. War demands preparation and armaments. Are you ready?

May 25-31. **Shelley Houston** *is a freelance writer living in Eugene, Oregon, with her husband of 37 years and her extended family.*

May 26

He Will Lift You Up

*When pride comes, then comes disgrace,
but with humility comes wisdom*
(Proverbs 11:2).

I resigned my job and was cleaning out my desk when my secretary came into my office. "You'll be able to find another job so easily with this position on your resumé," she said. I kindly dismissed her words, but secretly thought she was right.

In the following months, wearing my executive wardrobe, I carried a powerful resumé in my leather briefcase . . . to interview after interview. Two years later, I gave up, feeling like a failure.

Then, for weeks, I cried out to God. (One day I even scared off a salesman coming to the door as I wailed in anguish.) My agony left me broken, like a wild horse finally submitting to its master. Humbled, I finally gave over to God's leading.

And God opened a new career for me: writing. This was my heart's dream, but one I never thought I could afford to pursue. I'm paid little for such offerings and gain less in esteem. But God provides for me and the family as He always has. When we walk in humility, we can experience God leading us to our heart's desire.

Lord, *thank You for loving me so much that You are unwilling to let me wallow in self-importance. Your greatest blessings are waiting on the sidelines. Help me see them more clearly. In Christ's name I pray. Amen.*

Scripture: Proverbs 11:1-10
Song: *"Humble Yourself"*

From this meditation today, I will pray . . .
Adoration _____

Confession _____

Thanksgiving _____

Supplication _____

From this meditation today, I will . . .
Think _____

Say _____

Do _____

SEARCH THE WORD

Pride opens a wide door to disgrace; humility keeps that door closed.

May 27

What's the Good Word?

How beautiful on the mountains are the feet of those who bring good news, who proclaim peace, who bring good tidings, who proclaim salvation, who say to Zion, "Your God reigns!" (Isaiah 52:7).

Scripture: Isaiah 52:7-12
Song: *"Our God Reigns"*

From this meditation today, I will pray...

Adoration _____

Confession _____

Thanksgiving _____

Supplication _____

From this meditation today, I will...

Think _____

Say _____

Do _____

One night, in 1814, Francis Scott Key sat imprisoned on a British ship during an attack on Fort McHenry. Sleepless, he watched the battle, writing notes of his thoughts. Imagine his anxiety as he saw the rockets in the night, fearing not only his own fate but that of his country. As morning broke he strained to see the American flag. Did it still wave over the fort?

Yes! Ecstatic, he penned "The Star Spangled Banner," now America's national anthem, which reflects the good news he received.

What sort of good news are we looking for these days? Every day the battles in our lives raise the question, "Who's winning now?" A wayward child, a broken promise, a lost investment, a life-threatening illness—all can pull us into fearing a chaotic future. But remember this: Jesus Christ already stands as victor. His news is, "Your God reigns!" There is no better news.

Almighty and ever living God, *how glad I am to know of Your victory over all forces that oppose You. I praise You to the highest heavens and in all the earth as my king and Lord, my champion to the end. In the name of the Father, the Son, and the Holy Spirit, I offer my worship. Amen.*

SPOTLIGHT
Next Week's Lesson

The best answer to the question, "Who's winning?" is "Our God reigns!"

May 28

He Is the One Who Keeps

We are not of those who shrink back and are destroyed, but of those who have faith and keep their souls
(Hebrews 10:39, *Revised Standard Version*).

My husband was recalled to active duty for Desert Storm. Our family became instant celebrities in our little city. Many people reached out to us, but some didn't know what to say. They would often mumble, "Keep the faith," even though they did not believe in God themselves.

Ten years later, I listened to a woman who grew up as a pastor's daughter in Latvia while it was under Russian rule. She and her family suffered many torments because of their faith in Christ. She admitted that at times she wanted to give up. But then she'd recall her young father's words on his deathbed: "Your faith in Christ must endure to the end! Then we will meet again." He understood the supreme importance of their faith as the key to their salvation.

Unlike the faith that was suggested to me—to keep a contrived "faith" in *general*—the Latvian pastor and his family placed their trust in a *person*: the Lord Jesus Christ. May we keep our faith in the same manner, knowing that He is actually the one who keeps us.

Lord God, let me never be ashamed of the way I walk with You, serve You, and continue to believe in You for all things. Help me to keep the faith as You keep holding me in Your mighty arms. In Jesus' name, amen.

Scripture: Hebrews 10:35–11:3
Song: *"Faith in Jesus"*

From this meditation today, I will pray . . .
Adoration _____
_____
_____

Confession _____
_____
_____

Thanksgiving _____
_____
_____

Supplication _____
_____
_____

From this meditation today, I will . . .
Think _____
_____
_____

Say _____
_____
_____

Do _____
_____
_____
_____

SEARCH THE WORD

*"Keeping the faith"
or "living in faith"—
that's my choice.*

May 29

What to Say?

Give thanks to the LORD, *call on his name; make known among the nations what he has done, and proclaim that his name is exalted* (Isaiah 12:4).

Scripture: Isaiah 12:1-6
Song: *"Great Is the Lord"*

From this meditation today, I will pray . . .
Adoration _____
_____
_____

Confession _____
_____
_____

Thanksgiving _____
_____
_____

Supplication _____
_____
_____

From this meditation today, I will . . .
Think _____
_____
_____

Say _____
_____
_____

Do _____
_____
_____
_____

Early this morning I looked out on towering mountains covered with new snow and capped in billowing robes of pinkish clouds. *God's majesty*! I wondered that anyone seeing such wonders could think anything less. And the sad thought came to me: If people see but don't recognize such wonders as the work of a creator's hand, what effect can my simple words of witness have?

Later in the day I heard an international news account of atrocities committed for political gain. As I sat gaping at the television, I realized what the people of the world need to hear. They can see the beauty of the world, it's true. But they experience it tinged with the horror of human sin. Any of us could become deeply convinced pessimists amidst such horrors—if we hadn't come to see the "big picture" of God's redeeming plan. Some day He will put all things right: "The creation itself will be liberated from its bondage to decay" (Romans 8:21). In the meantime, we give thanks for glimpses of His glory, wherever and whenever they come to us. That's what the people need to know, and that's what I can tell them.

Creator and Redeemer, *loosen my tongue and help me proclaim Your perfection in beauty, justice, and holiness. In Christ's name I pray. Amen.*

SPOTLIGHT
Next Week's Lesson

Will you "fearlessly make known the mystery of the gospel"?
(Ephesians 6:19).

May 30

Memorizing the Map

Though I constantly take my life in my hands, I will not forget your law (Psalm 119:109).

In planning to attend a concert in a city about 50 miles from home, I pulled up a map on the Internet. The city had a complicated downtown with many one-way streets. So I studied the route before I got in my car, and then tucked the map into the glove compartment.

When I left, I thought I had plenty of time to get to the concert. But when I entered the downtown area I immediately became disoriented. I couldn't remember the names of neighboring streets—and that valuable map just wasn't within arm's reach. Soon I was driving in circles.

I finally pulled over and got out the map—which led me straight to the concert. (Late, of course!)

How often do I do the same with God's Word, the "life map" He's given me? Oh, I study the Word, but then I tuck it away, sometimes for days. I set out to live life as I think I remember Him directing, only to find myself straying from the pathway of peace and joy.

What great reasons we have for hiding His Word in our hearts! Not only does God promise to guide our footsteps; He promises sweet companionship along the way.

Dear Heavenly Father, *pull me to your Word daily, that I might know the blessed fellowship of Your presence. How I need Your constant wisdom and encouragement! I pray through Christ my Lord. Amen.*

SEARCH THE WORD

If I study God's Word, the lamp to my feet, I can see where I'm going.

Scripture: Psalm 119:105-112
Song: *"Thy Word Is a Lamp Unto My Feet"*

From this meditation today, I will pray . . .
Adoration _____
Confession _____
Thanksgiving _____
Supplication _____

From this meditation today, I will . . .
Think _____
Say _____
Do _____

May 31

Endless and Powerful Prayer

Pray in the Spirit on all occasions with all kinds of prayers and requests. With this in mind, be alert and always keep on praying for all the saints (Ephesians 6:18).

Scripture: Ephesians 6:10-18
Song: *"Soldiers of Christ, Arise!"*

From this meditation today, I will pray . . .

Adoration _____

Confession _____

Thanksgiving _____

Supplication _____

From this meditation today, I will . . .

Think _____

Say _____

Do _____

Dreams are strange, aren't they? Sometimes they're just the result of a too-spicy dinner or a day filled with unresolved problems. But I think God occasionally speaks to me in my dreams. Here's an example: I walked down a hall with many doors on each side. As I walked, something appeared in the distance. A large mattress rolled into a tight bundle filled the entire hall! I couldn't pass, and yet, I must. I ran hard, jumped and dove into the middle of the roll. I pushed and kicked, seeking to worm my way through. But I could not.

Silent darkness came, and then I again walked the same hall and approached the same mattress. "How can I do this, Lord?" I asked. "I tried my best before." Then, as I walked, the mattress dissolved around me. It seemed that God was ready to do battle for me—I only had to ask.

Our text says, "Be alert!" When we arm ourselves for spiritual battle, then proceed without prayer, we walk in our own strength. But God wants to unleash His omnipotence. What better reason to pray in His Spirit?

Dear Lord, *I am weak, but You are strong. How can I conquer the impossible before me, except by Your power and grace? Go before me, Lord, and make my path straight. In Jesus' name, amen.*

SPOTLIGHT
Next Week's Lesson

The soldiers of Christ need my prayers, and I need theirs.

June

CALLED OUT OF EGYPT

Encourage one another daily.
—Hebrews 3:13

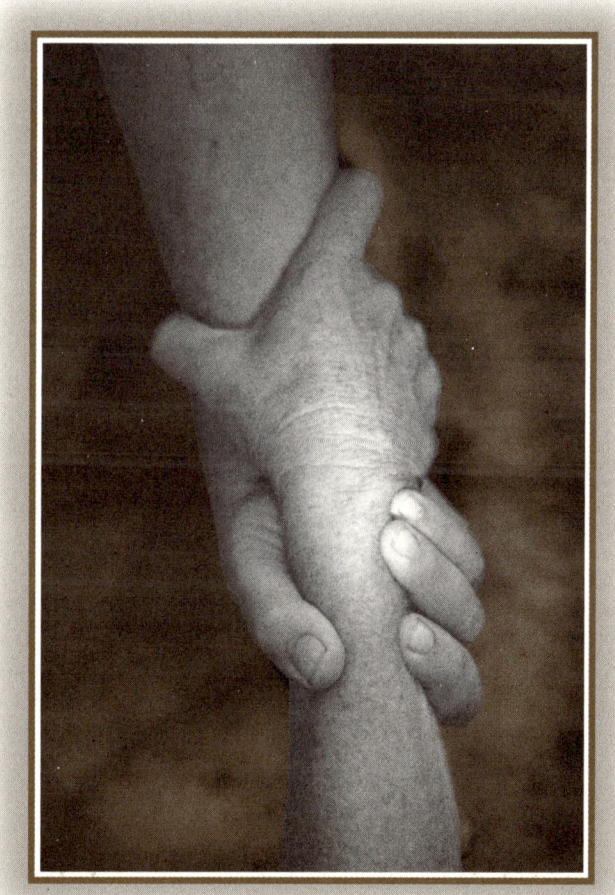

Photo © iStock

June 1

Enjoy Each Time

His sister stood at a distance to see what would happen (Exodus 2:4).

Scripture: Exodus 2:1-10
Song: *"Thy Will Be Done"*

From this meditation today, I will pray...

Adoration _____

Confession _____

Thanksgiving _____

Supplication _____

From this meditation today, I will...

Think _____

Say _____

Do _____

June 1-7. **Donna Clark Goodrich**, *of Mesa, Arizona, is a freelance writer and instructor at Christian writers seminars.*

In his late 30s, our son-in-law felt a call to preach, so he went to school to get his theological education. Thrilled with this turn of events in his family's life, I prayed for God's will, adding a P.S. to my prayer—that God would open up a church nearby.

Shortly before his graduation, he received an invitation to submit his profile . . . to a church in Oklahoma, over a thousand miles away. "No, Lord," I wept. "I can't bear for them to move that far away. When will I ever see our two granddaughters?"

I prayed often that week and was finally able to put this beloved family in God's hands. Then I wrote and told them that, just as I gave our daughter to the Lord when she was born, I was giving her back to Him. I would rejoice with them, no matter where God led.

Moses' mother gave up her son, for a time, and then was allowed to raise him, for a time. Let us be ready to rejoice amid each blessed "time" God gives us.

Lord, *help me to enjoy every moment with my family. I pray for Your perfect will for each one—no matter what the sacrifice may be for me. Then let me stand at a distance to see what blessings will occur! In Christ, amen.*

SPOTLIGHT
Next Week's Lesson

At 80, Moses knew age was no excuse for refusing God's call.

June 2

Is Someone Watching?

Moses was afraid and thought, "What I did must have become known" (Exodus 2:14).

Whenever one of our children did something wrong, I could always detect the guilty party. No, I didn't have eyes in the back of my head (as they sometimes thought). But as soon as I asked who was at fault, our youngest—if guilty—would immediately begin to cry. Our middle child would say, "I have to go to the bathroom," or our eldest would take off running, his hands covering his back end.

Moses glanced "this way and that and seeing no one, he killed the Egyptian and hid him in the sand" (Exodus 2:12). He thought he was safe, but later a Hebrew man asked him, "Are you thinking of killing me as you killed the Egyptian?" (v. 14). *Someone saw!*

My mother used to tell me, "God sees everything you do and hears everything you say." Lest this thought make you feel paranoid, however, there is also a positive side. When we help someone in need, when we visit a sick friend, when we prepare a meal or encourage someone who is going through a rough time, we may think no one sees. But God does. Nothing we do is hidden from Him.

Father, *remind me today that people are watching what I do and listening to what I say. Let my words and my deeds be acceptable in Your sight. And may people see Your Son, Jesus, in me. Through His name, I pray. Amen.*

SEARCH THE WORD

Our loving Father is in on all our "secrets."

Scripture: Exodus 2:11-22

Song: *"You Cannot Hide from God"*

From this meditation today, I will pray . . .

Adoration _____

Confession _____

Thanksgiving _____

Supplication _____

From this meditation today, I will . . .

Think _____

Say _____

Do _____

June 3

Reward: Here or There

Moses thought that his own people would realize that God was using him to rescue them, but they did not (Acts 7:25).

Scripture: Acts 7:23-29
Song: *"It Pays to Serve Jesus"*

From this meditation today, I will pray . . .
Adoration _____
_____
_____

Confession _____
_____
_____

Thanksgiving _____
_____
_____

Supplication _____
_____
_____

From this meditation today, I will . . .
Think _____
_____
_____

Say _____
_____
_____

Do _____
_____
_____
_____

I needed a job. My rent was due, and other bills had to be paid. Then a friend told me of an opening where she worked, and I went for an interview. The work sounded interesting, the pay acceptable, but I would have to sell alcohol and also work on Sundays.

I wrestled with the decision, but then I remembered one of my mother's sayings, "If in doubt, leave it out." I turned down the job, feeling I'd done the right thing.

Moses must have felt he was doing right when he killed the Egyptian who mistreated his fellow Israelites. His own people turned against him, however, saying, "Who made you judge and ruler over us?" Moses ended up fleeing to another country.

But what happened in the end? He found forgiveness—found a wife too—fathered two sons, and later led his people out of Egypt. And my situation? The next week I found a job closer to home, with better wages, and I didn't have to compromise my convictions.

I believe this: If you'll do what is right today, God will reward you—if not in this life, then in the next.

God, *today I face many decisions. Help me look beyond material benefits to the peace that comes from doing right. Give me strength to bypass immediate gratification for the promise of eternal reward. Through Christ, amen.*

SPOTLIGHT
Next Week's Lesson

Only God will know
the right time for us to "Go!"

June 4

If God Sends You . . .

I have indeed seen the oppression of my people in Egypt. I have heard their groaning and have come down to set them free. Now come, I will send you back to Egypt (Acts 7:34).

It was a hard decision. I had over two hundred income tax customers, many second generation. But I felt the Lord calling me to give more time to writing (and encouraging other writers). So I sold the business.

A few years later a former customer said, "I wish you were still doing taxes." Driving home, I thought, *Why not? The money is good, and I'd be helping people.* Then it seemed as if the Lord were saying to me, "Why do you want to go back to Egypt?"

Moses wrestled with this kind of decision. He left Egypt because his people were being mistreated. And when he stepped in to help, they railed against him. But now God was telling him to go back. His chosen people were being oppressed, they were groaning, and God was saying, "Go back, Moses." And Moses went.

Thirteen years after selling my tax business, I am preparing about 30 tax returns a year, and it feels right. God has sent struggling people my way, folks who need help with life issues as well as taxes. I realize now it's OK to go back to Egypt . . . *if* God sends you.

Lord, *I know that my ways are not Your ways. Your Word tells me that whatever state I'm in, I should be content. Help! Through Christ, amen.*

Scripture: Acts 7:30-34
Song: *"Far Off I See the Goal"*

From this meditation today, I will pray . . .

Adoration _____

Confession _____

Thanksgiving _____

Supplication _____

From this meditation today, I will . . .

Think _____

Say _____

Do _____

SEARCH THE WORD

What ways are you finding to help the hurting?

June 5

Glad Reunion Day

There on the mountain that you have climbed you will die and be gathered to your people, just as your brother Aaron died on Mount Hor and was gathered to his people (Deuteronomy 32:50).

Scripture: Deuteronomy 32:48-52

Song: *"Heaven Is Here, Where Hymns of Gladness"*

From this meditation today, I will pray . . .

Adoration _____

Confession _____

Thanksgiving _____

Supplication _____

From this meditation today, I will . . .

Think _____

Say _____

Do _____

"They said it'd be any time," my daughter said over the phone. I assured her of our prayers, but when I hung up, I was still concerned for her. She had never been around someone who was dying, and this was her husband's grandmother, whom we all dearly loved.

An hour later came the second call. Grandma Addie was gone, and when we talked to our daughter that evening, I asked her how she had handled it. "Oh, Mom, I'm so glad I was there," she said. "She had a faraway look in her eyes and was nodding and saying, 'Yes, OK, OK.' Then her face lit up, she said, 'Ohhh, yes-s-s-,' and she was gone. It was so beautiful."

When we lose a loved one who has walked with the Lord, Heaven becomes more real to us. This is what God was reminding Moses. Even though there were times when he and his brother Aaron disobeyed God's commandments, at his death he was still considered a "servant of the Lord" (Deuteronomy 34:5). Isn't that how we all would like to be remembered?

Lord of All, *may I so live today that when it's time to join those who have gone before me, I may be considered Your servant. In Jesus' name, amen.*

SPOTLIGHT
Next Week's Lesson

Like Moses may we report for duty and complete our mission.

June 6

Will You Take My Place?

Now Joshua son of Nun was filled with the spirit of wisdom because Moses had laid his hands on him
(Deuteronomy 34:9).

There aren't many people I consider saints, but Claramae Bostwick is one. Not a blood relative, she was known to everyone as "Aunt Clara." My Sunday school teacher when I was a teenager, she also helped plan my wedding ceremony and continued as my friend and mentor for the next 47 years. Now 101 years old, and residing in an assisted living center, her mind is still keen.

She always ends her letters with, "Always live for Him," but one letter that I received a year or so ago really startled me. "You must hang on for when I am gone, Donna. Will you take my place?"

Oh my, take Aunt Clara's place? Who can fill her shoes? A godlier woman I have never met.

Perhaps that's how Joshua felt when he learned he was to be the one to lead the children of Israel into the promised land. Take Moses' place? Fill his shoes? But just as Joshua had the same promises God had given Moses, so I today have the same promises that have sustained Aunt Clara for over a hundred years.

O God, *help me be willing to do the work You have for me, even when it means taking up the ministry of one who has led me. I dedicate my gifts to Your kingdom's service—with no strings attached. In Jesus' name, amen.*

Scripture: Deuteronomy 34
Song: *"Let Thy Mantle Fall on Me"*

From this meditation today, I will pray . . .
Adoration _____

Confession _____

Thanksgiving _____

Supplication _____

From this meditation today, I will . . .
Think _____

Say _____

Do _____

SEARCH THE WORD

When filling someone else's shoes, foot size is less important than heart size.

June 7

Standing on Holy Ground

Moses! Moses! . . . Take off your sandals, for the place where you are standing is holy ground (Exodus 3:4, 5).

Scripture: Exodus 3:1-12
Song: *"Holy Father, Bless Us"*

From this meditation today, I will pray . . .
Adoration _____

Confession _____

Thanksgiving _____

Supplication _____

From this meditation today, I will . . .
Think _____

Say _____

Do _____

Many years ago a lady by the name of Ina Ogdon gave up a brilliant professional career to care for her father, who struggled with a disability. It was difficult for her, one who was accustomed to appearing before thousands, to minister in private to just one person. However, instead of pining away in self-pity, unable to follow her chosen career as a concert singer, she penned the words to the Song, "Brighten the Corner Where You Are."

Moses was a well-educated man, raised as a prince in Pharaoh's palace. But 40 years later he was tending sheep in the desert, a place the Lord told him was holy ground.

Young mother, weary of all the never-ending tasks that fill your day, you're standing on holy ground.

Factory worker, tired of doing the same repetitious routines, hour after hour, you're standing on holy ground.

Retired grandfather or grandmother, wondering if your days of usefulness are over, you're standing on holy ground.

And, as He did with Moses, God is calling you by name today.

Heavenly Father, *the place You've called me to may not be of my choosing. Sometimes it feels like a desert. But if it is where You want me, help me to take off my shoes and bring light to my corner. In Jesus' name, amen.*

SPOTLIGHT
Next Week's Lesson

Just when you least expect it, the ground becomes holy and God calls your name.

June 8

Because I Said So!

God said to Moses, "I AM WHO I am. This is what you are to say to the Israelites: 'I AM has sent me to you'" (Exodus 3:14).

"Because I said so," my parents often responded when I was a young child questioning them about doing what I was told. Instead of giving me a reason, they just repeated that infamous line one more time.

As a child, truth be told, it rather bugged me! Why should I do something simply because I was *told* to? And further, I vowed in my heart never to repeat that dreaded mantra to my own kids.

A few decades later, of course, "Because I said so" came suddenly from my lips! But something strange had occurred. Now I understood those words from a different perspective. As a parent I realized I wasn't telling my children to do something just for the sake of being told to do it. The emphasis was on the "I"! Just like my parents, I now had the authority to declare something be done. And it was for the child's own good.

God gave Moses a directive. And being a perfect parent, He reminded Moses that He had the authority to commission him to the task.

Dear Lord, help me to obey You willingly, knowing that all Your commands have my best interest at heart. In the name of Jesus I pray. Amen.

Scripture: Exodus 3:13-18

Song: *"O How Happy Are They Who the Savior Obey"*

From this meditation today, I will pray...

Adoration _____

Confession _____

Thanksgiving _____

Supplication _____

From this meditation today, I will...

Think _____

Say _____

Do _____

SEARCH THE WORD

"Who says?"
"God says."
"Well, OK then."

June 8–14. **Karen Morerod** lives in Kansas with her family. She enjoys bringing God's Word to life through writing and drama.

June 9

By All Means!

Then the Lord *said to him,
"What is that in your hand?" "A staff," he replied*
(Exodus 4:2).

Scripture: Exodus 4:1-9

Song: *"Leaning on the Everlasting Arms"*

From this meditation today, I will pray . . .

Adoration _____
_____
_____

Confession _____
_____
_____

Thanksgiving _____
_____
_____

Supplication _____
_____
_____

From this meditation today, I will . . .

Think _____
_____
_____

Say _____
_____
_____

Do _____
_____
_____
_____

When teaching Sunday school or telling others about God, wouldn't it be great to have a visual aid like the one given to Moses? Wouldn't it be great, through God's power, to make an inanimate object come to life? Or to call down some great healing power over a disease or a physical infirmity? Surely people would believe in God after seeing that!

But wait a minute. While God can work His will through whomever He chooses, His question raises an important point. God asked Moses, "What is that in your hand?"

Isn't God asking the same of you and me? "Karen, what is in your hand? What are the gifts and talents I've given you? What special circumstances have I placed before you? And how will you use these things for my glory?"

God can use us—all that we are and have—to do wonderful things in His kingdom. Therefore, let us affirm His greatness, give witness to His faithfulness, and bring people before the throne of His mercy—with every means at our disposal.

Lord, *You have blessed me with spiritual gifts to use in advancing Your kingdom and building up Your church. Help me to use these gifts in the most practical ways today for Your glory. In Jesus' name, amen.*

SPOTLIGHT
Next Week's Lesson

Rely on the Lord's resources
to accomplish the Lord's work.

June 10

Just Keep Witnessing

*The L*ORD *said to Moses, "When you return to Egypt, see that you perform before Pharaoh all the wonders I have given you the power to do. But I will harden his heart so that he will not let the people go"* (Exodus 4:21).

Janie and I worked at the same office. We became good friends and talked often of our faith. I soon realized her belief in God was, well, . . . *nonchalant.* She lightheartedly admitted she wasn't too committed to living a God-honoring life. In spite of our differences and my leaving that workplace, we remained close.

Several years after my departure, I sensed God prompting me to talk to Janie about her faith. The urging was persistent, so I called, and we met at a local park one day.

I mustered up some courage and asked: "Janie, what do you think will happen to you when you die?"

"We're all going somewhere, I guess," she said. "But, Karen, I'm not ready to give up certain things in my life right now. So, I guess I'll just take my chances." She has yet to make a firm commitment to living in God's will.

When the Lord asks us to reach out to others, we have no guarantee they'll respond the way we hope they will. But our responsibility is just to be faithful in our witness. God will take control of the results.

Lord, *today I ask for the courage to let Your light shine through me—even if Your presence receives a cool reception. Through Christ I pray. Amen.*

SEARCH THE WORD
Sometimes our success is measured by obedience, not results.

Scripture: Exodus 4:18-23
Song: *"What Are These in Bright Array?"*

From this meditation today, I will pray . . .

Adoration _____

Confession _____

Thanksgiving _____

Supplication _____

From this meditation today, I will . . .

Think _____

Say _____

Do _____

June 11

Forgiven to Forgive

These are the things you are to do: Speak the truth to each other, and render true and sound judgment in your courts
(Zechariah 8:16).

Scripture: Zechariah 8:11-17
Song: *"Gracious God, My Heart Renew"*

From this meditation today, I will pray . . .
Adoration _____
_____
_____

Confession _____
_____
_____

Thanksgiving _____
_____
_____

Supplication _____
_____
_____

From this meditation today, I will . . .
Think _____
_____
_____

Say _____
_____
_____

Do _____
_____
_____
_____

"I'm available if you need help," Kathy said to Denise, who was experiencing all kinds of stress as mother of the bride. Besides the wedding preparations, Denise faced conflict within a close circle of friends over another situation. Sadly, she had already alienated some of those friends with criticism and harsh words.

Kathy phoned to talk to Denise about the situation. But Denise verbally attacked Kathy—and hung up on her! She also asked someone else to take over the wedding tasks that Kathy had agreed to do. A 20-year relationship seemed to have evaporated overnight.

Several weeks passed, and Denise finally called Kathy. While she never said "I'm sorry," Denise seemed apologetic. Kathy paused, wondering how to respond. "Lord, give me the right words," she quickly prayed. Then Kathy knew what she should do: She simply extended grace and forgiveness in order to restore the relationship.

Kathy dealt kindly with her friend because she was so familiar with the undeserved forgiveness of God in her own life. Is it the same for you?

Dear Lord, *Your unmerited favor is the greatest motive for extending grace to others. Help me do it! In Jesus' name I pray. Amen.*

SPOTLIGHT
Next Week's Lesson

Even when we're filled with fear, God forgives and provides.

June 12

No Rejection Here!

I took you from the ends of the earth, from its farthest corners I called you. I said, "You are my servant"; I have chosen you and have not rejected you (Isaiah 41:9).

John felt called to pastoral ministry in his mid 50s. He gave up a successful business and enrolled in seminary. His career change would mean a huge salary cut, but God's call was clear to him. He graduated and began serving a small but thriving congregation.

The church grew and seemed to be doing well. Then, after several years, some discontented members began trying to force their minister to resign. Overhearing some gossip, John heard about the discord. Specific reasons never came forth, but the tragic undercurrents persisted. After a few months, he resigned.

"I was devastated," he said later. "It was the lowest point of my life; it seemed no one wanted me." Yet John did go on to serve another church, enjoying a fruitful ministry there. (Some years later, the first church closed.)

God calls each of us to serve, using whatever gifts He's given us. Often we will run up against opposition and rejection. But let us constantly hold in our hearts these blessed words: "'You are my servant'; I have chosen you and have not rejected you."

Heavenly Father, *I am so privileged to be Your servant. Help me persevere in this calling, no matter the opposition. In Christ's name, amen.*

Scripture: Isaiah 41:8-13
Song: *"The Service of the King"*

From this meditation today, I will pray...

Adoration _____

Confession _____

Thanksgiving _____

Supplication _____

From this meditation today, I will...

Think _____

Say _____

Do _____

SEARCH THE WORD

*We're selected—
not rejected.*

June 13

Information . . . or Wisdom?

Whoever listens to me will live in safety and be at ease, without fear of harm (Proverbs 1:33).

Scripture: Proverbs 1:20-33
Song: *"Step by Step"*

From this meditation today, I will pray . . .
Adoration _____

Confession _____

Thanksgiving _____

Supplication _____

From this meditation today, I will . . .
Think _____

Say _____

Do _____

I'm so amazed at the vast amount of information available on the Internet. Is the expiration date on my eyeglass prescription legally binding? What, exactly, is *roseola*? How many planets are there? Where should I plant my hyacinths? How far is Kansas City from Denver? What's the process of refining silver? Can mold from old pancake mix really kill you? It's all there for me, just a click or two away . . .

There's even a Web site to confirm whether something you've read on the Internet is true or not! With all of this knowledge at our fingertips, should we ever be heard replying, "I don't know"?

Having a vast "storage bin" of facts is helpful, but there is something greater than just possessing information. We must learn to put our information to practical use in God's service. This is what the Bible means by "wisdom." And the truest, most reliable source of wisdom is God's Word. Following God's wisdom makes all the difference in how our lives unfold.

O God, *I know I can choose to immerse myself in Your wisdom each day. Help me to long for Your words and hide them in my heart. Remind me that "listening" to You in this way will make a real difference in all my attitudes and actions. All praise to You, in Christ's name. Amen.*

SPOTLIGHT
Next Week's Lesson

When we say
what God says,
we'll say a mouthful.

June 14

Knocking—with Knocking Knees

Now go; I will help you speak and will teach you what to say (Exodus 4:12).

I knocked at the assigned door. Linda and I were to visit some guests that had attended a recent church service. Mostly we simply wanted to let them know we were glad they'd visited. But we always anticipated a deeper conversation that might give us an opportunity to talk about Christ.

We'd just completed a series of lessons about witnessing to our faith—but we were still nervous. Been there? As I knocked, Linda whispered, "Dear Lord, please don't let them be at home." Her voice shook, and she clenched her hands together. (This wouldn't be our last visit together—or her last desperate prayer for an empty house!)

Looking back, I remember chuckling and teasing her about her fearful prayer. Thankfully, she was lighthearted through her anxiety.

It helps me to remember this: In those nervy situations, God promises us, as he did Moses, that when He sends us out, *He will go with us.* There's no better confidence builder than the great I AM, whether we're talking to Pharaoh or our neighbors.

Lord, You never promised me an anxiety-free existence. But You did promise Your constant presence amid all circumstances. So help me to rely on You when it's time to speak of Your goodness today. In Jesus' name, amen.

SEARCH THE WORD

"There is a friend who sticks closer than a brother" (Proverbs 18:24).

Scripture: Exodus 4:10-16, 27-31
Song: *"Be Bold, Be Strong"*

From this meditation today, I will pray...

Adoration _____

Confession _____

Thanksgiving _____

Supplication _____

From this meditation today, I will...

Think _____

Say _____

Do _____

June 15

Yes, We Can!

Now get to work. You will not be given any straw, yet you must produce your full quota of bricks (Exodus 5:18).

Scripture: Exodus 5:10-21
Song: "Take Your Burden to the Lord and Leave it There"

From this meditation today, I will pray . . .
Adoration _____
_____
_____

Confession _____
_____
_____

Thanksgiving _____
_____
_____

Supplication _____
_____
_____

From this meditation today, I will . . .
Think _____
_____
_____

Say _____
_____
_____

Do _____
_____
_____

On my first teaching job in the mid-1990s, I was charged with teaching kids how to use a computer keyboard. I entered my classroom to find the computer equipment piled in a heap, and no software in sight. For about two weeks, I taught kids how to type on those old machines. We did the best we could, but we fell far short of the mark. My attitude also fell short.

While it's easy for us to judge the Israelites for their harsh attitudes toward Moses and Aaron, suppose we examine our own attitudes amidst our struggles? When did you last encounter one of those seemingly impossible tasks? And how was your frame of mind?

Today I want to encourage all of us to see the opportunities that come packaged within the tough times. It's then that our witness to God's goodness can shine the brightest. It's easy to be a strong believer when everything seems to be going well. But when the quota of bricks is far too big, can we rely on the one who is greater than every man-made obstacle? (Let me hear you, now: "Yes!")

O Lord, thank You for Your help when the load seems impossible. Help me to do all things as if I'm working for You alone. In Jesus' name. Amen.

SPOTLIGHT
Next Week's Lesson

When we do it God's way, shouldn't it all work out? Yes, eventually.

June 15-21. **Von Mitchell,** *a school teacher and coach in Cedaredge, Colorado, is also a freelance writer and songwriter.*

June 16

He Is Sovereign

Ascribe to the L<small>ORD</small> the glory due his name
(Psalm 29:2).

I am amazed and humbled by the absolute sovereignty of God. As I read the psalm about how the voice of the Lord "is powerful" (v. 4), "breaks the cedars" (v. 5), and "strikes with flashes of lightning" (v. 7), I recalled an incident that occurred near our home last week.

You see, my wife and I are blessed to live in a beautiful little Colorado town at the base of the Grand Mesa. Just last week, we observed a fire, ignited by a bolt of lightning, which burned down two houses only a couple miles from where we live.

The name of our town? Cedaredge. We did indeed witness the powerful voice of the Lord strike and break the cedars in our little corner of the world.

Many pay homage to the powerful forces of nature around us, but it is the Lord God who deserves glory as the source of it all. Praise God! The same Almighty Lord who shows up in these spectacular natural displays also "gives strength to his people" and "blesses his people with peace" (v. 11). So I ask myself in this quiet moment: Will I live today as His humble servant?

Heavenly Father, *I come humbly before You and give You glory. You alone are worthy of all honor and praise. Though Your voice "strips the forests bare" (v. 9), yet I know that You love me and care for every concern in my life. Thank you, Sovereign Lord, in the name of Your Son, Jesus. Amen.*

SEARCH THE WORD

May we join our voices with those who cry, "Glory!"

Scripture: Psalm 29
Song: *"King of Glory"*

From this meditation today, I will pray . . .

Adoration _____

Confession _____

Thanksgiving _____

Supplication _____

From this meditation today, I will . . .

Think _____

Say _____

Do _____

June 17

Finding God

If from there you seek the LORD your God, you will find him if you look for him with all your heart and with all your soul (Deuteronomy 4:29).

Scripture: Deuteronomy 4:25-31
Song: *"Jesus My Lord, My God, My All"*

From this meditation today, I will pray . . .
Adoration _____
_____
_____

Confession _____
_____
_____

Thanksgiving _____
_____
_____

Supplication _____
_____
_____

From this meditation today, I will . . .
Think _____
_____
_____

Say _____
_____
_____

Do _____
_____
_____
_____

This Scripture passage is one of my favorites in the Bible. I love it because it's such a clear promise from God: You will find Him, if you sincerely seek Him.

I remember well the days in my life when I was searching for meaning, searching for truth. I am so thankful that God revealed himself to me as I pursued the answer to my heart's longings. Now, as a schoolteacher, I occasionally have the opportunity to share that experience with kids who are doing some serious searching of their own.

I once heard a wonderful preacher named Bryan Jarrett say, "Transparency before God is the highest form of reverence." I had to think about it for awhile, but then the statement really hit home with me. I don't think God is insulted when we have questions or doubts. He's surely not offended when we are honestly searching for the truth—because He *is* the truth. When we search wholeheartedly, we'll eventually find Him. (But don't take my word for it; take Him at His Word.)

Dear Heavenly Father, *thank You for revealing yourself to me when I was searching. I pray today for the kids I've met who are also searching. I pray that You would draw them closer to You each day. I pray this prayer in the name of Jesus, my merciful Savior and Lord. Amen.*

SPOTLIGHT
Next Week's Lesson

To the question,
"O Lord, why?" God replies,
"Now you'll see what I will do."

June 18

Where Would We Be?

*I will restore them because I have compassion on them. They will be as though I had not rejected them, for I am the L*ORD *their God and I will answer them* (Zechariah 10:6).

Where would we be without God's compassion? In Old Testament times we read about how the Israelites messed up before God. Many times I have wondered, "How could they? These people saw the sea part. They beheld the glory of God in a pillar of cloud and fire. Their food rained down from Heaven! How could they ever doubt God and turn away to worship idols?"

Then I think about the miracles I've witnessed, and how I too have drifted from God, more preoccupied with some ball game on TV than in spending time with Him. And I am ashamed. You see, God provides my food. His glory guides me by way of the Bible and the Holy Spirit. I've seen relationships restored that seemed as impossible as crossing the Red Sea on dry ground. And I've seen lives changed in ways that defy explanation except to say, "God did it." How could I ever lose sight of God? I am treacherous without excuse. Are you?

Yet we serve a compassionate God who restores us, just as He did the Israelites. His compassions never fail.

Dear God, please forgive me for ever losing fervor for serving You in light of all You have done in my life. Thank You for the Word and Your precious Holy Spirit. I give You thanks. In Jesus' name. Amen.

Scripture: Zechariah 10:6-12
Song: *"Love Found a Way"*

From this meditation today, I will pray . . .
Adoration _____
_____
_____
Confession _____
_____
_____
Thanksgiving _____
_____
_____
Supplication _____
_____
_____

From this meditation today, I will . . .
Think _____
_____
_____
Say _____
_____
_____
Do _____
_____
_____

SEARCH THE WORD

When I remember my blessings, can I give God less than my best?

June 19

The Real Lion King

He rescued me from my powerful enemy, from my foes, who were too strong for me. They confronted me in the day of my disaster, but the LORD was my support (Psalm 18:17, 18).

Scripture: Psalm 18:13-19
Song: "Strong Tower"

From this meditation today, I will pray . . .
Adoration _____
_____
_____

Confession _____
_____
_____

Thanksgiving _____
_____
_____

Supplication _____
_____
_____

From this meditation today, I will . . .
Think _____
_____
_____

Say _____
_____
_____

Do _____
_____
_____
_____

Like many people, I love C. S. Lewis's classic book series, The Chronicles of Narnia. In the film adaptation of one of the books, *The Lion, the Witch, and the Wardrobe*, comes an amazing closing scene. A witch is about to kill all that is good in the land of Narnia. It appears that all hope is lost. But then a resurrected Aslan comes a-roarin'! I get chills every time I see it. "It is finished," Aslan says, and order is restored.

Sometimes it seems that evil is about to take over, doesn't it? Maybe a trusted friend has suddenly spoken unkind words against you. Maybe your health takes a nosedive, or a coworker keeps taking advantage of your goodwill. Whatever the case, there is one who comes to "steal and kill and destroy" (John 10:10). He "prowls around like a roaring lion looking for someone to devour" (1 Peter 5:8). But thank God, the Lion of the tribe of Judah is the one true Lord and king. He comes a-roarin' in on the day of our disaster. He is our ever-present help in times of trouble (see Psalm 46:1).

Dear Jesus, *thank You for Your work on the cross when You said, "It is finished!" Thank You for bringing me "into a spacious place" because You "delighted in me" (v. 19). I give You praise for all You have done. Amen.*

SPOTLIGHT
Next Week's Lesson

In the depths of despair, look to the God who is always there.

June 20

Monsoon Time

If any of the peoples of the earth do not go up to Jerusalem to worship the King, the Lord Almighty, they will have no rain (Zechariah 14:17).

For weeks we had no rain. The wind would blow, and occasionally it would cloud up, but no rain. It was a definite dry spell—one we're not so used to where we live. Then, as if on some mysterious cue, it finally rained!

We were overjoyed. It seemed that our greenery sprang to new life overnight. The air was filled with that beautiful, clean smell and, for once, the temperatures cooled down. All of nature rejoiced (including the two residents of our household).

We go for stretches of time with "no rain," don't we? I mean that we tend to dry up, spiritually—and even become a little crusty—as we move away from the Lord with questionable priorities. I don't have any geographical explanation for this arid condition of our hearts, but it sure seems as if Scripture does: Maybe we dry up because we spend so little time worshiping the king.

Friends, if that's all it takes to unleash the clouds of Heaven in our souls, then let's worship God with all our hearts today. Take a moment and lift up a thankful heart for all He's done in your life. Bring on the monsoon.

Father, *please forgive me for not spending more time worshiping You. You alone are the source of my soul's renewal. In Jesus' name, amen.*

SEARCH THE WORD
Drive away the dry-as-dust clouds with a rain dance of praise!

Scripture: Zechariah 14:12-19
Song: *"Grace Like Rain"*

From this meditation today, I will pray . . .

Adoration _____

Confession _____

Thanksgiving _____

Supplication _____

From this meditation today, I will . . .

Think _____

Say _____

Do _____

June 21

Keep the Faith

"Ever since I went to Pharaoh to speak in your name, he has brought trouble upon this people." . . . Then the Lord said to Moses, "Now you will see what I will do to Pharaoh: Because of my mighty hand he will let them go" (Exodus 5:23; 6:1).

Scripture: Exodus 5:1-9, 22, 23; 6:1
Song: *"Here Am I, Send Me"*

From this meditation today, I will pray . . .
Adoration _____
_____
_____

Confession _____
_____
_____

Thanksgiving _____
_____
_____

Supplication _____
_____
_____

From this meditation today, I will . . .
Think _____
_____
_____

Say _____
_____
_____

Do _____
_____
_____
_____

The Lord was calling the Israelites to draw closer to Him, and Moses had just delivered God's order to Pharaoh: "Let my people go." But this Egyptian ruler, who had significant power at the time, decided to make things even rougher yet on God's people.

Has that ever happened to you? You decide to tithe . . . but the car breaks down. You set up family devotions for 8:00 every night . . . but hectic schedules prevent you from following through. You want to draw closer to God . . . but countless obstacles rise up in your way.

Well, keep the faith. Our hope comes in God's answer to Moses in our Scripture passage for today. We may encounter difficulties when we move to draw closer to God. (The forces of evil certainly don't want to see us get closer to the Lord.) But take heart! Our Savior has overcome the world (John 16:33) and will help us do the same.

My Lord God, *I pray that You will help me press in and draw closer to You. Help me overcome any of the obstacles that will surely get in the way. Remind me, again and again, that with You all things are possible. In the name of the Father, the Son, and the Holy Spirit, I pray. Amen.*

SPOTLIGHT
Next Week's Lesson

Hard hearts bring on hard times—
for themselves and others.

June 22

Legacy? Begin Now!

Moses took the bones of Joseph with him because Joseph had made the sons of Israel swear an oath. He had said, "God will surely come to your aid, and then you must carry my bones up with you from this place" (Exodus 13:19).

The great 19th-century evangelist D. L. Moody determined to impart a legacy of faith that would reach beyond the grave. He said, "Some day you will read in the papers that Moody is dead. Don't you believe a word of it! At that moment I shall be more alive than I am now. I shall have gone up higher, that is all—out of this old clay tenement into a house that is immortal, a body that death cannot touch." On his deathbed he made assignments for work still to be done. That work continues, a hundred years later, at the Moody Bible Institute in Chicago, Illinois.

Joseph, while on his deathbed, gave an assignment to his brethren, promising the help of God. This patriarch lived a legacy of faith until his dying day, constantly showing confidence in his promise-keeping God. That is the kind of legacy I, too, would like to leave behind some day. But I can begin now, today, with the smallest step of faith. Thanks be to God!

Father, grant me the fortitude to live out a legacy of faith that brings honor to Your name. I pray in the precious name of Jesus. Amen.

Scripture: Exodus 13:17-22
Song: *"Faith of Our Fathers"*

From this meditation today, I will pray...

Adoration _____

Confession _____

Thanksgiving _____

Supplication _____

From this meditation today, I will...

Think _____

Say _____

Do _____

SEARCH THE WORD
Hoping in the hereafter makes living in the here and now more rewarding.

June 22–28. **Kathy Hardee,** *a writer in Mendota, Illinois, is married with two children and one grandchild. She strives to glorify God through her writing.*

June 23

Destined for Glory

I will harden Pharaoh's heart, and he will pursue them. But I will gain glory for myself through Pharaoh and all his army, and the Egyptians will know that I am the Lord (Exodus 14:4).

Scripture: Exodus 14:1-9
Song: *"Glorious Is Thy Name, O Lord"*

From this meditation today, I will pray . . .
Adoration _____
_____
_____

Confession _____
_____
_____

Thanksgiving _____
_____
_____

Supplication _____
_____
_____

From this meditation today, I will . . .
Think _____
_____
_____

Say _____
_____
_____

Do _____
_____
_____
_____

Steve and I had been dating for four years and were engaged. He was working toward his medical degree, and I was starting nursing school in the fall.

Our lives seemed to be moving forward at a comfortable pace . . . until the car accident. Just past midnight a drunk driver sped through a red light and smashed into the side of our car. Steve was unharmed, but I suffered broken bones, needed several surgeries, and faced months confined to a wheelchair. Yet I'll never forget the sense of God's presence with me during those long hospital nights and quiet mornings. Through pain I found a peace with God I hadn't experienced before.

Within a month after the accident, Steve and I broke up, and I decided not to pursue nursing. What many considered a "bad news" situation, God redeemed for my good—steering me onto a new and better path. Yes, God used a drunk driver to show me—and the hardness of Pharaoh's heart to show the Israelites—the glory of His power and presence.

Dear Lord, *thanks for always working for my good. I trust Your plan for my life, and I give you all the glory for the results. In Jesus' name, amen.*

SPOTLIGHT
Next Week's Lesson

Even with their enemies breathing down their necks, the Israelites were safe in God's care.

June 24

Point Them to God

Moses answered the people, "Do not be afraid. Stand firm and you will see the deliverance the LORD will bring you today" (Exodus 14:13).

"Mom, I think I'm pregnant," my daughter said one morning before school. My heart broke. In that moment, all the wonderful dreams I'd cherished for my daughter seemed to vanish. It was hard to see how God could work this out for good. I could have said any number of hurtful things, but I saw the fear in her eyes. All I could do was love her and assure her that God would see us through.

When the Israelites turned on Moses at the first sign of trouble, he looked beyond their anger. Pharaoh's army was indeed chasing them with a vengeance. And, yes, things looked bad. "What have you done to us by bringing us out of Egypt?" the people cried.

Moses could have said, "Have you so soon forgotten the misery of Egyptian bondage? You stubborn and forgetful people!" But he didn't say any of those things. He saw the fear in their eyes. He was moved to compassion. All he could do was assure them that God would see them through. (And that is what God did.)

Great God of Glory, *help me to see hurting and fearful people as You see them. Use me to point them to You—the one who fights for and protects His own. In the name of Jesus, Lord and Savior of all, I pray. Amen.*

Scripture: Exodus 14:10-14
Song: *"The Battle Is the Lord's"*

From this meditation today, I will pray . . .

Adoration _____

Confession _____

Thanksgiving _____

Supplication _____

From this meditation today, I will . . .

Think _____

Say _____

Do _____

SEARCH THE WORD

Strengthen the shaky with gentle, encouraging words.

June 25

Our Fortress

The LORD *Almighty is with us; the God of Jacob is our fortress*
(Psalm 46:11).

Scripture: Psalm 46
Song: *"A Mighty Fortress Is Our God"*

From this meditation today, I will pray . . .
Adoration _____
_____
_____

Confession _____
_____
_____

Thanksgiving _____
_____
_____

Supplication _____
_____
_____

From this meditation today, I will . . .
Think _____
_____
_____

Say _____
_____
_____

Do _____
_____
_____
_____

The alarm rang, and Mrs. Anderson rushed us into the hallway. We sat in a row next to our lockers, legs crossed, heads down, arms wrapped over our heads. The tornado ripped off the gymnasium roof, shattered windows, and frightened several hundred children and their teachers. But we were huddled in the hallway, the safest place in the school.

Today's Scripture tells us about the safest place in the world. When calamity shakes the earth and nation rages against nation, we have a place to go. That "place" is Almighty God. He is waiting. Strong. Secure. Fortified. No enemy is allowed entrance. No harm will come to those dwelling in His presence.

I sometimes forget that God is not only my heavenly Father, He is my fortress. The Lord is my strong tower. When I run to Him, I am safe.

Inspired by this psalm, Martin Luther wrote the hymn, "A Mighty Fortress Is Our God." Whenever he heard discouraging news, he had been known to say, "Come, let us sing the 46th Psalm." May that be the song filling our hearts today.

Lord, *I run to You. Please wrap me in the arms of Your love and renew me in the power of Your strength. Thank You, in Jesus' name. Amen.*

SPOTLIGHT
Next Week's Lesson
The double-sided cloud plunged the Egyptians into darkness, but shone a path for God's people.

June 26

A Grandmother's Legacy

Trust in the Lord with all thine heart; and lean not unto thine own understanding. In all thy ways acknowledge him, and he shall direct thy paths (Proverbs 3:5, 6, King James Version).

With every note or greeting card I send, I include a verse of Scripture. I hope those words from the Lord will bring encouragement to the person receiving them. I often spend more time contemplating which verse would be best than I spend writing the note.

I learned this habit from my grandmother. On every birthday card, book, or Bible she gave me—and there were many—I'd find a verse or two written in her perfect penmanship. But Grandma didn't spend much time deciding which verses to write. Nine times out of ten, she inscribed Proverbs 3:5, 6, always in the *King James Version*.

Grandma must have known that if I spent all my days obeying just those two verses, I would live a joyful and successful Christian life (also see Psalm 1:1-3).

Has God written a verse on the tablet of your heart? Suppose you were to share with others those precious words of encouragement from the Lord?

Dear Lord, *help me to trust You today with more of my heart—and to lean only on Your wisdom and understanding—so that my footsteps will always be following Yours. And as You guide me, may I ever be open to sharing Your wisdom and goodness with others around me. I pray this prayer in the name of Jesus, my Savior and Lord. Amen.*

Scripture: Proverbs 3:3-10
Song: *"Trust and Obey"*

From this meditation today, I will pray . . .
Adoration _____
Confession _____
Thanksgiving _____
Supplication _____

From this meditation today, I will . . .
Think _____
Say _____
Do _____

SEARCH THE WORD
What Bible verse will you use to brighten someone's day?

June 27

Problem Solved

Who among the gods is like you, O Lord? Who is like you—majestic in holiness, awesome in glory, working wonders?
(Exodus 15:11).

Scripture: Exodus 15:1-13
Song: *"Victory in Jesus"*

From this meditation today, I will pray . . .
Adoration _____
_____
_____

Confession _____
_____
_____

Thanksgiving _____
_____
_____

Supplication _____
_____
_____

From this meditation today, I will . . .
Think _____
_____
_____

Say _____
_____
_____

Do _____
_____
_____
_____

Shirt-tags drove my 2-year-old grandson crazy. He often came running to me, pulling on the collar of his shirt, crying, "Bugging me, Gram. Bugging me." I'd scoop him up in my arms, give him a hug and assure him that I'd take care of his problem. Although shirt-tags might seem a huge problem to a 2-year-old, to me it was no big deal. One snip; problem solved.

The ancient Israelites faced a much more formidable foe. When they looked up, there were the Egyptians, marching after them, and God's people were terrified. They cried to the Lord and complained to Moses: "Why didn't you just let us stay and serve the Egyptians?"

But their problem was puny to an all-powerful God. After He delivered them, they expressed their astonishment and praise as they sang: "You blew with your breath, and the sea covered them. They sank like lead in the mighty waters" (v. 10). Pharaoh's great army was no match for the breath of God. One blow; problem solved.

Heavenly Father, *thank You for reminding me: All of my problems are small compared to Your omnipotent power. Help me to praise You now, even as I wait on You. In the name of Your Son, my Savior, I pray. Amen.*

SPOTLIGHT
Next Week's Lesson

"The Lord is my strength and my song; he has become my salvation"
(Exodus 15:2).

June 28

God Used . . . Whom?

I will harden the hearts of the Egyptians so that they will go in after them. And I will gain glory through Pharaoh and all his army, through his chariots and his horsemen (Exodus 14:17).

This is what I want on my headstone: *Kathy Hardee—A Champion for God's Glory.* That's why I became excited one morning after reading Romans 9:17, "I raised you up for this very purpose, that I might display my power in you and that my name might be proclaimed in all the earth."

"Yes, Lord," I prayed, "that's what I want for my life. Display Your power and glory in me!" When I finished praying and looked back at the page, I realized I'd missed the first part of the verse, "For the Scripture says to Pharaoh . . ."

I had to reread that phrase several times? Unbelievable! God spoke these words to the great enemy of Moses and God's people?

Of course, God wasn't surprised by Pharaoh's attack on the Israelites. Nor did Pharaoh rise to a place of leadership purely of his own volition. God raised him up for His own purposes. God uses whomever He pleases to accomplish His plan and glorify His name.

I just hope He uses me, starting this very moment . . .

Dear God, *I'm awed by the thought that You, the creator of the universe, might work in me to glorify Your name. Even so, use me, Lord God, use me today for Your purposes. I pray in Jesus' holy name. Amen.*

SEARCH THE WORD
God can gain glory from willing servants or willful enemies.

Scripture: Exodus 14:15-25, 30
Song: *"Glorify Thy Name"*

From this meditation today, I will pray . . .
Adoration _____
_____
_____
Confession _____
_____
_____
Thanksgiving _____
_____
_____
Supplication _____
_____
_____

From this meditation today, I will . . .
Think _____
_____
_____
Say _____
_____
_____
Do _____
_____
_____
_____
_____

June 29

Not Safe!

The Mighty One, God, the LORD, *speaks and summons the earth from the rising of the sun to the place where it sets* (Psalm 50:1).

Scripture: Psalm 50:1-6
Song: *"I Sing the Mighty Power of God"*

From this meditation today, I will pray . . .
Adoration _____
_____
_____

Confession _____
_____
_____

Thanksgiving _____
_____
_____

Supplication _____
_____
_____

From this meditation today, I will . . .
Think _____
_____
_____

Say _____
_____
_____

Do _____
_____
_____

The *Seattle Post-Intelligencer* reported in 1997 that wild animal attacks were on the rise, including attacks by American bison in Yellowstone National Park. The article said, "In the last 15 years, more than 56 people have been injured and two killed by these seemingly placid beasts. . . . Nearly all attacks result from provocation, often when someone approaches to get a good photo."

Approaching great power with unthinking nonchalance—it made me think: although God is my friend, He is also the creator and sustainer of the universe. He, of all that is powerful, deserves the utmost respect.

In one of my favorite passages in C. S. Lewis's *The Lion, the Witch, and the Wardrobe,* beavers explain to the human children that Aslan, the Christ figure, is a lion. When Lucy asks, "Then he isn't safe?" Mr. Beaver responds, "Who said anything about safe? Course he isn't safe. But he's good. He's the King, I tell you."

God of the Universe, *Your powerful wildness demands my veneration. I bow in reverence and acknowledge Your kingship over my life. In the name of Jesus, Lord and Savior of all, I pray. Amen.*

SPOTLIGHT
Next Week's Lesson

Beware of taking
God for granted.

June 29-30. **Bonnie Doran** *lives in Denver, Colorado, with her husband of 24 years. She works part-time as a bookkeeper for her church.*

June 30

Out of Water

Repent, then, and turn to God, so that your sins may be wiped out, that times of refreshing may come from the Lord, and that he may send the Christ, who has been appointed for you —even Jesus (Acts 3:19, 20).

I participated in a 9 kilometer race several years ago. The course followed a dirt path around Boulder Reservoir on a warm morning in May.

The inaugural race during the previous year had been rather sparsely attended, so the large number of participants for the second annual race caught the planners by surprise. By the time I reached the water stations, along with the back of the racing pack, the stations were dry—and so was I! Although I'd carried some water with me, I couldn't wait to cross the finish line where a friend waited with an ice-cold bottle of refreshment.

My own efforts at spiritual growth sometimes feel like that hot, dusty race course. I try to do everything in my own strength and wonder why I'm so tired and discouraged. Yet God calls to me (and you) every day: "Come, all you who are thirsty, come to the waters; and you who have no money, come, buy and eat! Come, buy wine and milk without money and without cost" (Isaiah 55:1).

Source of Living Water, *let me submerge myself in Your ocean of strength and love before I put on my running shoes for the course You've set for me. In the precious name of Jesus I pray. Amen.*

Scripture: Acts 3:17-25

Song: *"The Waves of Salvation"*

From this meditation today, I will pray . . .

Adoration _____

Confession _____

Thanksgiving _____

Supplication _____

From this meditation today, I will . . .

Think _____

Say _____

Do _____

SEARCH THE WORD

For those who know Jesus, the "times of refreshing" are here.

> **I** will sing to the LORD,
> for he is highly exalted.
> —Exodus 15:1

July

CALLED TO BE GOD'S PEOPLE

I am the Lord *your God.*
—Deuteronomy 5:6

July 1

Joy: More Than a Feeling

*I will clothe her priests with salvation,
and her saints will ever sing for joy* (Psalm 132:16).

Scripture: Psalm 132:11-18
Song: *"Joyful, Joyful, We Adore Thee"*

From this meditation today, I will pray . . .
Adoration _____
_____
_____

Confession _____
_____
_____

Thanksgiving _____
_____
_____

Supplication _____
_____
_____

From this meditation today, I will . . .
Think _____
_____
_____

Say _____
_____
_____

Do _____
_____
_____

In the story of Batman, one of the villains is the Joker, so-called because a surgical mistake left him with a permanent, grotesque smile. And that smile is anything but genuine.

Unlike the Joker, I don't walk around town with a grin glued to my face. Circumstances can depress me. I allow minor irritations to balloon into personal affronts. I answer one too many telephone calls from solicitors. Or I try to cope with the day's demands with only a few hours of sleep (and way too much caffeine).

Sometimes I feel far from the teensiest bit of joy, let alone being able to show it in word and deed. However, I do have a deep satisfaction in God that transcends temporary happiness. God has proved faithful in keeping His promises to me and my family down through the years. I know I can rely on Him . . . even when I don't feel like it.

My Lord and King, *sometimes I feel I have the emotional excitement of a teaspoon! But I thank You for Your goodness to me, day by day—and for Your promise of eternal joy still to come. Please keep my heart singing today—and if I need a nap, give me some time for that wonderful joy as well! I pray in Jesus' name. Amen.*

SPOTLIGHT
Next Week's Lesson

Find joy in keeping the Commandments.

July 1–5. **Bonnie Doran** lives in Denver, Colorado, with her husband of 24 years. She works part-time as a bookkeeper for her church.

July 2

Heavenly Amnesia

I will forgive their wickedness and will remember their sins no more (Hebrews 8:12).

As I grow older, it seems my short-term memory needs more and more help. One little trick has been around for ages, and it apparently works for most people—tying a string around a finger. However, I've never tried this because I can't tie a bow with one hand (and I'm afraid the string might get caught in my computer's keyboard).

My method? I usually try, as soon as possible, to write down what I want to remember. Problem is, later on, I often can't decipher my own hurried handwriting!

One weight-loss program uses what they call an "anchor." A member uses an object, such as a key ring, to spark the remembrance of former successes and to be encouraged to continue following the program.

Well, here's my point: God untied the string and lost the anchor regarding our sins. He has not only forgiven us, but forgotten we ever disobeyed Him.

It may seem strange that Almighty God chooses long-term (lasting for eternity) memory loss. But that's the power of His love. And that heavenly amnesia is the source of all my praise.

Lord God, *I thank You for the power of Your awesome love. You forged the true meaning of "forgive and forget." Help me do the same toward others who may wrong me this day. I pray in Christ's name. Amen.*

SEARCH THE WORD

God has forgiven you and forgotten your sins. Have you?

Scripture: Hebrews 8:6-12
Song: *"Love Lifted Me"*

From this meditation today, I will pray . . .

Adoration _____

Confession _____

Thanksgiving _____

Supplication _____

From this meditation today, I will . . .

Think _____

Say _____

Do _____

July 3

A One-Way Pact

This is my covenant with them when I take away their sins (Romans 11:27).

Scripture: Romans 11:25-32
Song: *"O the Deep, Deep Love of Jesus"*

From this meditation today, I will pray . . .
Adoration _____
_____
_____

Confession _____
_____
_____

Thanksgiving _____
_____
_____

Supplication _____
_____
_____

From this meditation today, I will . . .
Think _____
_____
_____

Say _____
_____
_____

Do _____
_____
_____
_____

I never learned all the nuances of proper etiquette. I know, however, that receiving a wedding invitation means I need to buy a present for the happy couple. A potluck implies I'll bring a dish to share. If I've helped someone move, I hope I can ask them to help me when I'm loading my own truck. And when someone invites me to dinner, it's politely expected that I'll reciprocate before too long.

These unwritten rules of social interaction remind me of the old adage, "You scratch my back, and I'll scratch yours." Approached in the right way, this rule of thumb can create a friendship based on mutual assistance. Used wrongly, it can also create excess guilt if we're wired to feel obligated every time someone does us a favor.

God doesn't dump guilt on us when He draws up a contract. His back-scratching pact works only one way. We can't do anything to earn it or deserve it, but He lavishes His love on us anyway. His promise of forgiveness doesn't depend on how well we perform, but entirely on His mercy. Hallelujah!

Dear Lord, *thank You for Your great love in spite of my unloveliness. I respond in reverence and awe to the pure grace of Your salvation. I pray this prayer in the name of Jesus, my merciful Savior and Lord. Amen.*

SPOTLIGHT
Next Week's Lesson

Doing things God's way
makes our way
much smoother.

July 4

Spirit of the Law

All the Law and the Prophets hang on these two commandments (Matthew 22:40).

Scripture: Matthew 22:34-40
Song: *"My Country 'Tis of Thee"*

My new stove has a Sabbath setting. I can program it to bake up to 73 hours ahead of time. Apparently the European manufacturer wanted to assist Orthodox Jews and others in their observance of the Old Testament law. (No cooking allowed on the Sabbath!)

The Pharisees insisted on strict adherence to the law and debated endlessly on how its regulations should be observed. Jesus turned their tome of regulations into two: Love God and love your neighbor. That proclamation must have come as a shock.

But we, too, like to measure our spiritual progress by tangible means. Did we pray for 20 minutes today? Read our three chapters in the Bible? Tithe exactly 10 percent? Often we want to get out the clipboard and check off our activities on a kind of spiritual to-do list.

Love for God and others can't be measured that way, though. My husband, John, tried to help a neighbor with car trouble. When they were unsuccessful in fixing the problem, John offered the use of his truck for the evening. At that moment, was his generosity closer to God's ideal than attending a church service or singing in a choir?

Lord, help me demonstrate love for You and for my neighbor with a sincere heart. Keep me true to the spirit of Your law! In Jesus' name, amen.

SEARCH THE WORD

Are these two items on your to-do list for today?
— Love God.
— Love others.

From this meditation today, I will pray . . .

Adoration

Confession

Thanksgiving

Supplication

From this meditation today, I will . . .

Think

Say

Do

July 5

Freedom

I am the Lord *your God, who brought you out of Egypt, out of the land of slavery* (Deuteronomy 5:6).

Scripture: Deuteronomy 5:1-9, 11-13, 16-21
Song: *"O Lord of Life, and Love, and Power"*

From this meditation today, I will pray . . .
Adoration _____
_____
_____

Confession _____
_____
_____

Thanksgiving _____
_____
_____

Supplication _____
_____
_____

From this meditation today, I will . . .
Think _____
_____
_____

Say _____
_____
_____

Do _____
_____
_____
_____

My husband created a design based on the abstract art of Piet Mondrian. A grid of heavy black lines enclosed squares of primary colors on a white background. One green square lay outside these lines. He titled it "Out of Bounds." Friends suggested other titles, such as "Thinking Outside the Box" and "Freedom."

God brought the Israelites out of slavery—but not out of bounds. They had freedom, but that freedom was tempered with certain clear-cut rules of conduct. Not "The Ten Guidelines" or "The Ten Suggestions," but "The Ten Commandments."

Yes, they were rules, but God intended them as a blessing, not as a burdensome list of do's and don'ts. We do the same with the people we love. For example, when we admonish a toddler, "Don't touch the stove—it's hot," we lay down a rule for the child's own good.

We have been brought out of slavery to sin into the freedom Christ bought for us on the cross. That freedom doesn't give us license to do anything we want. It does give us the power—and the gratitude—to do what pleases God.

Lord, *I stand amazed at the price You paid for my freedom from sin. Thank You for giving me the desire to serve You gladly. In Jesus' name, amen.*

SPOTLIGHT
Next Week's Lesson

"You have been set free from sin and have become slaves to righteousness" (Romans 6:18).

July 6

Successful Mediocrity?

However many years a man may live, let him enjoy them all. But let him remember the days of darkness, for they will be many. Everything to come is meaningless (Ecclesiastes 11:8).

Would you rather be great . . . or just happy? Writer Henry Longfellow once said: "Most people would succeed in small things if they were not troubled with great ambitions." The idea makes me think of a friend of mine who once told me: "You know, Carol, I actually began to relax and enjoy my life—when I finally accepted that I was going to be a fairly mediocre person."

Bottom line: I am not under some cosmic mandate to be "great" in life. But I am called to see all of my life as resting in God's hands—my existence begun by Him and my life headed back to Him. The important thing is to live each day with the creator's reputation in view, rather than my own.

With this outlook, I know that I can enjoy each moment of my life. But, as Solomon (the writer of Ecclesiastes) reminds us, God is in charge of the Success or Failure Department. As He guides me, my so-called mediocrity will become an eternal success.

Lord, help me enjoy each day as it comes and to live it to the fullest. May I give thanks to You amid every situation. In Jesus' name, amen.

Scripture: Ecclesiastes 11:7–12:1
Song: *"Joyfully Sing"*

From this meditation today, I will pray . . .
Adoration _____

Confession _____

Thanksgiving _____

Supplication _____

From this meditation today, I will . . .
Think _____

Say _____

Do _____

SEARCH THE WORD

Give your creator joy as you delight in the life He's given you.

July 6–12. **Carol Wilde** is a pastor's wife and freelance writer living in Moultrie, Georgia. For exercise, she loves walking her Yorkshire terrier, Robbie Burns.

July 7

He's Still There

Will the Lord reject forever? Will he never show his favor again? . . . [But] I will remember the deeds of the LORD; yes, I will remember your miracles of long ago (Psalm 77:7, 11).

Scripture: Psalm 77:3-15
Song: *"Seek the Lord Who Now Is Present"*

From this meditation today, I will pray . . .

Adoration _____
_____
_____

Confession _____
_____
_____

Thanksgiving _____
_____
_____

Supplication _____
_____
_____

From this meditation today, I will . . .

Think _____
_____
_____

Say _____
_____
_____

Do _____
_____
_____
_____

I've been to plenty of meetings where people were "seeking God." I've heard many sermons, too, about what it takes to find God, and what needs to be done to stay close to Him. All of it seems like so much hard work. Really, a bit discouraging.

No doubt there is a place for discipline in pursuing spiritual growth. But it is not the starting point. For God is the one who first began the search, and He has found us.

The psalmist fears that he has grown far from God's presence, that somehow God has chosen to reject Him. Then he remembers: God's presence is woven into the fabric of his personal and communal history. He can discern God by reading back through his own life's story, by journeying back through the halls of memory and tracing the gracious hand that reached out to guide and bless, sometimes miraculously. I love how C. S. Lewis once summed it up: "While in other sciences the instruments you use are things external to yourself, . . . the instrument through which you see God is your whole self."

O Lord, keep me alert to Your blessings at all times. Yes, help me to see Your hand at work in the most mundane unfolding of each day. In the precious name of Jesus I pray. Amen.

SPOTLIGHT
Next Week's Lesson

By remembering and celebrating the past, we more fully live in the present.

July 8

Remember God's Wonders

*Remember the wonders he has done,
his miracles, and the judgments he pronounced*
(Psalm 105:5).

Have you found that it takes a good memory to be truly happy? How hard it is for us to accept: Happiness comes after the fact; it is a result rather than a goal. Usually it is the result of striving for a goal that focuses attention away from our own selves and circumstances.

To become totally involved in pursuing our passions, rather than our happiness, brings us to the point, later, in which we realize that we have reached a state of peace and contentment. The poster on my husband's office wall, with words by Nathaniel Hawthorne, puts it so well:

> Happiness is like a butterfly;
> The more you chase it,
> The more it eludes you.
> But when you turn your attention
> to other things, it comes,
> And sits softly on your shoulder.

As I go about my day today, I would like to let happiness land where it will, in its own time and place. Each instance will create a memory for me of God's goodness.

Dear God, help me to dedicate myself to doing Your will—and to make some good memories today! In Jesus' name I pray. Amen.

Scripture: Psalm 105:1-11
Song: *"Happy the Souls to Jesus Joined"*

From this meditation today, I will pray . . .

Adoration _____
_____
_____

Confession _____
_____
_____

Thanksgiving _____
_____
_____

Supplication _____
_____
_____

From this meditation today, I will . . .

Think _____
_____
_____

Say _____
_____
_____

Do _____
_____
_____

SEARCH THE WORD

"That is happiness; to be dissolved into something completely great."
—Willa Cather

July 9

Mistakes? Learn!

*Not since the days of the judges who led Israel,
nor throughout the days of the kings of Israel and the kings of Judah,
had any such Passover been observed* (2 Kings 23:22).

Scripture: 2 Kings 23:1-3, 21-23
Song: *"The Mistakes of My Life"*

From this meditation today, I will pray . . .
Adoration _____
_____
_____

Confession _____
_____
_____

Thanksgiving _____
_____
_____

Supplication _____
_____
_____

From this meditation today, I will . . .
Think _____
_____
_____

Say _____
_____
_____

Do _____
_____
_____
_____

Oops! What a mistake! God's people had simply forgotten—for many long years—to abide by His Word. They'd even let the all-important Passover celebration slip into oblivion.

Individuals, even whole nations, do "mess up," regularly. So, have I got you thinking about all your own mistakes at the moment? Rather than wallow in guilt, probably the best thing we can do now is to "reframe" our mistakes. That is, instead of seeing them as terrible disasters, we begin to view them as normal and natural results of the courage to make decisions and take risks. For the Christian, that is simply a good definition of determining to live by faith, each day.

Actually, a mistake can serve as a welcome call to slow down and look more closely at the direction we're traveling. What adjustments can we make? How can we avoid this in the future?

Dear Heavenly Father, *remind me today that my mistake need not grow into a moral frame-up in the court of personal self-condemnation. Help me remember that, like any other human experience, I can invite a mistake to become my teacher. I pray this prayer in the name of my precious Lord and Savior, Jesus Christ. Amen.*

SPOTLIGHT
Next Week's Lesson

Memories of our mistakes will either immobilize or energize us. The choice is ours.

July 10

It Actually Worked Out!

They left and found things just as Jesus had told them
(Luke 22:13).

Scripture: Luke 22:7-13
Song: *"Still, Still with Thee"*

Peter and John were given a set of clear-cut, but rather elaborate, instructions to follow. Did they believe, at the outset, that everything would fall into place?

Actually, I think they simply had to step out in faith. I see them having to take a risk. But then what joy when they found that the plan had unfolded "just as Jesus had told them"!

Could I live like that? Suppose I choose to live a life of faith (which will involve plenty of risky decisions), and I thereby miss out on all kinds of fun, fulfilling, satisfying experiences? Surely I would regret such a decision! That thought has crossed my mind occasionally. Are God's plans for us always in our very best interest? Couldn't we devise a more self-fulfilling life on our own?

But to be convinced of God's good will toward me is the only way I can be moved to live a life of holy risk—of faith in God. Here's something that helps: to come to the blessed place in which I finally see that "what God commands" is exactly the same as "what is the very best for me."

O Lord, *I celebrate Your involvement in the unfolding drama of my life's adventure! Help me to step out in faith, quickly, when You call me to do Your will. In Your precious name I pray. Amen.*

From this meditation today, I will pray...
Adoration _____
_____
_____

Confession _____
_____
_____

Thanksgiving _____
_____
_____

Supplication _____
_____
_____

From this meditation today, I will...
Think _____
_____
_____

Say _____
_____
_____

Do _____
_____
_____
_____

SEARCH THE WORD

Trust God to know what's best for me? It's a risk worth taking.

July 11

For Joy: Remove the Sin

It is actually reported that there is sexual immorality among you
(1 Corinthians 5:1).

Scripture: 1 Corinthians 5:1-8
Song: *"Print Thine Image, Pure and Holy"*

From this meditation today, I will pray...
Adoration _____

Confession _____

Thanksgiving _____

Supplication _____

From this meditation today, I will...
Think _____

Say _____

Do _____

The silly little cartoon showed Moses speaking, just returned from Mt. Sinai with the Ten Commandments in his hands. He's reporting to his people about his encounter with God on the mountaintop. He says: "It was hard bargaining—we get the milk and honey, but the anti-adultery clause stays in."

Of course, the topic of sexual immorality is serious business, as the apostle stressed to the Corinthians. But the practical question remains: Must a life of faith be a series of hard-bargaining rounds, as the cartoonist believes?

It's true that some things are clearly wrong, and a number of "anti" clauses must stay put (the real Moses would never have questioned that). Yet some people view God as quite disappointed when His creatures seem to be having a little fun.

That's a contrast to my sense of who God is. For example, I've been surprised to find out how much joy flows from the pages of Scripture—pure fun: singing, dancing, shouting, playing, making music. Surely God smiles at our joy. And that, of course, is why He commands against every self-destructive behavior.

Dear Father in Heaven, *help me to see Your commands as an invitation to live a happier life. In the name of Christ I pray. Amen.*

SPOTLIGHT
Next Week's Lesson

Whose idea was it to get the family together and have a celebration? God's.

July 12

Help Me Focus!

Observe the month of Abib and celebrate the Passover of the Lord *your God. . . . For six days eat unleavened bread and on the seventh day hold an assembly to the* Lord *your God and do no work* (Deuteronomy 16:1, 8).

On television one evening, my husband and I watched a Japanese tea ceremony and marveled at the "attitude of awareness." The participants in the ceremony sit still and silent on a straw mat, facing each other, waiting for the hissing sound of boiling water in the pot before them. They listen to the water seethe. Then one man drops in the tea, whisks it, and presents the pottery bowl to his friend. The receiver looks at the bowl, inspects it, feels it, comments about its beauty, and then slowly drinks. Everything is done slowly; awareness reigns. Of course, they are not just drinking the tea, but, if it doesn't sound too strange, they are "being there with" the tea.

I believe the Lord calls for a similar kind of attentiveness when He commands the Israelites to observe an entire month—and one day per week—with special devotion to Him. Perhaps with these commands, they will learn the habit of staying attuned to His presence, even in the "ordinary" days.

Dear Father, *can I even do one thing without a multitude of other things screaming for my attention? Help, Lord! Give me special times of peace and quiet that I might focus on Your loving presence. In Jesus' name, amen.*

Scripture: Deuteronomy 16:1-8
Song: *"Listen to the Blessed Invitation"*

From this meditation today, I will pray . . .

Adoration _____

Confession _____

Thanksgiving _____

Supplication _____

From this meditation today, I will . . .

Think _____

Say _____

Do _____

SEARCH THE WORD

Mental focus and a quiet setting help us center our thoughts on God.

July 13

No Generation Gap

Shout for joy to the LORD. . . . *For the* LORD *is good and his love endures forever; his faithfulness continues through all generations* (Psalm 100:1, 5).

Scripture: Psalm 100
Song: *"Great Is Thy Faithfulness"*

From this meditation today, I will pray . . .
Adoration _____
_____
_____

Confession _____
_____
_____

Thanksgiving _____
_____
_____

Supplication _____
_____
_____

From this meditation today, I will . . .
Think _____
_____
_____

Say _____
_____
_____

Do _____
_____
_____

Our family gathered at the dining room table to decorate pumpkins one autumn Sunday evening. Grandson Nathan (about 7 years old) took time out to lead us in song. His arms waving wildly, he caught his reflection in the window and smiled at himself, pleased with his conducting skills.

During his college years, Nathan directed from the back of his dad's church, manning the sound system. Now a graduate, he plans to work on a master's degree while living in Israel. Some form of ministry in his future proves God's faithfulness through at least five generations of our family. Nathan's father, grandfather, great-uncle, and great-great grandfather served in pastoral ministry.

Tracing our spiritual heritage back through the generations is an exciting and God-honoring activity. (Try it, even though it may take some research!) God's faithfulness extends backward and forward, while rewarding us with a grateful heart.

Faithful God, *I am so grateful for Your kindness to me through years past. And I sing Your praises as I move into the future. In Christ's name, amen.*

SPOTLIGHT
Next Week's Lesson

We are to support those who are set aside for the Lord's service.

July 13-19. **Ann L. Coker,** Terre Haute, Indiana, *directs a crisis pregnancy center. She's married to her favorite preacher and has 4 children and 12 grandchildren.*

July 14

Return to the Lord

Blow the trumpet in Zion, declare a holy fast, call a sacred assembly (Joel 2:15).

From various e-mails I began to see that many people around the world are serious about revival. One e-mail alerted Messianic Jews to blow their shofars at an appointed time—to call the nation to repent. A second e-mail came from prayer groups around the world announcing a Global Day of Prayer planned in key cities. A third e-mail, from my friend and her husband, told about their decision to hold days of fasting during each week. This will help them prepare for their upcoming short-term mission trip to China. They're inviting others to join them.

Blowing shofars, gathering to pray, and even fasting doesn't guarantee revival. But these are surely steps in the right direction. However, let's remember, God is as close as our next breath. I like the way writer Tim Stafford put it: "You can worry that your relationship with [God] has gone cold. . . . You can think it will take a lot of time, a month or so of spiritual discipline, to get going again with Him. Then you sit down and discover, in just minutes, that you don't have to do a thing—except take some time. Be alone with him. In what feels like no time you are caught up again in your love."

Dear Father, *I am prone to wander. Change my heart, O God; renew me by Your Spirit; help me make the return trip home. In Jesus' name, amen.*

SEARCH THE WORD
Blow a horn, fast, pray—do whatever it takes to draw closer to God.

Scripture: Joel 2:12-16
Song: *"Come, Thou Fount of Every Blessing"*

From this meditation today, I will pray . . .
Adoration _____

Confession _____

Thanksgiving _____

Supplication _____

From this meditation today, I will . . .
Think _____

Say _____

Do _____

July 15

Serving Is the Reward

This service that you perform is not only supplying the needs of God's people but is also overflowing in many expressions of thanks to God (2 Corinthians 9:12).

Scripture: 2 Corinthians 9:6-12
Song: *"In the Service of the King"*

From this meditation today, I will pray . . .
Adoration _____
_____
_____

Confession _____
_____
_____

Thanksgiving _____
_____
_____

Supplication _____
_____
_____

From this meditation today, I will . . .
Think _____
_____
_____

Say _____
_____
_____

Do _____
_____
_____
_____

We hear it repeatedly. The one who visits a shut-in feels she's the one receiving the blessing. A carpenter or bricklayer helps with renovation of houses damaged after a hurricane, and he returns with a renewed sense of thankfulness. We give of ourselves in service, and yet we are the ones who receive such joy in return.

A couple from our church has taken several mission trips to Haiti. They offer their professional skills, dentistry and pharmacy, to meet the medical needs of the village folk. But hearing this couple tell their story, I sense that they were on the receiving end. They overflow with gratitude for the opportunity to give in Christ's name.

When we help supply what others need, whether they "deserve" it or not, we are truly serving in the name of Jesus. The rewards we receive are eternal, but we are also rewarded *in the very act of service.* Just talk with those in ministry and ask about the personal benefits. Then look around you and plug into some of your church's outreach efforts.

Lord, *I want to serve You and Your people with a grateful heart. May my service honor You as I seek to help meet needs around the corner and around the world. May my reward be found in You alone. In Jesus' name, amen.*

SPOTLIGHT
Next Week's Lesson

Anointed and sanctified, Aaron accepted the call to serve God's people.

July 16

Right Answer, Wrong Response

*John came to you to show you the way of righteousness. . . .
And even after you saw this, you did not repent and believe him*
(Matthew 21:32).

At the crisis pregnancy center where I work, most of our clients are single yet sexually active. The peer counselors tell them about the physical, emotional, and spiritual benefits of abstinence. Some will quickly agree to wait until marriage, yet we see most of these girls again. Broken vows reap the consequences of pregnancy and/or sexually transmitted diseases.

Those clients who keep a commitment to wait express a sense of regret, remorse, and guilt about their former lifestyles. I think their sense of guilt is a good thing, however. It leads to repentance and right actions. For these girls and guys, there is hope.

There is only hope when we agree with God about our sinful and self-destructive attitudes and actions. When the truth bears down on our consciences, we accept the truth. Then, and only then, do we have hope.

In other words, we can have the right answer but the wrong response. Unless we act out our decision to follow Christ, we continue to run around in circles of confusion.

Heavenly Father, *I know that You are pleased when my actions agree with my words. Help me not to turn a deaf ear to You but to act according to Your perfect will. I pray through my deliverer, Jesus. Amen.*

Scripture: Matthew 21:28-32
Song: *"Just As I Am"*

From this meditation today, I will pray . . .
Adoration _____

Confession _____

Thanksgiving _____

Supplication _____

From this meditation today, I will . . .
Think _____

Say _____

Do _____

SEARCH THE WORD

Let your walk match your talk.

July 17

Caught in the Expectation Trap?

*Do not be conformed to this world,
but be transformed by the renewing of your mind*
(Romans 12:2, *New American Standard Bible*).

Scripture: Romans 11:33–12:2
Song: *"May the Mind of Christ, My Savior"*

From this meditation today, I will pray . . .
Adoration _____
_____
_____

Confession _____
_____
_____

Thanksgiving _____
_____
_____

Supplication _____
_____
_____

From this meditation today, I will . . .
Think _____
_____
_____

Say _____
_____
_____

Do _____
_____
_____
_____

Freshmen girls asked me to lead their late-night devotional. I talked about the difference between *conforming* and being *transformed*. We can conform to the good life but in a wrong way.

This was a Christian college; these girls came from Christian homes and attended church. Such teens can easily abide by the rules of house or dorm, doing what's expected. But have their minds been transformed?

All of us believers must choose whether to be transformed from within or simply to conform to outside pressures. Christ makes the inner transformation possible.

Counselors at the crisis pregnancy center look for red flags in their clients. Surprisingly, one group of risk factors actually involves *good* behavior—attending church, getting good grades, being athletic, and having a college scholarship. In the environment of success, these girls may rationalize that this is not the time to have a baby. Thus, they merely conform to the world. Their basic need is to be transformed by kingdom values.

O God, *You have revealed Your perfect and acceptable will. Show me the areas where I need to move away from mere conformity. Instead, transform me, renewing my mind daily. Through Christ, I pray. Amen.*

SPOTLIGHT
Next Week's Lesson

Moses conformed to God's instructions and helped transform Aaron into the high priest.

July 18

Two Teachers or One?

So that with one accord you may with one voice glorify the God and Father of our Lord Jesus Christ (Romans 15:6, *New American Standard Bible*).

Never have I seen such a smooth process of speaker and interpreter working together. My husband, Bill, was speaking on holiness at a seminary in Malang, Indonesia. The interpreter was a student who had previously studied in the United States. As soon as Bill completed one sentence, the student spoke the translation. Actually, they seemed to speak with one voice. They even found Scripture passages and read together without hesitation.

The Lord was glorified as students and faculty heard the message in their own language. We knew God was in control, for a clear sense of His presence prevailed in that auditorium. We could have sung: "Our God has made us one; His glory is displayed."

We know that God's glory filled the tabernacle in the wilderness. And on the Day of Pentecost the disciples were of one accord. Those who listened to the disciples' message heard it in their own and varied languages. Even today, can we not expect God to move among us when we serve Him with one mind and voice?

Lord, *I want You to move within me and show me Your glory. You desire this even more than I do! So I humbly ask that You begin the change in me. Bring me into one accord with Your will and Word. In Jesus' name, amen.*

SEARCH THE WORD

"My way or the highway" is the wrong way in Christ's church.

Scripture: Romans 15:1-6
Song: "Our God Has Made Us One"

From this meditation today, I will pray . . .
Adoration _____
_____
_____
Confession _____
_____
_____
Thanksgiving _____
_____
_____
Supplication _____
_____
_____

From this meditation today, I will . . .
Think _____
_____
_____
Say _____
_____
_____
Do _____
_____
_____

July 19

Say It; Do It

Moses said to the assembly, "This is what the Lord *has commanded to be done"* (Leviticus 8:5).

Scripture: Leviticus 8:1-13
Song: *"Lead Us, O Lord"*

From this meditation today, I will pray...
Adoration _____
_____
_____
Confession _____
_____
_____
Thanksgiving _____
_____
_____
Supplication _____
_____
_____

From this meditation today, I will...
Think _____
_____
_____
Say _____
_____
_____
Do _____
_____
_____
_____

The minister of a rural church called the children up front. He asked them, "Who is your neighbor?" All together they answered with names of their friends who live nearby. Then the tougher question, "How are you supposed to treat your neighbor?" Silence. The 4-year-old son of visiting missionaries spoke loud and clear, "I have to share." That was a typical first answer. "And what else?" Again the visitor was the first to respond, "I have to forgive." That answer went deeper.

Why was he ready to respond? He was taught that precept over and over, and he practiced it. He also saw that it worked for his good. He heard it said by his parents, and his part was to obey. Saying it was as good as doing it.

How does this simple lesson connect to the story in Leviticus about the anointing of priests? Over and over, Moses heard God speak His commands. Over and over, Moses and the Israelites were instructed to obey. When they did obey, they benefited. When they disobeyed, well . . . that's another story.

Father, *I cannot address You as Sovereign Lord without acknowledging Your rule over me and all things. Through Your Word, I know who You are and how You want me to live. May all I do be a testimony to the joys of obedience. In the name of Your Son, my Savior, I pray. Amen.*

SPOTLIGHT
Next Week's Lesson

"I seek you with all my heart; do not let me stray from your commands" (Psalm 119:10).

July 20

Headline News Makers

News about him spread through the whole countryside
(Luke 4:14).

The aftermath of 9-11 brought the name of a man, and his organization, to the forefront of newscasts throughout the whole world. We do not need to mention his name, but most people could tell you if asked. People also remember where they were when the infamous news-creating act of this man's organization was thrust upon the world.

Our verse today speaks of another man, a man in the process of founding a life-changing opportunity for every man, woman, and child that would ever live. News of him also spread throughout the whole country. But that man, and the news of him, centered in love and truth. His words and actions produced life rather than death. And people praised Him for the power and the truth that flowed from Him as He taught in their synagogues.

Two men, two news-creating circumstances. Yet, what contrasting realities! What differing effects! It makes me wonder: What kind of "news" will I bring to my own world this day?

Heavenly Father, *help me to spread only goodwill in my world and to pass along the wonderful news of Your salvation to others. And keep the fire of Your presence real in my life. In the name of Christ I pray. Amen.*

Scripture: Luke 4:14-19
Song: *"Pass It On"*

From this meditation today, I will pray...
Adoration _____
_____
_____

Confession _____
_____
_____

Thanksgiving _____
_____
_____

Supplication _____
_____
_____

From this meditation today, I will...
Think _____
_____
_____

Say _____
_____
_____

Do _____
_____
_____

SEARCH THE WORD
Living in a dark corner of the world? Light it up with news about Jesus.

July 20–26. **Mary Louise DeMott** *is a wife and grandmother who loves to teach and write about the most important thing in her life—her Lord and Savior.*

July 21

Needing to Forgive?

"Lord, how many times shall I forgive my brother when he sins against me? Up to seven times?" Jesus answered, "I tell you, not seven times, but seventy-seven times" (Matthew 18:21, 22).

Scripture: Matthew 18:21-35
Song: *"The Joy of the Lord Is My Strength"*

From this meditation today, I will pray . . .
Adoration _____
_____
_____

Confession _____
_____
_____

Thanksgiving _____
_____
_____

Supplication _____
_____
_____

From this meditation today, I will . . .
Think _____
_____
_____

Say _____
_____
_____

Do _____
_____
_____
_____

A recent family misunderstanding caused many hurt feelings, much weeping, and frequent cries of "You don't understand!" The situation could have been avoided with better communication. And, of course, much forgiveness could have helped heal the many wounded hearts in this battle.

Our verse today challenges me in my relationships with others. It is so easy to "say" I forgive you without truly meaning it. The reality is that my enemy, and yours, does his best to use such unforgiveness as a wedge between us and our Lord.

Here's something that helps me. I find a verse that speaks to my heart. Then I meditate upon it (sometimes for days) until I arrive at true forgiveness and peace. Nehemiah 8:10 is such a verse: "The joy of the Lord is your strength." I have found that as I begin to praise the Lord, I am reminded how much He has forgiven me. That tends to melt my heart toward anyone whom I feel has wronged me.

Father, *help me to remember all that You have forgiven me when I am distressed about a perceived wrong. In the name of Jesus I pray. Amen.*

SPOTLIGHT
Next Week's Lesson

What joy there is in forgiveness—
both given and received.

July 22

Know, Do, Live

"What is written in the Law?" . . . "You have answered correctly," Jesus replied. "Do this and you will live" (Luke 10:26, 28).

A mother whale gives birth to her baby under water. It seems that God has given her an inborn knowledge that her baby must be helped to the surface for that first life-giving breath of air. By the time that baby has grown to adulthood, it will have learned to take a huge gulp of air that will give it almost an hour of underwater swimming. We might say the baby whale is blessed to have a "knowledgeable" mother give birth to him.

Knowledge is important, but Jesus stresses something much more important—that Christians should both *know* and *do* His Word. The Parable of the Good Samaritan simply reinforces the idea by means of a practical example.

You see, we can't claim allegiance to powerful spiritual precepts without "getting our hands dirty" with their interpersonal implications. Love is, ultimately, an action word! As Bible commentator William Barclay said: "It will always be true that the outsider will have no use for an alleged faith which is demonstrably ineffective. Long ago, Nietzsche, the atheist philosopher, issued the challenge: 'Show me that you are redeemed, and then I will believe in your Redeemer.'"

Lord, help me not only to love the concepts of the Bible but also to love doing them. Guide me in ministry this day! Through Christ, amen.

SEARCH THE WORD

To whom can you be a Good Samaritan today?

Scripture: Luke 10:25-37
Song: *"Thy Way, Not Mine, O Lord"*

From this meditation today, I will pray . . .

Adoration _____

Confession _____

Thanksgiving _____

Supplication _____

From this meditation today, I will . . .

Think _____

Say _____

Do _____

July 23

Send Out Workers

The harvest is plentiful but the workers are few. Ask the Lord of the harvest, therefore, to send out workers into his harvest field (Matthew 9:37, 38).

Scripture: Matthew 9:35-38
Song: *"Send the Light"*

From this meditation today, I will pray . . .

Adoration _____
_____
_____

Confession _____
_____
_____

Thanksgiving _____
_____
_____

Supplication _____
_____
_____

From this meditation today, I will . . .

Think _____
_____
_____

Say _____
_____
_____

Do _____
_____
_____
_____

The evening service was especially moving to our minister and his wife. Their son, Logan, and Kendra, his wife, were the speakers. That evening they told about New Tribes Mission. They had just graduated from the first section of training and were preparing to begin the final two years.

Those two years would be harder and more intense than anything they had experienced so far. Furthermore, they were told they couldn't work at a "paying" job; they would have to raise their own support. This would help prepare them for their years of missionary service.

It was obvious to all of us that this young couple found it difficult to ask for support. But it was also obvious to us that God wanted this work done in His kingdom. What a blessing to be part of such a great endeavor!

Each of us must "support" through finances and prayer, if we cannot "go." Some do not have finances, but all should be participants in prayer for missionaries doing God's work. Let us be God's hand extended to a lost and dying world.

Lord, *help me to support financially—and with daily prayer—those You send to places I can't go with the gospel message. In Jesus' name, amen.*

SPOTLIGHT
Next Week's Lesson

In God's economy
wealth hoarded
is wealth wasted.

July 24

He Watches Over You!

When the Lord saw her, his heart went out to her and he said, "Don't cry" (Luke 7:13).

Tears filling his eyes, the weary man sat outside the main gate to the White House. His ragged clothes gave evidence of a long journey. A young boy stopped and asked why he was crying. The man's son was to go in front of a firing squad and be killed for desertion. "The guards will not let me see the president," said the man as he rubbed his eyes. "Mr. Lincoln is so kind that, if he heard the full details, I feel sure he would pardon my son."

"I can take you to the president," said the young boy.

"You?" asked the old man, surprised.

"Yes, he's my father. He lets me talk with him whenever I want to."

True to his word, president Lincoln's son brought the man to the Oval Office. And, indeed, when the president heard the full story, he pardoned the condemned soldier.

Lincoln, known for his great compassion, is only a shadow picture of our great God and His compassion for every man, woman, and child that has ever lived. Even now, He invites you to open Your hurting heart to Him.

Dear Father in Heaven, *when I am hurting and discouraged, You are there. You care for me and constantly oversee my needs. Let me always trust You, even in the times when my tears are flowing freely. I pray this prayer in the name of Jesus, my merciful Savior and Lord. Amen.*

SEARCH THE WORD

Jesus has the power to heal our deepest hurts.

Scripture: Luke 7:11-17
Song: *"His Eye Is on the Sparrow"*

From this meditation today, I will pray . . .

Adoration _____

Confession _____

Thanksgiving _____

Supplication _____

From this meditation today, I will . . .

Think _____

Say _____

Do _____

July 25

God's Bidding

I tell you the truth, whatever you did for one of the least of these brothers of mine, you did for me
(Matthew 25:40).

Scripture: Matthew 25:31-40
Song: *"Do Something for Jesus"*

From this meditation today, I will pray . . .
Adoration _____
_____
_____

Confession _____
_____
_____

Thanksgiving _____
_____
_____

Supplication _____
_____
_____

From this meditation today, I will . . .
Think _____
_____
_____

Say _____
_____
_____

Do _____
_____
_____
_____

One of the most moving experiences of my life happened one Christmas season. A heavy workload had kept me from completing my shopping. During one lunch hour I raced into a store, planning on grabbing lunch afterwards.

Finished shopping, I spotted a checkout line where I would be next. Others crowded behind me, and then . . . the clerk's phone rang. Turning away, she whispered, but I heard desperation in her voice as she said, "My tire went flat on the way to work, and I'm almost out of gas. I'm out of money until Friday; no, I can't get to church tonight. Please, can you help?" A look of desperation, and then she whispered, "That's OK, I'll find someone." As the young lady rang up my purchase, I saw her fighting to keep tears from falling.

I've never felt God speak to my spirit so clearly. I grabbed what money I had and pressed it into her hand. "I believe God wants me to give you this," I whispered. Turning, I hurried out the door, hoping I had done God's bidding.

Dear Father, please help me stay alert to Your voice, and let me act on what You are telling me to do. Let me be Your hand extended to one of Your hurting creatures in my world. In the name of Christ I pray. Amen.

SPOTLIGHT
Next Week's Lesson

Jubilee was a time for restoration, rejoicing, and reaching out to others.

July 26

He's Coming!

Have the trumpet sounded everywhere
(Leviticus 25:9).

The first time I heard the song "The King Is Coming," I felt chills. I was at a concert, and as the houselights darkened for the second half of the program, the Gaither Trio stood there ready to sing a new song. But before the music started, shockingly, from the back of the auditorium a blaring trumpet fanfare sounded. The Gospel Brass came up the center aisle, playing. As they neared the front the Gaithers began singing:

> *"The King is coming,*
> *the King is coming,*
> *I just heard the*
> *trumpet sounding,*
> *And now His face I see."*

The audience stood in awe. What a beautiful experience it was for all of us.

I've never forgotten that moment, and every time I read about the trumpets sounding in the Bible, I recall that concert so many years ago. It intensified the reality of my coming king. For one day God's trumpets will sound everywhere, and all peoples will bow down to the Lord of lords.

Almighty and everlasting Father, *help me always remember that Your Son is coming back again at any moment. May I stay ready—and looking up. In the name of the Father, the Son, and the Holy Spirit, I pray. Amen.*

SEARCH THE WORD

We await the trumpet blast loud enough to wake the dead.

Scripture: Leviticus 25:8-21, 23, 24
Song: *"The King Is Coming"*

From this meditation today, I will pray...

Adoration _____

Confession _____

Thanksgiving _____

Supplication _____

From this meditation today, I will...

Think _____

Say _____

Do _____

July 27

My Portion: The Best

I cry to thee, O LORD; *I say, Thou art my refuge, my portion in the land of the living . . . for thou wilt deal bountifully with me* (Psalm 142:5, 7, Revised Standard Version).

Scripture: Psalm 142
Song: *"Jesus, My All in All"*

From this meditation today, I will pray . . .
Adoration _____
_____
_____

Confession _____
_____
_____

Thanksgiving _____
_____
_____

Supplication _____
_____
_____

From this meditation today, I will . . .
Think _____
_____
_____

Say _____
_____
_____

Do _____
_____
_____

My grandfather loved telling about "the good ole days." One summer day he told me of working in the watermelon fields of Oklahoma. He said he walked to the field in the dark of the day and chose a large watermelon. He carried it to the creek and placed it deep in the stream. The sun rose high overhead, and the heat and humidity pressed hard upon him as he worked.

"By noon, I was all but dead," he said. He dragged to the river and plunged into the cool water to retrieve his melon. After cracking it open on a rock, he'd used his pocket knife to slice out the middle. He said that the juicy, red sweetness ran down his chin and throat to cool him inside and out.

"But Grandpa, you ate just the middle?" I asked.

"It was my portion," he said, smiling. "When you work in a melon field, you eat the very best of the melon."

God provides similarly for His tired workers. He refreshes with the very best—himself.

O Lord, refresh my commitment to serve You today, even when I feel pressed down. Let the joy of my salvation sustain me. In Christ, amen.

SPOTLIGHT
Next Week's Lesson

Even manna from Heaven couldn't quiet Israel's complainers.

July 27-31. **Shelley L. Houston** *lives in Eugene, Oregon, with her husband of 37 years. She writes for various secular and Christian publishers.*

July 28

Maudlin Murmurings

Moses said to Aaron, "Say to the whole congregation of the people of Israel, 'Come near before the Lord, for he has heard your murmurings' " (Exodus 16:9, Revised Standard Version).

Scripture: Exodus 16:1-12
Song: "Guide Me, O Thou Great Jehovah"

It was hot. The moving truck we'd rented had no air conditioning. I was six months pregnant, and our two toddlers squirmed nonstop between us. Half of the 16 hour trip lay ahead.

"Could things be any worse?" I complained to my husband . . . just before the truck broke down. Hours later, a mechanic told us it would be a three-hour repair. He suggested we walk to a restaurant two miles away, since there was no cool place to wait. On the way out of his yard, I tripped on an old car part and gashed the top of my foot.

We had to walk under a freeway overpass. The shaded concrete felt cool as we sat to spell ourselves. Soon, my husband wanted to go, but I balked.

"I'm not moving . . . ever. I'm going to sit here until I die," I moaned, watching the blood ooze from my foot.

I felt justified in my complaining that day, just as the Israelites must have felt in the wilderness so long ago. But the truth is, our merciful God knew where we were. He heard not only my words but my aching heart.

Lord God, *forgive my moaning, my whining, and my wanderings. But thank You for caring when I hurt and knowing what to do when I cry out with a deep need. I pray through my deliverer, Jesus. Amen.*

From this meditation today, I will pray . . .

Adoration _____

Confession _____

Thanksgiving _____

Supplication _____

From this meditation today, I will . . .

Think _____

Say _____

Do _____

SEARCH THE WORD

Although we give Him static, God never tunes us out.

July 29

Bread of Heaven

Truly, truly, I say to you, he who believes has eternal life. I am the bread of life (John 6:47, 48, Revised Standard Version).

Scripture: John 6:41-51
Song: *"Bread of the World"*

From this meditation today, I will pray...
Adoration _____
_____
_____

Confession _____
_____
_____

Thanksgiving _____
_____
_____

Supplication _____
_____
_____

From this meditation today, I will...
Think _____
_____
_____

Say _____
_____
_____

Do _____
_____
_____
_____

"Bread is sacred in France," our French exchange student explained to our family. "Children are never allowed to play with their bread, and a loaf of bread is placed carefully on the table, right side up, so as not to cause it to be dishonored."

"Why is that?" I asked.

"During WWII there was a shortage of bread, and so our grandparents have taught us not to waste. But also, bread is traditionally thought to be the body of Christ."

I was stunned by his reply, since he and his parents were atheists. His words about a national tradition had an empty ring to me, as they seemed to mimic a time of heartfelt reverence for Christ. The difference between the two eras was faith. One generation believed, the next two only go through the motions of respect out of tradition.

This all caused me to wonder. To what extent do we honor the Christ, the bread of life? Do our own children understand the sacredness of the bread, the body of Christ? And more importantly, do they know and believe in the Christ whom it represents?

Heavenly Father, *fill me with Your presence today. Make me aware of Your nurturing Spirit who teaches us and our children to believe. Thank You, Father, in the name of Your Son, the bread of life. Amen.*

SPOTLIGHT
Next Week's Lesson

God, who likes to make us glad, is sad to hear, "If only I had..."

July 30

Relying on the Spirit

Simon Peter answered Him, "Lord, to whom shall we go? You have the words of eternal life" (John 6:68, New King James Version).

I live in a small town, but we do have our own airport. However, since so few people use the service, only one carrier can afford to operate flights from here. So when I want to take a flight from home, I must use this carrier.

When Simon Peter confessed Jesus as his Lord, he made a statement that seems similar, at first blush, to my situation of having only one air travel provider. But that's not what Peter was saying when he asked, "to whom shall we go?" It's not that there was no one else who claimed to have knowledge of true religion. Many people in Jesus' time offered answers to the people's spiritual needs. And there were even numerous pretenders in those days claiming the title of Messiah.

Peter realized, instead, that what Jesus provided was the true Way—Jesus himself as the sacrifice for sin. Peter might not have understood the full significance of Jesus' blood and body yet, but he surely knew that Jesus' very words held the key to eternal life. In Peter's time, and in our own, there truly is no other way.

Lord, I thank You for Your great gift of salvation by the sacrifice of Jesus' body and blood. He has released us from the sentence of death and from the power of sin. May I live out this truth today! In Jesus' name, amen.

SEARCH THE WORD

Jesus has the monopoly on words that lead to eternal life.

Scripture: John 6:60-68
Song: *"No Not One"*

From this meditation today, I will pray . . .

Adoration _____

Confession _____

Thanksgiving _____

Supplication _____

From this meditation today, I will . . .

Think _____

Say _____

Do _____

July 31

Look to the Rock

Let any one who thinks that he stands take heed lest he fall
(1 Corinthians 10:12, *Revised Standard Version*).

Scripture: 1 Corinthians 10:1-11
Song: *"Rock of Ages"*

From this meditation today, I will pray...
Adoration _____
_____
_____

Confession _____
_____
_____

Thanksgiving _____
_____
_____

Supplication _____
_____
_____

From this meditation today, I will...
Think _____
_____
_____

Say _____
_____
_____

Do _____
_____
_____
_____

I went on vacation recently and visited a church in another state. It was a large, well-established congregation. The sermon theme was the necessity of doing good works, a theme repeated in the bulletin and on posters in the halls. But to this church "good works" meant providing services and programs *for each other*—such as mowing the church lawn, hosting ladies luncheons, leading men's retreats, and offering child care. There seemed to be no thought of the church having any ministries in their community at large nor in global missions.

My visit to this seemingly self-serving church caused me to rethink my own service to God. A minister once urged our congregation to think of our church not as a country club where we come to fellowship, but as a hospital where the weak and wounded can be received, comforted, and healed. I realized that lately my own "service to God" consisted of meeting my own needs, mainly for social interactions.

How easily our religion slips into pleasure-seeking idolatry, with our own needs as the focus. May we keep our eyes on the rock, our Savior, so that we don't fall.

O God, please forgive my sin of "self service." Lead me into paths of true service for Your glory. In Christ's holy name I pray. Amen.

SPOTLIGHT
Next Week's Lesson
How quickly God's people forgot all His blessings! So, how's your memory?

August

CALLED TO OBEY

*I lift up my voice to the L*ORD*. . . .*
Set me free . . . that I may praise your name.
—Psalm 142:1, 7

Photo © Comstock

August 1

Holy Vacations

Keep yourselves in God's love as you wait for the mercy of our Lord Jesus Christ to bring you to eternal life (Jude 21).

Scripture: Jude 1:14-23

Song: *"What a Friend We Have in Jesus"*

From this meditation today, I will pray . . .

Adoration _____
_____
_____

Confession _____
_____
_____

Thanksgiving _____
_____
_____

Supplication _____
_____
_____

From this meditation today, I will . . .

Think _____
_____
_____

Say _____
_____
_____

Do _____
_____
_____

When our children were growing up we took many modest vacations. The family sometimes planned all year for a special time away, but we often took short trips of a day or two as well. These times built great memories and relational bridges among us.

There were many other children in our neighborhood, but we never included them in our vacations. Why? They weren't a part of our family. Members are privileged to whatever bonuses the family offers, from extras—like vacations—to basics, like room and board.

God fashioned the family after the structure of His relationship with us. We Christians also benefit from being seated in His circle, a position that those who "follow their own ungodly desires" (v. 18) cannot enjoy. As we spend time with our Father, we develop a stronger relational bond along with great memories that we can share with the rest of the family. So, today, let's take some "vacation time" with our Father.

Heavenly Father, *may I see and hear You with new ears and heart. Refresh my cold soul with the warmth of Your love, like an Arizona sun on our Alaskan backs. I love You, Father, in Jesus' name. Amen.*

SPOTLIGHT
Next Week's Lesson

The benefits of being part of God's family belong to all of us who believe.

August 1, 2. **Shelley L. Houston** *lives in Eugene, Oregon, with her husband of 37 years. She writes for various secular and Christian publishers.*

August 2

Troubling the Servants?

Why have you brought this trouble on your servant? What have I done to displease you that you have put the burden of all these people on me? (Numbers 11:11, 12).

Do you ever get your way at church? Many decades ago, I thought my church was out of touch with what was relevant to life, especially concerning standards of dress. I decided to help them out of the "stone age" by wearing pants to church on a Sunday night. This action didn't have the effect I hoped—Mom cried, and a woman verbally shamed me. However, in time, the church did consent to women wearing pants to services.

A victory? Not mine. I have learned there is little worth fighting about in church. However, I continue to be amazed at the large number of Christians who selfishly torpedo the work of God over disappointments about their fairly trivial preferences. Things like the style of music, architectural aesthetics, parking lot spaces, or a myriad of other personal opinions are raised to church-splitting levels.

Some members tend to "bury" the true servants of the Lord in trivialities and foil their worthy efforts to witness to the message of God's grace. (So tell me: How are we different from the meat lovers' grumblings in the desert?)

O God, *forgive my foolish ways. Cause me to see my brother's needs as more important than my own. Help me respond to the higher calling of Your work in me, on behalf of others. In Jesus' name, amen.*

Scripture: Numbers 11:1-6, 11-15
Song: *"Father, Make Us One"*

From this meditation today, I will pray . . .

Adoration _____

Confession _____

Thanksgiving _____

Supplication _____

From this meditation today, I will . . .

Think _____

Say _____

Do _____

SEARCH THE WORD
Destroying unity over trivialities dishonors the Lord who makes us one.

August 3

It's a Privilege

They forgot what he had done, the wonders he had shown them (Psalm 78:11).

Scripture: Psalm 78:5-17

Song: *"Trusting in Thee"*

From this meditation today, I will pray . . .

Adoration _____
_____
_____

Confession _____
_____
_____

Thanksgiving _____
_____
_____

Supplication _____
_____
_____

From this meditation today, I will . . .

Think _____
_____
_____

Say _____
_____
_____

Do _____
_____
_____

"Don't you remember?" my friend said. "We talked about this before."

I did remember . . . vaguely. That is, I remembered talking, but I couldn't remember the particulars. "Sort of," I said. "But could you refresh my memory?"

Forgetfulness, I'm learning, is a natural by-product of growing older. I once could recall all sorts of random trivia. Now I'm lucky to remember what I ate for dinner yesterday. Usually, forgetfulness is merely inconvenient or embarrassing. In matters of faith, however, forgetfulness can be disastrous.

Many mornings I study the Bible, only to forget what I've learned by noon. Or God answers a prayer in a remarkable way, and within weeks I've forgotten about it. Perhaps one of the main reasons God gave us the Bible is so that we could go back over it, again and again, and refresh our memories. What a privilege He gives us!

Lord, *my memory dims with each passing year, and I forget things I want to remember. Should I forget all else, help me to remember You and Your faithfulness. Help me to remember what You've done, both in the grand scope of history and in my own personal history. In Jesus' name, amen.*

August 3-9. **Sarah Overturf** *lives in Longmont, Colorado, with her husband and three children. She is a writer and a school librarian.*

SPOTLIGHT
Next Week's Lesson

What memory aids do you use to remind yourself of God's goodness?

August 4

Lost, Not Forgotten

Although they have sold themselves among the nations, I will now gather them together (Hosea 8:10).

Scripture: Hosea 8:1-10

Song: *"Bringing in the Sheaves"*

I love browsing antique stores and rummaging through the old artifacts that speak of lives lived and passed. But I'm always saddened when I come to the inevitable box of black and white photographs. I look at the pictures of families, young couples, children, and babies, and I think, "Someone should have these." But how do you identify the "someone" who's connected to these lives? We live in a scattered society where we rarely know the names of our forbears, let alone their faces.

In God's family, however, there are no unknowns. There is no box of people He can't place. He knows our names, and He knows our faces. Even when we stray far away from His care, He does not forget us. He is ever waiting to gather us back to himself, to reclaim us as His own. "This one here—he is mine. And that one there—she belongs to me."

Are you praying today for someone who is "lost"? Keep praying. That person may be lost, but he or she will never be forgotten.

Father, *thank You for bringing me back to yourself. Thank You for claiming me, for calling me Your child and allowing me to call You Father. Thank You for reminding me that though I may be forgotten in this world, I matter to You for eternity. Amen.*

From this meditation today, I will pray...

Adoration _____

Confession _____

Thanksgiving _____

Supplication _____

From this meditation today, I will...

Think _____

Say _____

Do _____

SEARCH THE WORD

If God carried a wallet, your picture would be in it.

August 5

Too Much to Ask?

He has showed you, O man, what is good. And what does the Lord *require of you? To act justly and to love mercy and to walk humbly with your God* (Micah 6:8).

Scripture: Micah 6:1-8
Song: "He Has Shown Thee, O Man"

From this meditation today, I will pray . . .
Adoration _____
_____
_____

Confession _____
_____
_____

Thanksgiving _____
_____
_____

Supplication _____
_____
_____

From this meditation today, I will . . .
Think _____
_____
_____

Say _____
_____
_____

Do _____
_____
_____
_____

I wasn't asking for much. Laundry folded. The dishwasher emptied. Bathrooms tidied. And no bickering. What I got instead were grumblings, sharp words, and shoddy work. Was it too much to ask for a few simple tasks to be completed with good attitudes?

Yet I have to admit that sometimes my own attitude and work can be less than exemplary. I groan when the phone interrupts an important project. I scowl at the dryer when it buzzes—again. Sometimes I wonder whether God looks at me and says, "Is it too much to ask—?"

Really, God doesn't ask that much of us. Just three things: justice, mercy, and humility. What would my life look like, I wonder, if I kept those three things at the fore of my thoughts? What if my children saw actions from me today that were truly just? What if my coworkers heard words of mercy from me? What if my neighbors saw me walking humbly? I wonder what good such a life might do. Surely finding out is not too much to ask.

Lord, *You have shown me what is good and what You require of me. Help me now to live it in the most practical ways. May my life be marked by these three things: justice, mercy, and a humble walk with You. I pray this prayer in the name of Jesus, my Savior and Lord. Amen.*

SPOTLIGHT
Next Week's Lesson

After all God did for them, was it too much to ask for the Israelites to trust Him?

August 6

Understanding Comfort

This is why I weep and my eyes overflow with tears. No one is near to comfort me, no one to restore my spirit (Lamentations 1:16).

My neighbor looked at me through her filmy blue eyes. "There aren't many left," she said.

I nodded as though I understood, but I didn't. Not really. She was near the end of her life. Her husband, her siblings, and most of her friends were gone. I was in a very different place, busy with little kids at home. I had no idea what it was like to be one of the last in an ever-shrinking circle of relationships. But my neighbor didn't need me to know that. She just wanted someone to know that she was in a hard and lonely place. I didn't have to be nearing the end of my own life to give her understanding. I could be right where I was.

When someone is going through a hard time, often what they need most is just someone who is near. A listening ear, the touch of a hand, a hug, an arm around their shoulders—these things bring both comfort and restoration to their spirits. And the only cost is a little of our time.

Father, *Your Holy Spirit is the Comforter within me. And yet You often choose to bring Your comfort through Your people. Help me to be a channel of comfort today. Help me see who is hurting and to be a human touch for Your heavenly warmth. I pray in the name of Christ. Amen.*

Scripture: Lamentations 1:16-21
Song: *"The Comforter Has Come"*

From this meditation today, I will pray . . .

Adoration _____

Confession _____

Thanksgiving _____

Supplication _____

From this meditation today, I will . . .

Think _____

Say _____

Do _____

SEARCH THE WORD

"The elderly need so little, but they need that little so much."
—Author unknown

August 7

Test Time

Let us examine our ways and test them, and let us return to the LORD (**Lamentations 3:40**).

Scripture: Lamentations 3:39-50
Song: *"I Am Thine, O Lord"*

From this meditation today, I will pray . . .

Adoration _____
_____
_____

Confession _____
_____
_____

Thanksgiving _____
_____
_____

Supplication _____
_____
_____

From this meditation today, I will . . .

Think _____
_____
_____

Say _____
_____
_____

Do _____
_____
_____
_____

Tests must be the bane of nearly every student who has ever sat at a desk. All that studying, all that work, and for what? Well, beyond basic knowledge, tests get us ready for life.

Tests don't end when school does. From the time we wake (will I hit snooze or get up and pray?) to the time we go to bed (will I go to bed angry, or will I make things right?), we're faced with one test after the other. Are we kind when others are rude? Are we gracious when someone else gets credit for a job we did? Are we patient, even when our last nerve is stretched thin?

Sometimes we fail at something we try, but there is zeal and passion in our motives. Sometimes we say the sweetest things, but our hearts are darkened with bitterness or envy. How will we know, unless we examine ourselves?

We won't pass every test with flying colors, but when we're consistently examining ourselves, we'll find that our tests bring us nearer to God. And that's better than an A any day.

Dear Father, *I need Your wisdom to examine both my ways and my heart. I don't see motives as clearly as You do, and I want them to be pure. I want the things I do, and the reasons behind them, to bring me nearer and nearer to You. In Jesus' name I pray. Amen.*

SPOTLIGHT
Next Week's Lesson

The 10 spies failed the test of courage, and the rest of Israel flunked too.

August 8

Pardon Me

Who is a God like you, who pardons sin and forgives the transgression of the remnant of his inheritance? You do not stay angry forever but delight to show mercy (Micah 7:18).

Anger covers quite a spectrum, including everything from being a little miffed to being blood-boiling, steam-rising furious. Anger is one of the strongest emotions we feel, and its energy powers many of our attitudes and actions. Strangely enough, it also seems to power some of God's actions.

What angers God? Sin. But because God also loves us, He does something about it. Through His anger comes a remarkable gift: pardon. He says, yes, what you did was wrong. But the debt has been paid. My Son paid it for you.

Scarcely a day goes by that we don't feel some form of anger. We can't keep anger from bubbling up, but we can choose what to do with it when it rises within us. We can fuel it, or we can let it lead to pardon and mercy.

Thankfully, God's anger doesn't last forever. He delights in pardoning us. And what a joy it is for us to receive and share both His pardon and His delight.

Who is a God like You, **Lord?** *Anger that leads to mercy—what an incredible gift! Help me when I am angry to remember to show mercy to those around me. Help me to pardon others as You have pardoned me. In the holy name of Jesus, my Lord and Savior, I pray. Amen.*

Scripture: Micah 7:14-20

Song: *"Grace Greater Than Our Sin"*

From this meditation today, I will pray...

Adoration _____
_____
_____

Confession _____
_____
_____

Thanksgiving _____
_____
_____

Supplication _____
_____
_____

From this meditation today, I will...

Think _____
_____
_____

Say _____
_____
_____

Do _____
_____
_____
_____

SEARCH THE WORD

"In your anger do not sin"
(Ephesians 4:26).

August 9

Running Scared?

Only do not rebel against the Lord. *And do not be afraid of the people of the land, because we will swallow them up. Their protection is gone, but the* Lord *is with us. Do not be afraid of them* (Numbers 14:9).

Scripture: Numbers 14:1-12

Song: *"Have Faith in God"*

From this meditation today, I will pray . . .
Adoration _____
_____
_____
Confession _____
_____
_____
Thanksgiving _____
_____
_____
Supplication _____
_____
_____

From this meditation today, I will . . .
Think _____
_____
_____
Say _____
_____
_____
Do _____
_____
_____
_____
_____

I was jogging through my neighborhood one winter night, bundled against the cold in a jacket, gloves, and a head warmer. Suddenly I heard footsteps behind me. Running footsteps. But they weren't passing, they were following me.

My already rapid heart rate raced as I tried to think of a plan. Ring someone's doorbell? Stop? Turn? Scream?

Ahead, a man was wheeling his trash can out to the curb. Surely here was help. But he only glanced quickly in my direction before going inside.

Then I felt something. Something I hadn't noticed before. My hair was bouncing against the head warmer as I ran. And the head warmer covered my ears, muffling the sound. There were no footsteps; it was only hair.

Isn't that how it often is with fear? Something that seems so terrifying turns out to be nothing. Sometimes there are real giants in the land, but sometimes they are only giants because we've let some unworthy thing grow too big in our own minds.

Lord, *this world is filled with frightening things. Help me to remember that when You are with me, I have nothing to fear. Through Christ, amen.*

SPOTLIGHT
Next Week's Lesson

No giant is too big
for God to vanquish.

August 10

Imperfect, but Honored

Take Aaron and Eleazar his son, and bring them up unto mount Hor (Numbers 20:25, *King James Version*).

Scripture: Numbers 20:22-29

Song: *"There's a Wideness in God's Mercy"*

The death of Israel's first high priest is typical of the death of many great, but flawed leaders. Three key words sum up Aaron's life.

Stripped: At his death, Aaron was divested of his honorable position and distinctive garments. He died humbly on a lonely mountaintop. Like Aaron, many of God's servants die peacefully, but sin leaves a dark cloud over their lives.

Gathered: Aaron was not "cut off" from his people like a rebellious sinner, but "gathered" to them like a repentant one (v. 26). God restored Aaron, and the passing of such a servant deserves a place of honor in the hearts of his countrymen.

Mourned: While his vital position was filled, Aaron's absence left a conspicuous hole (v. 29). After all, he and Moses were the original leaders of the Exodus. Like so many of God's servants, Aaron was valued more in death than in life. Death has a way of putting an imperfect career in its true light.

Dear Lord, *help me to honor the good that Your grace has accomplished in the imperfect lives of those who have loved You. In Jesus' name, Amen.*

From this meditation today, I will pray . . .

Adoration _____

Confession _____

Thanksgiving _____

Supplication _____

From this meditation today, I will . . .

Think _____

Say _____

Do _____

SEARCH THE WORD

May we be as merciful to our less than perfect leaders as God is to us.

August 10–16. **Richard M. Robinson** *is a Baptist minister in Denver, Colorado. He enjoys singing in a gospel quartet, writing, and collecting vintage Mac computers.*

August 11

How History Comes Alive

Blow up the trumpet in the new moon, in the time appointed, on our solemn feast day (Psalm 81:3, *King James Version*).

Scripture: Psalm 81:1-10
Song: *"O Praise Our God Today"*

From this meditation today, I will pray...
Adoration _____
_____
_____
Confession _____
_____
_____
Thanksgiving _____
_____
_____
Supplication _____
_____
_____

From this meditation today, I will...
Think _____
_____
_____
Say _____
_____
_____
Do _____
_____
_____
_____

Israel's celebrations were to be tributes to a loving God. Their religious holidays rested on historical reference points, especially their slavery in Egypt (vv. 5, 6) and survival in a barren wilderness (v. 7). Over time, this glorious history became academic and ordinary to the people. But holidays need history, or they will lose their power to inspire. To counteract this tendency, Asaph called up images from the past, as when their ancestors were released from heavy burdens and menial work (v. 6).

Short of a time machine, a little sanctified imagination is the next best thing to being there. After all, we should learn history to leap into it. So be creative.

Joseph Bayly, in his poem, *Psalm of Laughter for Easter,* compared history's greatest event with life's happiest moments. To jump-start his joy, he imagined this:

> Christ died and rose and lives.
> Laugh like a woman who holds her first baby.
> Our enemy death will soon be destroyed.
> Laugh like a man who finds he doesn't have cancer.

It's true! A little imagination makes history come alive.

Dear Lord, *sanctify my imagination as I study Your Word. Let it produce celebrations of joy in my life. Through Christ I pray. Amen.*

SPOTLIGHT
Next Week's Lesson

For Moses, disobedience changed the joy of God's miracle into sorrow and disappointment.

August 12

How Will You Respond?

It is a people that do err in their heart, and they have not known my ways (Psalm 95:10, King James Version).

Scripture: Psalm 95
Song: "Search Me, O God"

The Exodus Generation were eyewitnesses to history's greatest miracles. As the Lord declared, they "saw my work" (v. 9). But lacking the faculty of spiritual eyesight, they stumbled in unbelief like blind men. They were incredibly wrong-headed in their assessments and conclusions of God's dealings.

The real problem was their erring hearts. Verse 10 is quoted in Hebrews 3:10 with one addition: "They do always err in their heart." Chronic wrong thinking stems less from defective logic and more from diminished love. If they had only known God's heart, they would have understood His ways.

It's all in how you respond. In verses 1-7, hearts melt like butter. But in verses 8-11, they harden like clay. Some receive and others reject, but the love is the same.

This psalm ends in death. Hardened and hopeless, the erring ones must die in the wilderness (v. 11). As Thornton Wilder observed, "There is a land of the living and a land of the dead—and the bridge is love, the only survival, the only meaning."

"Search me, O God, and know my heart: try me, and know my thoughts: and see if there be any wicked way in me, and lead me in the way everlasting" (Psalm 139:23, 24). In Jesus' name, amen.

From this meditation today, I will pray . . .
Adoration _____
_____
_____

Confession _____
_____
_____

Thanksgiving _____
_____
_____

Supplication _____
_____
_____

From this meditation today, I will . . .
Think _____
_____
_____

Say _____
_____
_____

Do _____
_____
_____

SEARCH THE WORD

Belief doesn't depend upon the size of the miracle but on the condition of the heart.

August 13

A Tale of Two Trees

Blessed is the man that trusteth in the LORD, *and whose hope the* LORD *is* (Jeremiah 17:7, King James Version).

Scripture: Jeremiah 17:5-10
Song: *"Find Us Faithful"*

From this meditation today, I will pray . . .
Adoration _____

Confession _____

Thanksgiving _____

Supplication _____

From this meditation today, I will . . .
Think _____

Say _____

Do _____

To borrow a few lines from a classic Dickens story: "It was the best of times, it was the worst of times, it was the age of wisdom, it was the age of foolishness . . . it was the spring of hope, it was the winter of despair . . ."

The prophet Jeremiah would certainly agree. In his day, society was a study in contrast. The majority were morally decayed and spiritually stunted, the outgrowth of a godless culture. However, the faithful remnant experienced revival in the midst of national decline.

This disparity comes through in the prophet's picture of two trees. The unbelieving majority were like a "heath in the desert" (v. 6). Resembling the Dwarf Juniper, they were as Matthew Henry described, "a naked tree, a sorry shrub, the product of barren ground, useless and worthless." But there was a godly minority that spiritually prospered like "a tree planted by the waters" (v. 8). The happy result: they were stable, preserved, and fruitful.

Even in the worst of times, surrounded by fools with spirits chilled into despair, you can be God's paradox, flourishing by faith.

Dear Heavenly Father, may I trust You more fully today. And keep me rooted in Your Word so that I may show others the secret of abounding in You. In the name of Jesus, Lord and Savior of all, I pray. Amen.

SPOTLIGHT
Next Week's Lesson

An abundance of water gushed out in spite of, not because of, Moses' level of faith.

August 14

Diluting the Savior?

He saith unto them, But whom say ye that I am?
(Matthew 16:15, King James Version).

Back in 2001, a Kansas City pharmacist was charged with diluting the cancer treatment drugs, Gemzar and Taxol, in order to make a larger profit. Americans were shocked and outraged. Robert Courtney admitted to diluting the drugs over a five-month span.

Commentator Michael Owenby observed, "This man held life-saving power in his hands, and for the sake of personal gain diluted it to the point where it could not help people. We can do the same with God's life-saving truth."

With life and death implications, Jesus asked His disciples, "Whom do men say that I, the Son of man, am?" (v. 13). If they presented anything less than the truth, the gospel would be turned into a powerless placebo for dying sinners. This is the worst criminal act in the world.

Peter's bold, clear answer was the pure truth: "Thou art the Christ, the Son of the living God" (v. 16). This is the only cure for the cancer of sin. And if we are to save souls and escape Heaven's censure, we dare not dilute the Savior!

O Holy Father, keep me from ever carelessly or knowingly misrepresenting Jesus, the Son of God, to a sin-sick world. He is fully man, fully God, incarnate to save us by His cross. And I pray in His precious name. Amen.

Scripture: Matthew 16:13-18
Song: *"Our Great Savior"*

From this meditation today, I will pray . . .

Adoration _____

Confession _____

Thanksgiving _____

Supplication _____

From this meditation today, I will . . .

Think _____

Say _____

Do _____

SEARCH THE WORD

Let's administer a full-strength dose of gospel truth to those who are dying.

August 15

Is It Worth It?

He that sat upon the throne said, Behold, I make all things new. And he said unto me, Write: for these words are true and faithful (Revelation 21:5, *King James Version*).

Scripture: Revelation 21:1-7
Song: *"When We All Get to Heaven"*

From this meditation today, I will pray . . .
Adoration _____
_____
_____

Confession _____
_____
_____

Thanksgiving _____
_____
_____

Supplication _____
_____
_____

From this meditation today, I will . . .
Think _____
_____
_____

Say _____
_____
_____

Do _____
_____
_____
_____

As the Bible ends with John's final glimpse into the eternal future, it again answers one of life's biggest questions: "Is it worth it?" Yes, life is hard, often unfair, and sometimes tragic. But take heart, a new world is coming (v. 1). Overcomers down here won't be underwhelmed up there. That era will be as far ahead of our age as we are to worms crawling in the mud!

John's picture actually defies description. In describing these visions, Don Fleming wisely observes: "They are not pictures of the physical characteristics of the new heaven and the new earth. The heavenly city is not an improved version of the present earthly city . . . the present world is to be completely replaced by a new order."

God means it when He says, "Behold, I make all things new" (v. 5). Think of it. Everything and everyone made new, made pure, made perfect forever. And best of all, "God himself shall be with them, and be their God" Is it worth it? You be the judge.

Dear Father, *it's really true, "the best is yet to be." Thank You for all my present blessings, but I am most grateful that You saved the best for last! In the name of Jesus, my Savior, I pray. Amen.*

SPOTLIGHT
Next Week's Lesson

Just as Moses got a glimpse of the promised land, we can envision Heaven as we read Revelation.

August 16

Does Anger Really Work?

Moses lifted up his hand, and with his rod he smote the rock twice: and the water came out abundantly, and the congregation drank, and their beasts also (Numbers 20:11, *King James Version*).

Scripture: Numbers 20:1-13
Song: *"Teach Me Thy Way, O Lord"*

Scripture declares that maturity, experience, and position aren't in themselves sufficient against temptation. Some of the Bible's greatest heroes have sinned after reaching an advanced age. Noah, David, Solomon, and Hezekiah are all prime examples of failing after much success. And the list includes Moses.

When God told Israel's greatest prophet to bring water out of the rock by speaking to it, Moses never even hinted that he would do otherwise. But because he was slandered and provoked by the people, Moses secretly simmered in anger.

Feeling belittled and humiliated by a new generation not half his age, he decided to strike back—literally. Whack! Whack! Two dramatic blows, and water gushed out. But now Moses' career was about to dry up.

The whole sad episode was caused by anger. As James reminds us, "the wrath of man worketh not the righteousness of God" (1:20). All Moses really needed to do was "Speak softly and carry a big stick."

Dear Lord, *help me to be patient and forgiving with others. Remind me that meekness is a virtue that You look for and use. In Jesus' name, amen.*

From this meditation today, I will pray . . .
Adoration
Confession
Thanksgiving
Supplication

From this meditation today, I will . . .
Think
Say
Do

SEARCH THE WORD

Don't let an explosion of anger cause you to blow it.

August 17

The Lord Is at Hand

I will walk among you and be your God, and you will be my people
(Leviticus 26:12).

Scripture: Leviticus 26:3-13
Song: *"O Master, Let Me Walk with Thee"*

From this meditation today, I will pray . . .
Adoration _____
_____
_____

Confession _____
_____
_____

Thanksgiving _____
_____
_____

Supplication _____
_____
_____

From this meditation today, I will . . .
Think _____
_____
_____

Say _____
_____
_____

Do _____
_____
_____

Sometimes, life becomes truly hectic. Pressures of family, job, community, and church bear down. You hunger for quiet minutes, maybe with a friend over coffee.

Well, good news. That friend is nearby. Jesus' final instructions to His disciples closed with these words: "Surely I am with you always, to the very end of the age" (Matthew 28:20). You might call that promise the fourth dimension of the great commission.

We know well the first three dimensions. Go and make disciples (recruit new followers of Jesus). Baptize them (identify the new followers as part of Jesus' body, the church). Teach them (instruct new followers to practice Jesus' teachings, day by day). This is the mission statement for Christians in every age, but there is more.

You see, Jesus is no distant taskmaster we must report to someday. He promised to *remain with* His humblest servant, always to encourage and strengthen. And Jesus always keeps His word. So pause often in a quiet corner of your heart. He is there for you.

Thank You, Jesus, for being my constant companion. Teach me to follow You closely and openly share my heart with You. In Your name, amen.

> **SPOTLIGHT**
> *Next Week's Lesson*
>
> The better we get to know Him, the more we will love Him.

August 17, 18, 20–23. **Lloyd Mattson** is a retired minister and writer with 15 great-grandchildren. He lives in Duluth, Minnesota.

August 18

Priorities in Order

Your strength will be spent in vain, because your soil will not yield its crops, nor will the trees of the land yield their fruit (Leviticus 26:20).

A farmer named Anton Nelson attended the small, country church I served as a seminary student. He was not what you'd call religious, but he was kind, and he always took Sundays off. Hay down, grain ripe, corn ready to pick—it didn't matter. Come Sunday morning, Anton milked his cows then put on his white shirt. Sometimes his family included our young family in Sunday afternoon picnics on the nearby river. We fished with long cane poles.

Meanwhile, my more dedicated churchmen often rode their tractors on summer Sundays, from dawn to dusk. They worried about rain and hail. (Sudden storms can cost a farmer dearly, if grain is ripe and hay is down. The Lord understands, right?)

I talked with Anton about all of this one day. He spoke not a word against the Sunday workers, but smiled quietly. "Sure, I get rained on sometimes, but after farming a long time, I can't see that my neighbors are any better off than me." Anton raised good crops and a fine family. He seemed at peace with himself. He had his priorities right.

Heavenly Father, *give me a long-range view. Let me not be tempted to compromise spiritual principles for immediate gain. In Jesus' name, amen.*

Scripture: Leviticus 26:14-26
Song: *"God Will Take Care of You"*

From this meditation today, I will pray . . .
Adoration _____

Confession _____

Thanksgiving _____

Supplication _____

From this meditation today, I will . . .
Think _____

Say _____

Do _____

SEARCH THE WORD
No matter what others say, you'll be blessed doing it God's way.

August 19

Bending the Rules

*[Samuel said,] "Why did you not obey the Lord?" . . .
"But I did obey the Lord," Saul said* (1 Samuel 15:19, 20).

Scripture: 1 Samuel 15:17-26
Song: *"I Surrender All"*

From this meditation today, I will pray . . .
Adoration _____
_____
_____

Confession _____
_____
_____

Thanksgiving _____
_____
_____

Supplication _____
_____
_____

From this meditation today, I will . . .
Think _____
_____
_____

Say _____
_____
_____

Do _____
_____
_____

King Saul was absolutely flabbergasted. He'd done what the Lord had asked him to do, and now Samuel was telling him the kingdom would be taken away from him because of his disobedience? Samuel had said to completely destroy the Amalekites and he had—except for their king, Agag. Saul knew that God had commanded him, "Totally destroy everything that belongs to them" (v. 3) and he'd done that—except for the very best sheep and cattle, which he intended to sacrifice to the Lord. Of course, his soldiers had also taken some sheep and cattle, but that was their right of plunder. In Saul's eyes the punishment was much too harsh for the crime of bending the rules a little bit. But God didn't see it that way.

Before we condemn Saul too harshly, we may want to look at our own tendencies to bend the rules to our own advantage. Whether it's speeding so we're not late for church, revealing some (but not all) of our income on a tax return, or lying to make ourselves look better than we are, we are all tempted to adapt the rules to suit ourselves. May God give us hearts to obey His commands to the best of our ability.

O Holy Father, how easy it is to make excuses for ourselves for failing to obey You. Help us to see our sin for what it truly is: an act of rebellion. Give us the strength and desire to do it Your way today. In Jesus' name, amen.

SPOTLIGHT
Next Week's Lesson

Reading and following God's signposts will keep us on the straight and narrow path.

August 19. **Cheryl J. Frey** *runs an editorial service out of her home in Rochester, New York. She spends her spare time with family—especially her grandchildren.*

August 20

Harmony in the Trinity

The Father loves the Son and has placed everything in his hands (John 3:35).

A godly friend from a church other than mine worries about me. According to him, I neglect the Holy Spirit. He fears my grasp of biblical truth and style of worship fall short. My friend knows I love Jesus, but he says that's not enough.

I respect his faith and worship, but I am content with mine. I gently remind my friend that the Godhead knows no jealously. No one can honor the Father and Son yet grieve the Holy Spirit.

We can't fully grasp the mystery of the Trinity—Father, Son and Holy Spirit—three in one. Nor can we know the full meaning of the Incarnation—Jesus, true God and true man. Faith begins where human knowledge ends, so we thank the Father for sending His Son to redeem us, and we thank the blessed Holy Spirit for drawing us to the Son. When we worship one, we worship all.

Why should varying perceptions of the unfathomable truths divide us? As brothers and sisters in Christ, we serve together in the kingdom of God's infinite grace.

Thank You, Father Almighty, for the rich variety of Christian thought that broadens the gospel outreach. Bless each church fellowship in my community that honors Your Son, my Savior. In the name of the Father, the Son, and the Holy Spirit, I pray. Amen.

Scripture: John 3:31-36
Song: *"The Family of God"*

From this meditation today, I will pray...
Adoration _____

Confession _____

Thanksgiving _____

Supplication _____

From this meditation today, I will...
Think _____

Say _____

Do _____

SEARCH THE WORD

May there be a wideness in our mercy toward other believers.

August 21

How's Your Appetite?

*You would be fed with the finest of wheat;
with honey from the rock I would satisfy you* (Psalm 81:16).

Scripture: Psalm 81:11-16
Song: *"My Heart Is Yearning Ever"*

From this meditation today, I will pray . . .
Adoration _____
_____
_____
Confession _____
_____
_____
Thanksgiving _____
_____
_____
Supplication _____
_____
_____

From this meditation today, I will . . .
Think _____
_____
_____
Say _____
_____
_____
Do _____
_____
_____
_____

The finest banquet I ever ate was Spam baked with cloves and brown sugar, a generous serving of macaroni (lightly browned), and a tall glass of cold milk. I have often eaten more exotic fare, but that dinner was memorable . . . because I was *so hungry*.

I was on a walking kick. One hundred miles a month. And each week or so I would fast for 36 hours. I never felt better or enjoyed greater vigor. The weight loss was welcome, but I did it mainly for fun. I simply loved walking.

On that "banquet morning" I set out for Lakewood School, about three miles away, I figured. But I figured wrong. The distance was five miles. No problem. I'd phone Elsie. But the school was closed. Elsie's golf course was only three miles away. Likely she'd be there. But she wasn't. I phoned from the club house for a ride and heard my beloved say, "Hurry home. Lunch is about ready—baked Spam and macaroni." But I still had another mile to walk!

When you have a heart-deep appetite for God, the simplest gospel fare is honey from the Rock. What is your appetite for Him these days?

O God, *help me listen closely to my heart this day. What will it tell me of my hunger for You? In Christ's name I pray. Amen.*

SPOTLIGHT
Next Week's Lesson

Are you starving for affection?
Nourish your soul with the
love of God.

August 22

No Quick Study!

The LORD *gives wisdom, and from his mouth come knowledge and understanding* (Proverbs 2:6).

For several years my work called for writing books and articles on Christian camping. I was humbled one day to meet an adult Asian student who shook my hand warmly and said, "You are my guru." My philosophy and ideas on camping had resonated with him. He asked me to read his thesis. I did and heard familiar echoes.

My ideas, of course, came from others. Truly original thinkers are rare. I gleaned concepts from my own "gurus," which I digested, reshaped, and blended into my own writings. My Asian friend had shaped my second-hand ideas to fit his culture.

Another generation will probably find my borrowed wisdom obsolete, but God's wisdom remains timeless. And here is one place to find it: We turn too seldom to the early church fathers (Irenaeus, Polycarp, Augustine, and the others), who spent their lifetimes pouring over God's Word and defending the faith. They wrestled with many of the ideas that challenge Bible students today. We can learn from, and build on, their findings.

God's wisdom really doesn't lend itself to quick sound bites. Let us be ready to work hard at understanding.

Lord God in Heaven, *speak to my heart of Your timeless wisdom. And let me be still long enough to hear! In Jesus' name I pray. Amen.*

SEARCH THE WORD
Wisdom comes from a long soak, not a quick splash, in God's Word.

Scripture: Proverbs 2:1-11
Song: *"Lord, Speak to Me"*

From this meditation today, I will pray . . .
Adoration _____

Confession _____

Thanksgiving _____

Supplication _____

From this meditation today, I will . . .
Think _____

Say _____

Do _____

August 23

What's on Your Mind?

Talk about them when you sit at home and when you walk along the road, when you lie down and when you get up (Deuteronomy 6:7).

Scripture: Deuteronomy 6:1-9, 20-24
Song: *"Thy Word Have I Hid in My Heart"*

From this meditation today, I will pray . . .
Adoration _____
_____
_____

Confession _____
_____
_____

Thanksgiving _____
_____
_____

Supplication _____
_____
_____

From this meditation today, I will . . .
Think _____
_____
_____

Say _____
_____
_____

Do _____
_____
_____
_____

Where does your mind go when it's free? A member of a board I led could rarely get through a meeting without slipping away to check the stock market. He was a banker, and his subconscious continually scanned the ticker tape.

Ask a group of teens what is most on their minds. The boys will probably shout *Girls!* The girls will say *Boys.* Dating is big among adolescents.

In younger years I was given to trout fishing. The moment my mind was free, it wandered to a stream and calculated where to lay the fly.

Banking, dating, and fly fishing are worthy enough, but wouldn't it be great if a sense of God's presence became the background music of our soul? The blessed man of Psalm 1 knew about that: "On his law he meditates day and night."

Why not turn random thinking into conversation with God, rather than just a dialogue with yourself? Talk about ordinary things. Ask the Lord to help you plan your day, drive safely, and use your words wisely.

God, *fill me with thoughts of You today. Let my every thought become prayer. And when things go wrong, help me to let You in on my problems, trusting Your wisdom for the way through. In Jesus' name, amen.*

SPOTLIGHT
Next Week's Lesson

How soon after waking do your thoughts turn to God?

August 24

Joy at Lake Tahoe

He spread out a cloud as a covering, and a fire to give light at night (Psalm 105:39).

My wife, Juanita, and I were camping above Lake Tahoe in northern California. We'd just driven from Chicago, loaded down with everything we owned. We had no job, no place to stay. My anxiety was growing. What in the world were we going to do?

This must have been how the Israelites felt when they left Egypt and camped in the wilderness, loaded down with their silver and gold. What in the world were they going to do? They shouldn't have worried. As He had promised, God was with them—in the cloud, in the fire, in the bread and quail, and in water from the rock.

That night at Lake Tahoe, I remembered some Christian friends who lived near San Francisco. I hadn't seen them for 10 years. So what made me think of them? I have no doubt that God brought them to my mind. Through this miracle, He kept His promise to care for us. I called my friends the next morning from a pay phone. "Sure, you can stay with us," they responded. "Our home is your home."

Dear Father, *I praise Your faithfulness and constant presence. You always think about where I am and where I'm going. In Christ's name, amen.*

Scripture: Psalm 105:37-45
Song: *"God Is Working His Purpose Out"*

From this meditation today, I will pray . . .

Adoration _____

Confession _____

Thanksgiving _____

Supplication _____

From this meditation today, I will . . .

Think _____

Say _____

Do _____

SEARCH THE WORD
There's no better stroll down memory lane than recalling a time when God provided.

August 24–30. **Larry Brook** grew up in Cameroun, Africa, the son of missionaries. He is a tenor soloist with the Elgin Opera Company in Illinois.

August 25

Without a Doubt?

When they saw him, they worshiped him; but some doubted
(Matthew 28:17).

Scripture: Matthew 28:16-20

Song: *"I Need Thee Every Hour"*

From this meditation today, I will pray . . .
Adoration _____
_____
_____

Confession _____
_____
_____

Thanksgiving _____
_____
_____

Supplication _____
_____
_____

From this meditation today, I will . . .
Think _____
_____
_____

Say _____
_____
_____

Do _____
_____
_____
_____

A few weeks after my wife and I moved to California, we rented a small apartment near Berkeley. Juanita found a part-time job in a fabric shop, but I was still looking for work. Then we faced a real crisis. I developed a blood clot in my leg and was consigned to complete bed rest. The days passed, and the bills kept coming. I sat in the room feeling bleak and hopeless. To be honest, I was filled with doubt.

There were people in Jesus' day who doubted. But how could they? I honestly don't know. (But then, look who's talking—how could *I* doubt?)

I've come to think that belief and doubt live side by side in all of our hearts. Jesus must have known this. I picture Him making bold eye contact with the doubters and saying, "I will be with *you* always."

A few days later, as I was trying to pray on my bed, I sensed Christ's presence in a special way. It was as if He were in my face, saying "I will be with *you*." In that moment, I was filled with gratitude. How little room for doubt there was then!

Dear Lord of my life, *I believe in You. Please help my unbelief, as I thank You for the confidence You are building in my heart. Trusting in Your name, Christ Jesus, I pray. Amen.*

SPOTLIGHT
Next Week's Lesson

It's almost beyond belief
how much God longs
to bless us.

August 26

God Is Great!

You are a forgiving God, gracious and compassionate, slow to anger and abounding in love (Nehemiah 9:17).

British writer Christopher Hitchens has come out with a new book titled, *God Is Not Great*. Right now it's in the top ten of the *New York Times* best-seller list. I heard Hitchens recently on the radio scolding a Baptist preacher who had called in to share his faith. The preacher said he and many others had been witness to the miraculous healing of his daughter—after much prayer.

Hitchens' reply? "How can you be so egotistical to believe that there is a God who cares about you and responds to your personal needs? You are deluding the public with false hopes, and you ought to be ashamed of yourself." What I wonder is why there are so many people who want to buy Hitchens' book and read about how indifferent—and *not* great—God is.

It makes me appreciate so much more Nehemiah's solid telling of the truth. Despite the refusal of the Israelites to "listen" and to "remember," despite their "rebellion," that God, in fact, was great. He was "forgiving" and "compassionate," "slow to anger," and "abounding in love."

He still is all these things, Christopher Hitchens, no matter what you say.

O God, *I say this with complete joy and confidence—You are great! Thank You for Your love and care. In Jesus' name, amen.*

SEARCH THE WORD

"For you are great and do marvelous deeds; you alone are God" (Psalm 86:10).

Scripture: Nehemiah 9:16-20

Song: *"How Great Thou Art"*

From this meditation today, I will pray . . .

Adoration _____

Confession _____

Thanksgiving _____

Supplication _____

From this meditation today, I will . . .

Think _____

Say _____

Do _____

August 27

Rebel Behind the Stove

Fear the LORD *and serve him with all faithfulness. Throw away the gods your forefathers worshiped beyond the River and in Egypt, and serve the* LORD *(Joshua 24:14).*

Scripture: Joshua 24:14-24
Song: *"And Can It Be That I Should Gain?"*

From this meditation today, I will pray...
Adoration _____
_____
_____

Confession _____
_____
_____

Thanksgiving _____
_____
_____

Supplication _____
_____
_____

From this meditation today, I will...
Think _____
_____
_____

Say _____
_____
_____

Do _____
_____
_____
_____

Dr. Walter Wilson, medical doctor and evangelist, once preached in a small country church that was heated by a wood stove at the back. During each service, a young man named Everett sat hidden behind the stove to listen to the sermon. Everett was "rough, ungodly, and given to wicked practices." But though he showed up for each sermon, he never stayed to talk. Instead, he bolted out the door.

Joshua, like Dr. Wilson, also knew the hearts of his listeners. He knew the people of Israel were disobedient. He challenged them to choose to serve the Lord and throw away the false gods of the Amorites. The people responded in faith: "We too will serve the Lord, because he is our God" (v. 18).

One evening, Dr. Wilson arrived at the little church to find Everett on the front step reading "the largest Bible I have ever seen." Everett explained that during the night he had chosen to serve Christ. "I have this big Bible," he said, "because I want everybody to know that Everett has been converted and loves the Bible."

Thank You, God, for continuing to call people today to fear You and serve You in faithfulness. May I demonstrate Everett's commitment to openly share Your love. In Jesus' name I pray. Amen.

SPOTLIGHT
Next Week's Lesson

No choice in life will bless us more than giving our hearts to the Lord.

August 28

Fish Faith

Who is it that overcomes the world? Only he who believes that Jesus is the Son of God (1 John 5:5).

When I was in Cambodia leading a Christian writers workshop, a young man told me his amazing story.

During the time of Pol Pot and "the killing fields" of the communist Khmer Rouge army, the young man's guards forced him to go down to the river and catch them a fish for dinner. They said that if he failed, they would cut his head off. The young man knew that his time had come, because the river was swift, and he had nothing with which to catch a fish.

Nevertheless, when he reached the river bank, he prayed, "Jesus, I know You are with me, and I release myself into Your hands." At that moment, he heard a thrashing sound beside the trail. He looked down and found the largest fish he had ever seen.

In a time of terror and massacre, my young Christian Cambodian friend had simply taken the apostle John's words to heart. He believed that only those who believe in Jesus and obey God's commands will "overcome the world." Could this be true for us, too, as we face the challenges of today?

Dear Lord, I probably won't find a fish thrashing in the back yard, but I pray for the faith to believe that with Christ, I can face any fear or conflict—or danger—that I encounter this day. Thanks be to God in Christ! Amen.

SEARCH THE WORD

"We have to pray with our eyes on God, not on the difficulties."
—Oswald Chambers

Scripture: 1 John 5:1-5
Song: *"Turn Your Eyes Upon Jesus"*

From this meditation today, I will pray . . .

Adoration _____

Confession _____

Thanksgiving _____

Supplication _____

From this meditation today, I will . . .

Think _____

Say _____

Do _____

August 29

Identified with the Agony

The LORD *is my rock, my fortress and my deliverer*
(Psalm 18:2).

Scripture: Psalm 18:1-6
Song: *"Rock of Ages"*

From this meditation today, I will pray . . .
Adoration _____
_____
_____

Confession _____
_____
_____

Thanksgiving _____
_____
_____

Supplication _____
_____
_____

From this meditation today, I will . . .
Think _____
_____
_____

Say _____
_____
_____

Do _____
_____
_____
_____

In the mining village of Aberfan, South Wales, a million tons of man-made coal slag turned into an avalanche. Heavy rains cause the slag to plow over cottages, homes, and Pantglas Junior High School. Over 160 bodies were recovered from the rubble, most of them children.

A survey taken in a nearby town asked the people if they believed God still cared for them. One person wrote, "No, not after the Welsh disaster."

Given such events, what are we to make of the psalmist's confidence that the Lord was a fortress and deliverer? Maybe the Lord was the psalmist's deliverer, we are tempted to say, but He sure wasn't for those 11-year-olds under the tons of coal slag!

Our only comfort is in believing, like the psalmist, that our confidence in God cannot be superficial. We are compelled to believe that, somehow, He hears our cries even amidst terrible suffering.

During the Aberfan disaster, one local minister, who had lost his son, declared, "We found Christ in our distress. Christ was identified with the agony . . . with those who wept."

Father, *I love You. You are my strength, my rock in whom I take refuge, especially when destruction overwhelms me. Through Christ, amen.*

SPOTLIGHT
Next Week's Lesson

Lay all your confusions, fears, and frustrations at the feet of the Lord who loves you.

August 30

Obey—and Live!

The LORD *will again delight in you . . . if you obey the* LORD *your God* (Deuteronomy 30:9, 10).

German philosopher Friedrich Nietzsche didn't think much of obedience. "If you are too weak to give yourselves your own law," he declared, "then a tyrant shall lay his yoke upon you and say: Obey! Clench your teeth and obey!"

Contrast this defiance to Mother Teresa's calming words: "If I belong to Christ, then He must be able to use me. That is obedience. Then we give wholehearted help to the poor. That is service. They complete each other. That is our life."

Why do we struggle with obedience? Especially when God promises to "delight" in us if we obey Him? (What greater reward for obedience could there be?) God further tells the people of Israel: "When you and your children return to the Lord your God and obey him with all your heart and with all your soul . . . then the Lord your God will . . . have compassion on you and gather you again from all the nations where he scattered you."

To obey God is to come home—to become fulfilled in ways we can only imagine. Mother Teresa understood this. Can we?

God, *grant me the wisdom to see that obedience to You in no way stifles me, but rather brings terrific fulfillment and freedom. In Christ Jesus, amen.*

Scripture: Deuteronomy 30:1-10
Song: *"Here I Am, Lord"*

From this meditation today, I will pray . . .
Adoration _____
Confession _____
Thanksgiving _____
Supplication _____

From this meditation today, I will . . .
Think _____
Say _____
Do _____

SEARCH THE WORD
Obedience to God, far from stifling us, frees us to become our very best selves.

August 31

Sweet Substitue

[Christ Jesus] who gave himself a ransom for all, to be testified in due time (1 Timothy 1:6).

Scripture: 1 Timothy 2:1-6
Song: *"Nothing But the Blood"*

From this meditation today, I will pray . . .
Adoration _____
_____
_____
Confession _____
_____
_____
Thanksgiving _____
_____
_____
Supplication _____
_____
_____

From this meditation today, I will . . .
Think _____
_____
_____
Say _____
_____
_____
Do _____
_____
_____

Years ago I attended a retreat for ministers. What an interesting group! The fellowship was awesome, and the discussions wide-ranging, to say the least. In fact, these ministers came from various denominations, spanning the spectrum of theological beliefs. That made things quite *interesting*. The sad part, which sticks so firmly in my mind, was a particiular sermon delivered one evening. The theme was "why we can't believe in substitutionary atonement."

Substitutionary atonement. I know those are big words, but they refer to Paul's words to Timothy in our Scripture today. It's the fact that Jesus, on the cross, acted as a *ransom* for sin. There's just no way around it. Christ, as the substitute ransom for sinners, dying in our place, is clearly proclaimed in myriad Bible passages. I remain amazed, to this day, that anyone could preach otherwise.

Hold tight to this glorious truth. If we had to pay the price of our sins, we could never erase the debt. But our ransom—our sweet substitute—paid the price for us.

Dear Lord, *I am so thankful that salvation is a free gift of Your grace. Remind, me though, that it was not cheap. Jesus paid it's price in precious drops of His saving blood. In His name I pray. Amen.*

SPOTLIGHT
Next Week's Lesson
Following leaders who have strength and courage will result in victory over our enemies.

Gary Allen lives with his wife, Carol, and Yorkshire terrier, Robbie Burns, in Moultrie, Georgia. He is acquisitions editor for Devotions®.